ETHNIC BRANDING IN CONTEMPORARY CHINA

STUDIES ON ETHNIC GROUPS IN CHINA
Stevan Harrell, Editor

ETHNIC BRANDING IN CONTEMPORARY CHINA

Buyi and the Paradox of Difference

YU LUO

UNIVERSITY OF WASHINGTON PRESS

Seattle

This book will be made open access within three years of publication thanks to Path to Open, a program developed to bring about equitable access and impact for the entire scholarly community, including authors, researchers, libraries, and university presses around the world. Learn more at https://about.jstor.org/path-to-open/.

Copyright © 2025 by the University of Washington Press

Acknowledgment for previously published materials appears on pp. xxi–xxii, which should be considered an extension of the copyright page.

Design by Ani Rucki

Composed in Minion Pro, typeface designed by Robert Slimbach

All rights reserved. No part of this publication may be reproduced or transmitted in any form or by any means, electronic or mechanical, including photocopy, recording, or any information storage or retrieval system, without permission in writing from the publisher.

Photographs by the author. Maps by Ben Pease, Pease Press.

UNIVERSITY OF WASHINGTON PRESS

uwapress.uw.edu

LIBRARY OF CONGRESS CATALOGING-IN-PUBLICATION DATA

Names: Luo, Yu (Anthropologist) author

Title: Ethnic branding in contemporary China : Buyi and the paradox of difference / Yu Luo.

Description: Seattle : University of Washington Press, 2025. | Series: Studies on ethnic groups in China | Includes bibliographical references and index.

Identifiers: LCCN 2024056930 | ISBN 9780295753638 hardcover | ISBN 9780295753645 paperback | ISBN 9780295753652 ebook

Subjects: LCSH: Bouyei (Chinese people)—Ethnic identity | Ethnicity—China—Wuyang Xian | Heritage tourism—China—Wuyang Xian | Wuyang Xian (China)—Social life and customs

Classification: LCC DS731.P84 L87 2025 | DDC 305.800951/18—dc23/eng/20250311

LC record available at https://lccn.loc.gov/2024056930

♾ This paper meets the requirements of ANSI/NISO Z39.48–1992 (Permanence of Paper).

TO ALL WHO HAVE TAUGHT ME
THE BUYI WAY OF LIFE

CONTENTS

Foreword by Stevan Harrell   ix

Preface   xiii

Acknowledgments   xix

Notes on Transcription   xxv

Introduction   1

CHAPTER ONE
Becoming Buyi in a Multiethnic Hinterland   26

CHAPTER TWO
Mo Rituals, Buyi Experts, and Post-Mao Cultural Revivals   55

CHAPTER THREE
Female Performers and the Spectacular State   89

CHAPTER FOUR
Heritage and Identity Politics on Display in the Village Museum   128

CHAPTER FIVE
Modernizing Rural Infrastructure and Branding a Historical Village   157

Conclusion   195

Glossary of Chinese Characters   205

Notes   209

References   229

Index   251

FOREWORD / *Stevan Harrell*

THE BUYI OR BOUYEI PEOPLE of Wuyang Village in Guizhou describe themselves as "like water." Not only do they live in valleys, near rivers, but their lives and their identities are fluid, ever changing as they adapt to the rapid material and social changes of contemporary China that swirl around them. Yu Luo's *Ethnic Branding in Contemporary China: Buyi and the Paradox of Difference* deftly analyzes the multiple paradoxes that flow from the Buyi's unstable position: ethnically distinct yet fully Chinese, cultural preservationist yet culturally innovative, a patriarchal culture performed by women, full participants in state schemes of development while building their own niche in the modern nation.

Since tourism is an important development strategy for the Buyi, these contradictions rise to the surface in what Luo describes as attempts at "ethnic branding." The Buyi are not clearly "exotic" like their uphill neighbors, the Miao: they have long grown rice in lowland paddies, they participated in the Qing dynasty imperial examination system, they have adapted Chinese characters to their Tai language, and their rituals have absorbed elements of China's "three teachings"—Confucianism, Daoism, and Buddhism. But they are clearly not Han Chinese either. Even today older people still speak Buyi, women still make distinctive batik skirts (though they wear them almost exclusively on ceremonial occasions or to perform for tourists), and Mo ritual masters perform ceremonies in the Tai language.

How, then, do the Buyi market themselves to tourists? They could, perhaps, adopt a brand of one more culture for travelers to check off their lists—one more set of songs, dances, and costumes. This might satisfy some visitors, but it would not satisfy the Buyi themselves, who are also attached to an ethnic identity that includes their advanced material culture and integration into the Chinese nation. As *Ethnic Branding in Contemporary China* demonstrates, the Buyi are not just branding themselves to make money off visitors; they are also working out, on both a cognitive and emotional level, who they are in their own consciousness and their own practices. They are not ready to give up their distinctiveness in the interests of modernity and national participation, nor are they ready to become just one more exotic cultural group.

The successive chapters of *Ethnic Branding in Contemporary China* analyze a series of practices that demonstrate Buyi people's agency in adapting local cultural elements to a modern social milieu of travel, mixing, and media. The apotheosis of a culture hero in a huge banner and a monumental statue; women making and trading videos of their songs, dances, and batik making; paving over a concrete path with more picturesque flagstones — all are ways of expressing difference in an unashamedly, even proudly modern ethnic community.

Buyi communities present an important lesson for anyone aiming to understand China's state-minority relations in all their fluidity and complexity. Since Buyi and most other southwestern peoples — unlike Uyghurs, Kazakhs, Tibetans, or Mongols — present no threat to national unity, the central state appears to pay them almost no attention. Local and regional state actors, most of whom are Buyi themselves, fully support Buyi efforts to brand themselves as one tool for economic development in a poor province. Many local tourist enterprises are encouraged and sometimes initiated by retired Buyi low-level officials or schoolteachers. For these "memory entrepreneurs," as Luo labels them, truly *l'état, c'est nous*. Hence the dilemma of the Buyi is not separatism versus integration, but rather the terms of participation in China's continual nation-building process.

Luo can provide us with this lesson in ethnicity, identity, and branding because she spent years getting to know Wuyang, its people, and the outsiders with whom they interact. Moreover, because of Luo's own history, the book also offers an important lesson in how ethnography happens.

Luo is the child of a Buyi father and a Han mother, raised in Guiyang, the provincial capital, originally bilingual in local and standard varieties of Chinese. Like so many other eminent scholars from minority backgrounds in China, she was drawn to ethnography partly because of the desire to *xungen*, to look for the ethnic roots that she was barely aware of, growing up as a bright Chinese youth with a good education and promising career prospects. When she first arrived in Wuyang, introduced by Buyi officials, she was gently derided as "the Han girl," despite the "Buyi" designation on her identity card. How could she be accepted as a member of an ethnic community to which she was attached by descent but not by culture or language?

Luo's personal paradox of double identity as an "insider-outsider" native ethnographer thus parallels the Buyi community's paradox of double identity as modern yet different. In the process of field research and writing, Luo has come to understand this paradox through her third identity as a professional ethnographer. The result is a richness that would be difficult to achieve for any random outsider who decided to study the Buyi. Luo's vivid examples, whether of bureaucratic maneuvering, conflicts over solar-powered streetlights, or housewife choreography, along with her personal reflections on that strange process of learning that we call ethnography, teach us important lessons about ethnicity, about contemporary China, and about the ethnographic enterprise.

Much has changed in China since we started Studies on Ethnic Groups in China back in the 1990s. What has not changed is the complexity and fluidity of ethnic relations, even though the ethnographic analysis of those relations has, if anything, become even more complex. As one of the richest, most subtle, and most up-to-date presentations of this on-the-ground reality, *Ethnic Branding in Contemporary China* is a most valuable addition to our series.

PREFACE

LUNAR NEW YEAR, 2013. The Yang family had just moved to their new concrete house at the base of the hill built on the rice field they once owned in Wuyang, a quiet village nestled amid pointy limestone hills. I had stayed with the Yang family on and off during my time in the village, whenever my initial host left for the county seat to take care of family matters. Still tending to their farmland while taking on part-time work around the area, the Yang couple were in their midfifties and had eight daughters, who were between fifteen and thirty-two at the time. As a young female researcher who was there to learn Buyi language and culture, I tried to fit in as a fictive daughter of the Yang family, calling the Yang couple "mother" and "father."

One lazy afternoon, I was hanging out with the daughters in their bedroom. Two of the Yang sisters, both in their midtwenties, had recently returned from doing migrant labor in the coastal provinces of China and had just purchased new cell phones with their savings. Playing with the phones and trying to take selfies, one sister gestured to me and said in a bantering tone, "Let's take one for the Han girl [$mei^1 ha^5$]!"

"Stop calling her the Han girl, haha!" chimed in their female cousin, who was then in high school. "She is a Han-with-Buyi girl [$mei^1 ha^5 de^2 ʔi^3$] now!" The girls all burst into laughter, while I awkwardly giggled along.

The appellation $mei^1 ha^5$ (the Han girl) was how villagers referred to me when I arrived in Wuyang. There had been Han daughters-in-law who married into the village, but I was different. I was there purely for study

xiv PREFACE

purposes. I neither spoke much Buyi nor knew how to farm when I first started my fieldwork. A city girl who appeared to hail from somewhere else, I did not fit in. However, the uneasiness I experienced when my host sisters called me "the Han girl" derived not only from being labeled an outsider but from the fact that my Buyiness was not recognized. After all, I consider myself to be of Buyi descent.

Born to a Buyi father and a Han mother, I was raised in Guiyang, the capital of Guizhou. My paternal grandparents had moved to Guiyang in their early years, never speaking Buyi to my father and his siblings. I still remember short trips to the countryside during my elementary school years to pay respects to family ancestors at their tombs. My rural relatives were speaking a language entirely unintelligible to me. At the time, I thought they were conversing in some rural dialect. Not until much later did I realize how different their Buyi—a northern Tai language—was from standard Chinese (Mandarin).

This language loss resulted from my upbringing as an urban child whose closest family members no longer spoke Buyi, despite the *minzu* (roughly translated as "ethnicity" or "nationality") category "Buyi" definitively printed on my state-registered identification card from the day I was born. Growing up in Guiyang, I had taken for granted the wide variety of cultural groups inhabiting the region, as many of my classmates came from diverse *minzu* backgrounds. It did not occur to me until my college years that I knew nothing about the Buyi heritage from my paternal side. Driven largely by this motivation to understand who I am, I embarked on an intellectual journey—with the support of many fellow Buyi—as I decided to pursue the topic of contemporary Buyi identity for my graduate work in the United States.

For the first twenty-odd years of my life, I had not spoken a word of Buyi. Relatives like my grandaunt offered me my first lessons in Buyi language. As I stayed with her family on the outskirts of Guiyang during the summer of 2010, I grew conscious of intergenerational language loss at a time when a rapidly expanding cityscape was profoundly transforming my relatives' village. A Buyi village known to many of the older generations of Buyi in the region, its ancestral tombs had been relocated to make way for a new depot, and younger villagers no longer undertook agricultural activity but instead sought jobs in the city. My grandaunt's children could understand but not speak Buyi, while her grandchildren could not understand Buyi at all. Grandaunt, however, tried to maintain the lifestyle she was used to, still reiterating to me the old saying "Anyone fluent in all three languages — Han, Buyi, and Miao — would have no fear to go around the world." I tried to pick up basic Buyi vocabulary as I followed Grandaunt everywhere — as she picked vegetables planted in the small remaining patches of field to sell at market days nearby, as she brought me to a tailor and made me my first Buyi outfit, and as we walked through the village where many migrant laborers from distant parts of rural Guizhou had come to reside in properties villagers rented out for extra income.

As I continued to map out the heterogeneous Buyi cultural landscapes farther into the hinterland of Guizhou, many Buyi areas across Guizhou and even in Yunnan welcomed me under the recommendation of the Association for Buyi Studies (Buyi Xuehui), a semigovernmental research organization whose members include cultural workers from the provincial to the county level. The county cadres took great care of my safety and logistical arrangements. Their assistance was enormously helpful, facilitating access to archives, social networks, and especially transportation means that were crucial in the densely mountainous areas of the region.

In my travels, I noticed strikingly similar local endeavors that sought to preserve Buyi culture while improving rural well-being. With local officials and Buyi elites usually taking the lead, some villages were actively responding to the fad of heritage identification, seeking to discover and make known well-preserved minority cultural practices and scenic sites. Others were hoping to improve village economies by engaging tourism. Many Buyi villages, like those of other ethnic groups, were experimenting with various development projects: cooking rural fare for tourists, staging ethnic performances, setting up village museums, or paving better roads. At a time when ethnic rural China had turned to heritage, tourism, and other cultural industries as the most promising means to alleviate poverty,

xvi PREFACE

these local projects were aimed at attracting visitors and gaining outside attention, including state support.

This characterized the village of Wuyang in Zhenning Buyi-Miao Autonomous County, where I conducted doctoral dissertation fieldwork for eighteen months in 2012–13. Not far from major cities or known tourism sites in Guizhou, Wuyang was nonetheless considered "newly discovered" and branded as a "thousand-year-old" Buyi village. My first impression of Wuyang Village largely hinged on its old stone residences and relics, as well as its members' insistence on speaking Buyi, regardless of whether they were young or old, farmers or migrant workers. Introduced to the community by local cadres who worked for the county government while maintaining strong connections with their village kinship networks, I had the opportunity to observe the diverse lives of illiterate farmers who still relied on their land and agricultural produce, migrant workers who returned to the village from time to time, and well-educated elites who had left their natal community but remained deeply tied to their place of origin.

Educated Buyi elites supported my research, because for them, Buyi history and traditional knowledge were worth further investigation. They themselves had been collecting old clothing and ritual scripts, painstakingly researching Buyi folklore, and interpreting cultural symbols and historical meaning in Buyi legends, rituals, and handicrafts in the hope of salvaging traditions and retaining Buyi identity. Many villagers, however, remained puzzled as to why I was studying Buyi culture. To them, learning a language of such little use made no sense, unless I intended to become an interpreter when the village grew into a tourism site. Others presumed that I might be a journalist of some sort, to whom they could speak of their hardship as elder peasants in a socioeconomic quandary and who they hoped had connections with higher-ups. But even though they did not really understand why I was interested in Buyi history, some searched the village for elders who would be able to answer my questions.

As I navigated my relations with various people in the village, some awkward encounters were indicative of the complexity of local power dynamics in relation to gender, class, and age differences. When I was first invited

PREFACE xvii

to family feasts in the village, I sat with middle-aged men with whom I could communicate fluently in Han Chinese, which allowed me to solicit background information about the village and its people. However, some women did not understand why a young woman like me would actively socialize with male villagers whom I had only met for the first time. In turn, female villagers initially kept their distance from me when I was not accompanied by my host family. Often at social events, I found myself having to decide which table to eat at, or whom I should sit next to, or which crowd to join for chitchat.

This urge to take sides occurred on a daily basis. At the time, my host family had opened the one and only eatery in the village, where tourists and visiting officials regularly came to eat. Having provided the meals and services, my host family usually waited until the visitors had left and then ate leftovers. Many times, local Buyi officials who knew me as Dr. Luo would invite me to join them to eat. I was tempted to do so in order to hear their visions of the village and enrich my understanding of local state actors. But I almost always felt the need to politely turn down their offer by responding that the kitchen needed me, because I wanted to maintain a close relation with my host family and with the fellow villagers who came to help. I did not want them to see me differently or to make myself seem superior.

My fieldwork experience was thus transformative for my understanding of not only the changes in an ethnic rural community and the internal differences among village residents, but also my own position, especially my mixed background. No matter how hard I tried to justify my Buyiness based on my paternal heritage and national registration, it did not change the fact that I was different from locals. In my previous fieldwork trips, Buyi villagers had made sense of me by referring to me as a "pseudo-Buyi" (*jia Buyi*) or "more-advanced Buyi" (*geng xianjin de Buyi*)—a Buyi who had perhaps shed her culture and fast-forwarded into mainstream Han society. But villagers in Wuyang still unequivocally identified me as a Han girl who spoke little Buyi and hailed from the city.

It was, therefore, surprising when I became a "Han-with-Buyi girl,"

xviii PREFACE

signifying my gradual gain in familiarity with Buyi culture. Being referred to as "a Han-with-Buyi girl" on the one hand signified my incremental transition from outsider to insider in Wuyang Village as I gradually picked up the Buyi language and learned to immerse myself in village life. On the other hand, it posed an intriguing question about the formation and reconfiguration of Buyiness, considered fluid by nature yet fixed as a feature of identity.

After a year of fieldwork, it seemed as if I was finally able to claim my Buyiness. As I continued to observe and participate in agricultural activities, family banquets, and village events, elder women were amazed by my patience and attention. They thought of me as unlike other young women my age, whom they saw as mostly interested in pop culture. When I sat with them as they prepared song-and-dance performances for Buyi festivals and public events, my host family explained delightedly, "She is a girl of our village [$mei^1 zau^2 ?ben^3$]. . . . She likes to come!"

This ethnography thus started as a search for identity among ethnic populations in southwest China. My personal story serves as a point of entry into enduring cultural elements and practices prized by local Buyi. Being and becoming Buyi was for me a process of making sense of my newfound life-world.

This is also an intercultural project, as I traveled between cultures both physically and metaphorically: between my urban upbringing and Buyi roots, and between my Western academic training and cultural exposure and my mainland China identity. The question of representation, therefore, does not cease to exist. I could not speak for the Buyi, but I could speak of some Buyi from my peculiar position as both an insider and an outsider.

This book, then, is in one sense a self-reflexive endeavor. I navigate my own sense of belonging as I lived with the hard-working and kind-hearted villagers, worked with scholars enthusiastic about Buyi history and culture, and shared a nostalgia and sense of loss with my family, who often asked, "What if the Buyi disappear in the future?" This book is dedicated to the Buyi people I have spent time with and come to know, to whom I am tremendously indebted for their insights.

ACKNOWLEDGMENTS

THIS BOOK PROJECT FINALLY bore fruit after more than a decade of endeavor. I could not have made it this far without the support of many who have always been by my side.

My heartfelt appreciation goes to Helen F. Siu for her patience in guiding me through my graduate study. Having taken me on when I had little knowledge about anthropology, Helen has believed in me throughout my academic career. Kalyanakrishnan Sivaramakrishnan and Erik Harms, my advisory committee members, encouraged me to be intellectually adventurous and provided invaluable advice from their professional experience. I would like to express my special thanks to Deborah Davis, who offered me critical and persistent support. It was Debbie who led me to the vibrant academic community in New Haven, where my ideas flourished.

Other faculty members at Yale have offered constructive comments on my coursework and research, including William Kelly, Michael Dove, Peter Perdue, Anne Underhill, Carol Carpenter, Susan Brownell, Karen Nakamura, Sara Shneiderman, Joseph Errington, and Douglas Rogers. Over the years, my thinking and writing have benefited from the Environmental Anthropology Collective and many other workshops on the Yale campus.

During my postdoc year at the University of California, Berkeley, You-Tien Hsing gave me her unwavering support. Other scholars in Chinese studies and in anthropology with whom I crossed paths in the Bay Area, including Wen-Hsin Yeh, Xin Liu, Nelson Graburn, Li Zhang, and Rachel Stern, offered thoughtful suggestions on my research and career. At the City

University of Hong Kong, where I first took on a faculty position, Hsiao-t'i Li and May Bo Ching kindly mentored me.

In the past few years, the University of Puget Sound has provided me with the most collegial environment anyone could ask for. My colleagues in the Department of Sociology and Anthropology and the Asian Studies Program have made me feel at home, and they are always there when I need help. I thank Monica DeHart, in particular, who kindly took time to brainstorm ideas with me when I was revising this book's manuscript.

I am particularly thankful for the opportunity to work over the years with Louisa Schein and Tim Oakes, both of whom share a longtime commitment to engaging the lives of ethnic, rural residents in Guizhou through critical scholarship. I very much enjoyed and appreciated the trips with Louisa in Guizhou, which have given me a unique insight into an anthropologist's meaningful journey over several decades in a land I deeply care about. Jodi Weinstein, who worked on the history of the Buyi (or Zhongjia in late imperial China), has been a key interlocutor ever since I took the Buyi as my central focus of study. The conference panels we formulated in collaboration with the research group led by Jean Michaud and Sarah Turner have significantly informed my understanding of the Asian borderlands.

A China studies writing group, in which I worked with Cheow-Thia Chan, Wei Luo, Guojun Wang, and Pengfei Zhao, offered tremendous help on writing, publication, and academic life in general since our time at Yale. Every session with them has been inspiring and comforting, especially during the tough times as I approached the finishing line. In Hong Kong, Jun Zhang, Minhua Ling, and Yi Kang have been supportive in all aspects of my life. I am indebted to their great insights, courage, and optimism. Jun was particularly responsive and helpful when I needed a fresh pair of eyes on my work.

My research over time has benefited from the constructive comments I received at the Yale University Agrarian Studies Program; Rutgers University China Anthropology Group; the University of California, Berkeley, China's Worlds Lecture Series; the University of California, Berkeley, Tourism Studies Working Group; the University of California, Davis, China

Anthropology Group; the University of San Francisco Chinese Studies Research Group; the 2017 Penn State University Asian Studies Summer Institute; the Hong Kong Anthropological Society; the Hong Kong Institute of Humanities and Social Sciences at the University of Hong Kong; Guizhou University; the 2020 Summer Institute for Chinese Studies at the University of Pittsburgh; and the Chinese-English Keywords Project. I thank those with whom I have had the pleasure to share these spaces to think and reflect, as well as colleagues at the various panels and roundtables that took place at the annual meetings of the Association for Asian Studies and the American Anthropological Association.

The research and writing of this project were made possible by grants and fellowships provided by the Council on East Asian Studies, the MacMillan Center, and the Agrarian Studies Program at Yale. The Early Career Scheme offered by the Hong Kong Research Grants Council allowed me to refine this project and turn it into a book. With the generous support that the Trimble family has given to the Suzanne Wilson Barnett Chair in Contemporary China Studies position at the University of Puget Sound, I took advantage of the Whiteley Center at Friday Harbor Labs, which provided a tranquil and productive refuge to revise the manuscript.

The manuscript received critical advice from two anonymous reviewers whom I am grateful to. At the publishing stage, I am honored to have worked with Lorri Hagman, Caitlin Tyler-Richards, Justine Sargent, Joeth Zucco, Beth Fuget, Mindy Hill, and Molly Woolbright at the University of Washington Press. Ben Pease created the maps. Elizabeth Berg copyedited my manuscript, and Alja Kooistra offered assistance in proofreading. Doug Easton helped me with indexing. I thank them for their patience and professionalism. My series editor, Stevan Harrell, read through numerous versions of my manuscript and offered meticulous suggestions for editing and revision. Occasional exchanges on our fieldwork experiences in southwest China added joy to this process.

Earlier versions of parts of this book have appeared in the following publications: "Alternative Indigeneity in China? The Paradox of the Buyi in the Age of Ethnic Branding," *Verge: Studies in Global Asias* 4, no. 2 (2018):

107–34; "Resourcing Remoteness and the 'Post-Alteric' Imaginary in China" (co-authored with Tim Oakes and Louisa Schein), *Social Anthropology* 27, no. 2 (2019): 270–85; "The Domestic Life of Buyi Videos: The 'Home Mode' in Ethnic Rural Southwest China," *Ethnos* 89, no. 4 (2022): 634–56, doi: 10.1080/00141844.2022.2081237; and a forthcoming chapter titled "A Solo Effort? Collecting Ethnic Minority Artefacts of/for Local Communities Amidst Southwest China's 'Museum Fever,'" in *The Rise of Private Museums and Heritage in East and Southeast Asia*, edited by Graeme Were and Pieter ter Keurs (Amsterdam University Press). I would like to acknowledge the publishers for permission to use these materials.

My intellectual journey would not have been complete without the wonderful friends whom I know I can turn to. I am thankful for the inspiration and company of Luisa Cortesi, Elizabeth Miles, Aniket Aga, Andrew Carruthers, Hosna Sheikholeslami, Ana Lara, Amy Zhang, Rose Keimig, Caroline Merrifield, Heidi Lam, Adrienne Cohen, Ranran Wang, Jing Zhao, Angel Ryono, Peng Xu, Alison Marlin, Fang Xu, Thomas Patton, Jin Huan, Chia Hui Lu, Lik Hang Tsui, Virginia Chan, Yang Zhan, Tiantian Diao, Suzanne Barnett, Mengjun Li, Anna Valiavska, Rachel DeMotts, Nagore Sedano Naveira, Priti Joshi, Sam Kigar, Kirsten Coffman, Kevin Kirner, Jennifer Neighbors, Ameera Nimjee, Bee Vang, and Juan Zhang, among many others. Yingni Guo, Yahui He, Xiaoshen Ma, Ning Ning, and Yifeng Wu shared my joys and sorrows and offered illuminating insights from other disciplines and their own life-worlds. Being abroad alone, I am deeply grateful to Enrico Bonatti, Merry Cai, Joan Mencher, Frank Southworth, Tan Lei, Liu Shengqing, and Moisha and Robert Blechman for their generous support as my second family. My other friends, some of whom I have known since high school and college in China or met during graduate school and fieldwork, have also offered warm encouragement.

This book project brought me first physically away from but ultimately ever closer to my hometown of Guizhou. My earlier research received generous support from intellectuals at various levels of the Association for Buyi Studies in Guizhou, both logistically and institutionally. I owe a most important intellectual debt to Yang Tingshuo, an admirable senior scholar whose expertise about the past and present of southwest China continues to inspire emerging local scholarship. My continual conversations with Weng Naiqun, Luo Zhengfu, Zuo Zhenting, and Chen Zhengfu have given me wonderful food for thought.

Without the hospitable Buyi villagers whom I visited in Guizhou and elsewhere, my research would not have been possible. I would like to express my greatest appreciation to those residing in my primary fieldsite, Wuyang Village. I thank them for taking me in as their family member and for providing crucial insights about the Buyi. My life was enriched by their optimism even during times of unpredictability and hardship living in a marginalized area where some people still worry about everyday subsistence.

The Wu family—whose deep concerns about Buyi traditions occupy many pages of this book—offered enormous help in my field research. Discussions with Wu Zhonggang and Wu Zhongshi have been very insightful. My special thanks to the late Wu Zhonghui, who introduced me to his family and his hometown, Wuyang Village, and with whom I no longer have the opportunity to clarify the International Phonetic Alphabet (IPA) he deployed to denote Buyi vocabulary.

Words cannot express my gratitude toward my parents, Luo Ping and Wang Qing, for their unconditional love and support. Their foresight led me into an exciting world that I would have never thought of exploring. Their encouragement from near and far has helped me survive the early years of my graduate study, the fieldwork in Guizhou, and critical stages of dissertating and job hunting. During my most difficult moments, they still have every confidence in me.

This research also means a lot to my paternal family, whose Buyiness set me off on a journey to search for the meaning of my own identity. It is my deepest regret that I will not be able to show this book to my grandmother, who passed away around the time the manuscript was accepted for publication. Having spent most of her life away from her village, my grandmother barely remembered any Buyi vocabulary but nonetheless missed her time with fellow Buyi villagers. In her mideighties, it was not

xxiv ACKNOWLEDGMENTS

easy for her to make frequent trips back to her village to attend life-cycle ceremonies and communal feasts, but spending hours watching the Buyi videos I brought back from fieldwork gave her some comfort.

Last but foremost, I want to especially thank my husband, Isak. As I pushed this project through, he offered encouragement and help whenever he could, from reading multiple revisions to giving me advice on book illustrations and cover design. His positivity, kindness, and sense of humor brighten up my days. We welcomed our daughter Marina into this world as my manuscript approached completion. Watching her grow while this book takes its final shape is a most extraordinary experience.

NOTES ON TRANSCRIPTION

TO DEMONSTRATE the bilingual nature of my research in local Buyi areas, I have made an effort to distinguish Buyi (Bouyei) vocabulary from Chinese words in this book (the spelling "Buyi" was approved by the Guizhou Minzu Affairs Commission in 1953, while "Bouyei" was the transcription adopted for foreign publications in 1991 [Weinstein 2014, 136]). While I use pinyin for Chinese words, I follow Buyi intellectuals from my fieldsite in using the International Phonetic Alphabet (IPA) for Buyi words, denoting pitch and tone with superscript numbers. This transcription method is different from the contemporary Latin-based Buyi script that was officially developed during the 1980s, after the Buyi-Zhuang Script Alliance Policy promoted in the 1950s was abandoned. When I started visiting Zhenning County around 2011 and 2012 for fieldwork, local Buyi intellectuals were drafting a book about the Buyi culture in Zhenning and using IPA to present the Buyi dialect used in the region where my fieldsite is located. However, the only knowledgeable figure I knew who participated in developing this transcription method passed away soon after I conducted my fieldwork. I never had a chance to inquire of him the IPA for certain Buyi words other than those that his family members intended to include in the book they compiled. Instead, I have attempted to denote some Buyi words following the basic rules he recorded, while consulting existing publications on this matter (e.g., Wu, Snyder, and Liang 2000, 2007; Holm 2013; Wu Zhonggang and Wu Kaifeng 2014). Therefore, any errors or oversights are mine alone.

In this book, I use pseudonyms for the village itself and some informants following anthropological convention, while taking into account the local political context. For key informants whose works I cite throughout, I use their real names. In other cases, I use subject identities or positions, rather than full names, for attribution. The use of terminology such as "Grandma" and "Uncle" for my Buyi informants is intended to indicate my fictive kinship with them, even though they are not biologically connected to me. While this is not common for Western readers, I translated these appellations directly from Buyi and Chinese, a mix of which is used to address family members, to be consistent with local culture.

ETHNIC BRANDING IN CONTEMPORARY CHINA

INTRODUCTION

STROLLING THROUGH WUYANG Village during my fieldwork, I often stopped by the one and only store in this quiet village, nestled in a small basin amid karst limestone hills. A middle-aged couple had turned the front of their house into a store retailing daily necessities. Men and occasionally women gathered to chitchat about village life while watching a television hung inside the storefront. One afternoon in November 2013, I found Uncle Yang, a respectable descendant of the Yang lineage, watching TV in the store by himself. Once an elementary school teacher in the nearby Zhenning county seat, Uncle Yang had returned to Wuyang Village upon retirement.

As I sat with Uncle Yang, the Guizhou Provincial Television channel began to show a group of Miao dancers dressed in their festive costumes, performing at a cultural promotional event. I turned to Uncle Yang and asked him what Buyi thought of Miao, the other populous ethnic minority group inhabiting the multiethnic region. Uncle Yang reaffirmed the long-held bias against the Miao that other Buyi had expressed: "We barely intermarried with the Miao. . . . Don't know if we were foes with them or what. Miao daughters-in-law were unwanted, and the meals they cooked for New Year's and ritualistic events would not be touched or consumed by our ancestors. We used to despise them for not being clean."

Uncle Yang then lamented an ironic twist: "But now they are more advanced [*xianjin*]; the Miao are broadcast on the TV so much more. It is as if we Buyi are not as good as they are!"

In the summer of 2015, I returned to Wuyang Village two years after my initial eighteen months of fieldwork. Late one evening, I received a phone call from Kun, an artist friend teaching at a university in Guiyang, the capital of Guizhou. I had first met Kun in 2013, when she followed a team of professors from her alma mater, the Sichuan Academy of Arts, to visit the then out-of-the-way Wuyang Village in search of artistic inspiration. Having heard of Wuyang Village as the "thousand-year-old Buyi village" through its branding by local Buyi elites, officials, and media workers, the team of art professors was amazed by the old Buyi stone residences and surrounding landscapes, appreciating them first and foremost as a unique visual experience.

Kun sought my advice over the phone because she was confounded by a design project on which she was collaborating with other artists in a neighboring county of Zhenning. The project endeavored to manifest the distinctiveness of the Buyi ethnic group through a sculpture. "The sculpture, to be erected at the public square in the county seat, is part of an effort to attract more attention. It would help to promote the local tourism economy and to bring more profit, because this county in southwestern Guizhou with a predominantly Buyi population has been so chronically impoverished," she explained. "Earlier on, we tried to incorporate ethnic elements such as the bronze drum [*tonggu*] and the ox head [*niutou*] into the sculpture. But local government officials, many of whom were Buyi, were dissatisfied. They were concerned about such symbols being indistinguishable from other ethnic groups—for instance, from those of the Miao in southeastern Guizhou, which is famous for its ethnic tourism." She asked if I, a native of Guizhou who was both registered as Buyi on my official identification card and an academic studying the Buyi, could pinpoint something distinct about the group.

Two hundred kilometers from Wuyang Village, the county where Kun was helping erect a Buyi sculpture undoubtedly embraced a similar kind of endeavor to Wuyang in showcasing something readily distinguishable, something others would not have. On my end of the phone, I remained baffled and silent. Once again, I ruminated on my enduring skepticism that

MAP 1. Overview map of Zhenning County in Guizhou, southwest China.

specific Buyi features could be gleaned as distinct from those of similar Tai-speaking peoples, or of other populous and influential groups—such as those identified as Han and Miao—in highly multiethnic regions where people have mixed and mingled over time. Even if I could think of something unique about the Buyi inhabiting a particular locality, would that be adequate to represent a heterogeneous ethnic group scattered across Guizhou and other parts of the Sino–Southeast Asian borderland (map 1)?

4   INTRODUCTION

This contemporary investment in distinguishable cultural characteristics exemplifies what I call "ethnic branding" in this book. Ethnic branding is a means by which ethnic identities can stand out through cultural promotion and visual design; however, it is not just for the sake of local reputations or tourism income. As the above stories imply, the need and aspiration to brand oneself accentuates locals' self-awareness in light of ethnic difference.

The Buyi, in particular, constitute a case in which ethnic branding is deemed at once necessary and challenging. Compared to other ethnic groups, such as the Miao or the Dong, the Buyi—with a lower profile today—are less closely identified with the colorful images of multiethnic Guizhou. Even as the tenth largest of China's fifty-five non-Han groups, with a current estimated population of nearly three million, the Buyi are little known by ordinary Chinese (perhaps except residents of Guizhou and some neighboring provinces), let alone in Western scholarship.[1] Local Buyi thus hope to preserve certain markers of distinctiveness, both for emotional reasons of cultural pride *and* for economic reasons of tourist income. At the same time, their lives are becoming increasingly similar to the rest of the society outside the limited cultural domains that mark their difference. Illustrating this critical juncture and situating it in a long historical process, this book documents the endeavor to brand cultural identity among local Buyi who have been my informants, friends, colleagues, and (pseudo-)kin. In search of identifiable ethnic characteristics, Buyi perform a juggling act to overcome their relative lack of visibility in public culture and to highlight difference for cultural production and promotion. So, what does ethnic branding mean for the Buyi, and what does it do in and beyond contemporary China?

THE ART OF ETHNIC BRANDING

The active endeavor to identify signatures of uniqueness among ethnic and indigenous practices has intensified during my many years of living, traveling, and conducting research in Guizhou. As my family sometimes accompanied me on fieldtrips to various areas, we noticed how Guizhou's villages, towns, and counties with a predominantly Buyi population would designate themselves the first Buyi place to host a particular festival or the hometown of certain Buyi handicrafts or cuisines. Works to demonstrate visual symbols or to highlight spectacular landscapes, healthy food, intriguing folklore, and so on would ensue.[2]

The ability to be different, or characteristically special, is something my father often commented on. As a Buyi of rural origin who has lived in the city for decades, my father remained nostalgic about old villages, having traveled on his own and with me to many ethnic areas in southwest China. In his parlance, ethnic culture needs *gexing*, which can be literally translated as "individuality" or "character," usually indicating a person with a distinct personality. For him, naming Wuyang Village the "thousand-year-old Buyi village" does not suffice; the original feel of Buyi life is its *gexing*—something historically rooted and arising in a given environment—and that should be highlighted in cultural promotion and protected from the threat of modern transformation or commercial development.

Branding a distinct persona is of particular importance for a place like Wuyang. Much of my fieldwork captured a pre-tourism moment when Wuyang Village was first undertaking planning and branding efforts years after some of the Miao and Dong villages in southeastern Guizhou had made national and international fame as tourist destinations (see Oakes 1998; Schein 2000; Chio 2014; Cornet 2015).[3] Therefore, tourism had not reached a mass scale but was more like an aspiration, as locals hoped to raise incomes and living standards in order to pull themselves out of poverty. Ethnic branding, for the local Buyi I worked with at the time, was very much a new path, brimming with desire and potential but also uncertainty. The search for *gexing* might then contribute to the "seductions of place" that cater to tourist desires to experience situated, sensuous qualities of difference (Cartier 2005).

However, the more I tried to unfold what was transpiring in Wuyang and other Buyi villages, the more I realized that trying to develop and achieve tourism is only part of the story. It does not capture how Buyi individuals understand or describe what they do and the broader structural contexts

6 INTRODUCTION

that shape their decisions. While local Buyi often invoke terms such as "name card" (*mingpian*) or "image" (*xingxiang*) as ways to refer to presenting their identity or place, ethnic branding is not just about showcasing difference for tourists. For many Buyi, it is about restoring the past, about having that accessibility to one's culture and history. As my father likes to put it, "*Gexing* is something from the inside out."

Branding, in my analysis, involves a dynamic process of crafting and molding—or *dazao*, a Chinese term my Buyi interlocutors often use—ethnic images, cultural sites, artistic performances, and so forth. But with a critical part of that branding being meaningful self-making, it is not reducible to (self-)commodification or objectification.[4] Many fail to realize that success in branding can be fleeting, but for local Buyi it creates something that stays with them. *Gexing* thus does not equate to "special characteristics" (*tese*) and "special products" (*techan*), which Chinese tourism promotions and marketing like to promote (Chio 2014, 197, 199). Nor is it simply a "commodified persona" drawn from multiple cultural frameworks to shape the presentation of self (Bunten 2008). Rather, it is a sense of selfhood. This is because ethnicity, as a mode of self-conscious fashioning, has become increasingly implicated in the fabric of everyday life, related to not only economic income but also emotion, belonging, knowledge, and memory.

Ethnic branding thus rests on both an inward search for identity-as-difference and an outward desire to gain visibility and market success. The latter is not an end in itself, nor is the former simply a means. Ethnic branding, first and foremost, hinges on a historical anchor for locals to negotiate subjectivity and articulate a sense of belonging; it involves deep feelings, both personal and social. Second, ethnic branding characterizes how local peoples seek to outperform other groups or locales in the contemporary economy, which foregrounds culture as one of the most important markers of ethnic groups in China. With both inward searching and outward competition for unique character, ethnic branding does not stop at selling ethnic culture as commodity and experience but is an everyday practice in a context where locals are juggling their ethnocultural positioning and aspirations for a better life. It contributes to the affective ties with one's home place and ethnic identity, adding a sense of purpose to local experience.

As I looked into a moment when Wuyang Village was finding its way to becoming a cultural destination by tapping into its *gexing*, my father reminded me of my Buyi persona. He suggested that, as a scholar of Buyi, my research also has and needs its *gexing*. Trained as an anthropologist in the United States while searching for my own cultural roots and conforming to local expectations in Buyi areas, I have also embodied a Buyi identity alternating between a modern one of material and educational progress and a traditional one of ethnic distinctiveness. My maternal Han descent and my upbringing in an urban setting contributed to unfamiliarity with the Buyi part of me when I was young. Largely indistinguishable from the Han, I have accepted Han culture and spoken the Han language as a child of a Han-minority mixed marriage (Blum 2001, 31). However, as Bamo Ayi (2007), who grew up half Yi in Sichuan, aptly puts it, mixed ethnic background does not necessarily eliminate the ethnic consciousness of its members. In my case, the awareness of my own Buyiness emerged as both part of an intellectual reflection on minority cultures and of the tourism practices among urban Chinese in the early 2000s that reinforced ethnic branding. As I traveled to Buyi villages and learned about ethnic realities beyond state-designated identities, I grew connected to something that used to be distant from me. My association with the Buyi community thus evolved from a familial identification with paternal relatives and an academic enthusiasm for indigenous traditions to a concern for the survival of my own ethnic group positioned within the politics, economy, and culture of the Chinese nation.

By incorporating a range of local voices and lived experiences (including my own), this study not only reflects a moment of decolonizing anthropology but also sets itself apart from *minzu* studies from the West on Guizhou. I follow Tenzin Jinba's (2022, 14) call to take advantage of my native status—especially my layered, situational nativeness—for critical reflection.[5] Native anthropology, or being a native anthropologist, by no means equates to assuming an insider perspective or essentializing a dichotomy in opposition

8 INTRODUCTION

to the non-native (Tsuda 2015). What matters is to acknowledge the modes of knowing and representation by native anthropologists who are left betwixt and between, with often shifting and mixed identifications by virtue of migration, education, or parentage (Meyers 2019; Ryang 1997, 2005). The push and pull between emotional attachment to and intellectual distance from one's own ethnic group can be a productive motivation (Bamo 2007; Narayan 1993) when it helps bring out the affective side of identity construction and maintenance. As I navigate differences in various aspects of identity and make sense of my plural sense of selves, my story is also about how local Buyi craft themselves and their lives within shifting fields of power and meaning. Just like the self-branding of local Buyi, this book is derived from an inward search for who I am and an outward desire to let my Buyi experiences be known. Making the bifurcation of self and other less determinate in my ethnographic inquiry, my research of and with the Buyi therefore sheds light on a complex process of knowledge production that is neither emic nor etic but perhaps both at once.

In what follows, I highlight the paradoxical process of branding a Buyi identity in particular sociohistorical contexts. With its focus on ethnic branding of the Buyi, this book offers a diachronic perspective on cultural identity production in southwest China and chronicles a shifting paradigm wherein multiple forces, whether the state or market, have contributed to essentializing or deconstructing ethnic differences. Moreover, it makes the case that the Buyi experience in China's southwest brings out the subtlety and diversity of China's ethnic politics at a time when the international spotlight is on the country's more contentious regions.

CAUGHT IN THE MIDDLE

Two months after our phone conversation, my artist friend Kun showed me a sketch of the sculpture that had been designed after consulting Buyi cultural experts in that county. This proposal, having received approval from the local government, was undertaken as a major construction project for the county seat. Intriguingly, on the suggestion of local Buyi elites, the designers covered the entire sculpture with wavy and spiral patterns. These curves, as Kun informed me, were meant to symbolize whirlpools, ostensibly identifying the Buyi ethnicity as closely related to water.

Indeed, the Buyi—far from a monolithic group—are believed to have mostly lived along highly irrigated river valleys. A Guizhou proverb alludes to this stereotype: "The Han live in townships, the Buyi live by waters, and the Miao live on mountaintops."[6] Though this phrase oversimplifies ethnic groups as occupying distinct ecological niches, it nevertheless implies the Buyi's association with water in a multiethnic region that is densely mountainous. It also portrays a spatial relation in which the Buyi are positioned vis-à-vis the Han and the Miao as these groups constantly create, trespass, and remake boundaries. This sets up the backdrop for the Buyi's self-perception in relation to regional history and the multiethnic dynamic: as some Buyi contend, the Buyi's waterlike persona manifests its adaptability and fluid interactions with other ethnicities.

Heavily crisscrossed by mountains and rivers, the region where China today borders Southeast Asia has witnessed the economic and cultural symbiosis of upland and lowland societies over time. This huge border area and hilly zone, which scholars termed Zomia, enabled the existence of "ethnic amphibians" who had been capable of "social shape-shifting" within a broad spectrum of identities (Scott 2009, 241, 281).[7] Present-day Guizhou, occupying the eastern end of Zomia, was one of the multiethnic frontier regions at the fringes of Chinese state control well into the nineteenth century. And yet, the importance of this region for Chinese statecraft is undiminishable (Oakes and Zuo 2022). In the eyes of late imperial officialdom, which treated local populations as targets of civilizing discourse and policy (Crossley, Siu, and Sutton 2006; Harrell 1995), unintelligible languages, curious dress, peculiar rituals, and unusual lifestyles and habitats marked the unfamiliarity that came to characterize human "holdouts." Guizhou's ethnic inhabitants were in turn arrayed on a successively hierarchized gradient from wild to tamed, from strange to familiar, according to the extent to which they had adopted Confucian ideals of cultivated manners and morals.[8]

Rivers and riverside settlements, with which Buyi have been associated, not only contributed to the flourishing of rice paddy agriculture on imperial China's southwestern frontier but also enabled central authorities to gradually take control of sedentary populations and garner taxes. Agriculture has always carried a political and moral valence, as it contributes to social stability and advancement from the stance of state formation by rendering local inhabitants more legible to the center (Perdue 1987; Scott 1998). New military and civilian settlements established by the central authority to (re)claim land and civilize frontier populations sought to occupy fertile land and control sufficient water sources, which were easier to find in flat valleys and in small basins in the interior of hilly regions (Fei Huang 2014). As rice planters along highly irrigated river valleys, some Buyi communities may have come into closer contact with these immigrants and settlers who established towns and controlled trade routes over time.

Due to such interactive processes, whereby cultural influences from the Han were strong and persistent, some local populations strategically deployed instrumental and symbolic means to attach themselves to the center rather than remaining outside the firm grasp of the late imperial regimes. Having long negotiated terms of coexistence with each other, a range of betwixt-and-between ethnicities hence emerged (Tenzin 2017, 563). The Buyi's forebears, for instance, maintained a Janus-faced identity depicted in historical archives as "both Sinicized and intractable" (Weinstein 2014, 26–27) or at once pliable and stubborn. Similar to other Tai-speaking groups (Holm 2003; Kaup 2000), the Buyi's forebears are believed to have maintained patriarchal structures and developed a sense of cultural superiority, some inventing a mythical Han origin for themselves in the hope of gaining higher social status. Jean Michaud (2006) notes that the Buyi have been influenced by Chinese religions to such a degree that other non-Han groups often consider the Buyi to be Han.

As the Buyi have remained relatively open to adopting Han Chinese culture, they have also distanced themselves from the "mountaintop Miao," often stereotyped as having practiced swidden (slash-and-burn) agriculture, which is devalued by the state as more primitive than sedentary wet-rice cultivation.[9] Illuminating how some Miao shifted residence upon exhausting the fertility of their land in the hills, an old saying among Wuyang villagers was "The Miao move their villages around" ($pu^3 jiu^2 tiau^2 ?ben^3$). Furthermore, and perhaps perceived as a consequence, some Miao do not worship their ancestors and have no ancestral places to which they return. The Buyi, by contrast, highly valued ancestral worship (including the adoption of Han-style ancestral altars and genealogical writing), which aligned with the ideal of Confucian civilization.[10] Thus, in official and popular perceptions, the Buyi have historically been ranked above the Miao in a hierarchy based on the level of sinicization (*hanhua* in standard Chinese with no corresponding word in Buyi).[11]

This interethnic dynamic involves a contemporary twist that is central to this book: although the Buyi have long been regarded as having maintained previously favored "civilized" qualities, these same traits are now undesirable in the paradigm of a cultural market that prefers ethnically unique or exotic features. Historically perceived as similar to Han or almost Han but not quite Han (Unger 1997; Scott 2009; Michaud, Barkataki-Ruscheweyh, and Swain 2016), the Buyi are caught in the middle: distinct from (and othered by) the mainstream Han, yet not as unique as some other ethnic minority groups. Watching the Miao appear frequently in mass media — dressed in their vivid costumes playing emblematic musical instruments — Uncle Yang lamented, "Are we Buyi not as good as they are?" Some Buyi elites described the fluidity and adaptability of Buyi as "just like water," but this historical versatility also seems to have become a liability for the Buyi, making it easy to become acculturated and challenging to stand out for contemporary cultural branding.

MINZU CULTURE IN CHINA'S SOUTHWEST

Despite historically fluid ethnolinguistic distinctions and shifting cultural practices, the *minzu* scheme under which respective identity labels were

12 INTRODUCTION

assigned to China's enormously diverse populations under Mao has since taken on a life of its own.[12] As the only currently available frame and relevant category for talking about cultural difference (Yeh 2007), these *minzu* categories—"primordially framed" and yet "de facto constructed" (Joniak-Lüthi 2015, 23)—that locals have used and lived with laid the foundation for ethnic branding today. As one of the first thirty-eight minority groups (*shaoshu minzu*) identified in 1953–54, the Buyi (or Buyizu) have developed a group consciousness apace with nation building and socioeconomic integration; this is especially true among an emerging generation of minority cadres trained by socialist educational institutions and government organs.

In the earliest decade of socialism, as officials and scholars dispatched by the central authority conducted ethnolinguistic studies and consulted with local elites to classify *minzu* groups (Harrell 2001b; Mullaney 2010), the party-state pledged to allow minorities to practice their cultures. With a surge in Soviet-style ethnology (*minzuxue*) in the socialist academy (Kaup 2018), literature and arts collected and cataloged from the ethnic folk (*minzu minjian*) context were often revamped for revolutionary purposes and became tools for social change.[13] This terrain was significantly altered during the Cultural Revolution (1966–76), when customary practices in the realms of culture and religion were attacked as the "four olds" (namely, old ideas, culture, customs, and habits). As some Buyi elites recall today, those years were a source of guilt over not being able to protect their heirlooms from being destroyed and, in turn, the reason they fear for the loss of Buyi culture and why they are making every effort to salvage traditions.

Therefore, the desire to restore accessibility to one's culture and history that lies at the heart of today's ethnic branding can be traced back to the period that followed the end of the Cultural Revolution after Mao's death. This included a nationwide revival of interest in creating new ethnological institutions, journal publications, and festive events starting in the 1980s (Mueggler 2001). State discourse, scholarly study, and everyday ethnic markers all intersected as various languages of ethnic revival (Harrell 2001b; Litzinger 2000; Schein 2000). While many materials on Buyi culture, arts, and history were published as official documents and scholarly works during the socialist era, such publications increased in the post-Mao decades. With the resurgence of ethnological studies, local cadres, cultural experts, and media workers actively participated in semigovernmental associations organized for each minority group (*minzu xuehui*). This contributed to a process that was intended to bring along a wave of "cultural self-consciousness" (*wenhua zijue*) of one's identity and belonging as part of the Chinese whole.[14] However, it might also factor in the sense of loss related to sinicization, as Buyi elites and cadres who themselves benefited from official education and employment have wanted to articulate their own version of Buyi history and yet have to rely on the language of dominant forces, whether Han, state, or urban.

The culture fad (*wenhua re*) that emerged during the post-Mao reform years contributed to new celebratory perspectives on China's ethnic minorities, while ethnic difference as well as ethnic tension, which had been generally suppressed during the Cultural Revolution, came into sight (Schein 2018).[15] With Tibet and Xinjiang in the spotlight, China's ethnic politics—derived from the heavy-handed repression by the Chinese state that is often equated with the Han majority—have garnered much attention.[16] On the other hand, the lived experience of many ethnic populations in less contentious regions of China, where multiethnic settlement predates and complicates the bifurcation of Han and minorities, has much to tell about the state-society relations in China's variegated peripheries. In southwestern provinces like Guizhou and Yunnan, the party-state implements government policies that accommodate the relatively diverse cultural practices of the southern minorities (McCarthy 2009; Sautman 2012). This is particularly true for ethnic groups that have had limited transborder connections or have historically never had their own state formations. The Buyi, as introduced above, are among the groups that maintained their existence in ways that were not directed at or against the domination of mainstream power structures. Buyi strive to make claims for cultural difference in a framework of "communist multiculturalism," which Susan McCarthy (2009) describes as allowing expressions of minority identity to be ways of participating in the imagined community of the nation. This has similarly taken place beyond China, as Chinese construction of identity based on the Soviet model influenced neighboring countries, such as Vietnam and Laos, where minorities are able to maintain their traditions as long as they do not pose a threat to the country's socialist progress (Michaud 2013). State-backed minority cultural expressions that include benign and aesthetic activities have been encouraged particularly for the fast-growing tourist trade; as a result, intensive marketing and self-advertising of highland identities have come to signify newness of traditions and future-oriented ethnic revivals (Wouters and Heneise 2022).

Ethnic branding, in this case, is situated in a context in which *minzu* culture has become more entangled with economic growth, deemed both a goal and a solution. Especially for areas and populations with socioeconomic disadvantages, the revival of colorful cultural forms has been directly linked to policies around poverty alleviation (*fupin*) through the profitability of culture first and foremost as tourist attraction and commodity.[17] This has given rise to a number of minority members of various social strata, ages, and genders partaking in ethnic branding. From minority intellectuals and cultural experts to uneducated villagers, they test the waters in their own ways by engaging in related businesses and cultural sectors. They collect historical artifacts or display artistic performances of their ethnic groups for knowledge production and cultural promotion, often with an economically oriented purpose. Importantly, they are at once subjected to histories of the socialist present and to market logics that encourage the pursuit of individual self-interest (Ong and Li 2008). Attempting to answer the question of who they really are, not just for their audiences but also for themselves (Meiu, Comaroff, and Comaroff 2020, 23), they often seek new ways to restore lost traditions and narrate *minzu* history in the process of fashioning a culturally marked self.

This book hence documents a moment when the state is still important but less determinant than in earlier decades as it tries to implement economic stimulus while reining in market forces that have significantly affected rural lives in early twenty-first-century China. Ethnic branding provides one of the few viable avenues to construct and maintain a state-recognized representation of minority peoples in public discourse, media, and other realms. As long as expressions and claims of cultural difference are made within the bounds of national unity (Yeh 2007, 86), the valorization of *minzu* culture is encouraged both as a new model of local governance and as a resource for new forms of capital accumulation.

As ethnic groups join the race of consumerist ladder-climbing, the challenge for contemporary Buyi, who are not known for their exoticness, becomes evident. Since the first decade of the twenty-first century, a fad of *yuanshengtai* (literally translated as "original ecology") in China's southwest, hinging on the state-market mechanism delineated above, has resulted in a range of sponsored art and media events as well as packaged commodities and experiences. Resembling core features of indigeneity, *yuanshengtai* romanticizes ethnic rural peoples as authentic and natural because of the presumably unspoiled environment in which they originated (Yu Luo 2018a, 2018b). This association of minority cultures with a pristine and idyllic rural lifestyle situated in nature-laden settings also coincides with an emphasis on environmental sustainability and attention to safeguarding intangible cultural heritage at the national, regional (East Asia), and global levels.[18] Therefore, in Guizhou's recent branding schemes, which highlight *yuanshengtai* with purportedly timeless qualities (Kendall 2019), ethnic rural peoples previously deemed primitive are now valorized as environmentally conscious and as bearers of cultural heritage. However, as we see from the Buyi case, finding *gexing* and establishing cultural claims to uniqueness are not always straightforward.

THE PARADOX OF DIFFERENCE

While culture has become a particularly important marker of *minzu* in the sense of exotic customs in contemporary southwest China (Kendall 2019), locals are finding their lives increasingly similar to the rest of the society other than the few cultural domains that mark their difference. On the one hand, the processes of nation building in China have bridged local differences and resulted in increased commonalities in lived experience

16   INTRODUCTION

and communicative practice across the country (Kipnis 2012), especially under the Xi regime, which aims at strengthening national identity and unity.[19] On the other, as Beth Notar (2006, 46) notes in her research on Dali, a well-known tourist destination in Guizhou's neighboring province of Yunnan, globalization may facilitate the promotion of cultural diversity to some extent, but it also leads consumers to sample signs of identity that are designed and circulated in more or less the same ways.[20]

Throughout my fieldwork and travel in Guizhou, I witnessed ethnic branding in many generic forms designed to generate eye-catching features with symbolic meanings: materializing ritual beliefs and creating powerful images of deities, staging song-and-dance performances for festive events, showcasing old artifacts in exhibitions, and revamping the appearance of villages. Granted, the best terrain to make claims to uniqueness and increase markers of distinction would be historically constituted cultural artifacts and practices with special environmental characteristics, based on which places can find relative advantage (Harvey 2001, 404–5). Ethnic food with particular flavors and ingredients, batik crafts with patterns meaningful to local history, and old houses built with natural materials often serve as grounds for conjuring up a sense of one-of-a-kind features originating in particular settings. This, however, inevitably leads to loci of difference in increasingly similar areas, including bodies, clothes, dance, music, narratives about the past, and whatever else might be easily recognizable as culture (Meiu, Comaroff, and Comaroff 2020, 25).

A key strategy for ethnic branding, however paradoxical, is the common practice of learning from well-publicized models to find one's own *gexing*. It seems particularly telling that local officials encouraged the Buyi to emulate the Miao example as more advanced in branding and promoting their exoticness, even though historically the Miao ranked beneath the Buyi on the ethnic hierarchy. With years of state-financed propaganda and entrepreneurial promotion, Xijiang Thousand-Household Miao Village in southeastern Guizhou has been elevated as an exemplar of ethnic rural tourism with its iconic scenery and signature performances, despite having become somewhat commercialized. Local governments thus often organized field trips for select village cadres to visit Xijiang; cadres were then to reference such model sites in developing their own. For those in Wuyang Village who visited Xijiang, the experience was unhelpful at best. While a female representative from Wuyang Village recalled that "good-looking houses" in Xijiang offered a vivid visual experience and served as a primary attraction for tourists from afar, she and other villagers felt that Xijiang was not as scenic as Wuyang Village. However, they understood that Xijiang received much state funding and was the subject of large-scale planning because of its high-profile tourist attractions and ethnic practices. The cultural object-forms of the Buyi, villagers suspected, would be far from comparable to those of the Miao, which had been recognized as heritage and developed into souvenirs, spectacles, and sites.

For the Buyi, with their relative invisibility in contemporary times, both the condition and solution of ethnic branding seem paradoxical. During my interlocutions with Buyi informants, some even suggested that the Buyi's distinctive features include their relatively high level of sinicization. This points to a philosophical paradox between timelessness and progressivism that underlies China's national history, that is, the tension between the impulse to preserve roots of cultural purity and the drive for civilizational progress (Duara 1995). Spatially speaking, this paradox—manifested and reproduced in nation building and local development—then becomes a "frontier paradox" (Oakes 2012, 321–22). In symbolic and lived forms, frontiers are both peripheral and central to the identity construction of Chineseness; they are inhabited by ethnic populations emblematic of the exotic and the traditional. Frontiers are therefore paradoxical spaces—at once sites of indigenes and processes of transforming them into civilized Chinese. In more recent times, this temporal-spatial paradox manifests in the simultaneous derogation and celebration of Guizhou's remoteness. While remoteness is often seen as a historical disadvantage, it is being recuperated in highly visual and marketable ways in an age of socio-spatial compression and increased mobility (Luo, Oakes, and Schein 2019), as

18   INTRODUCTION

those positioned as ethnically exotic and socially remote tend to catch people's attention.

The Buyi thus exemplify the state of being caught in a double bind: a situation in which one cannot guarantee winning no matter what one does, because possible paths to overcoming a dilemma compete with one another, leading to no effective resolution.[21] Juggling the urge to search for cultural purity and distinctness with the need to become and advance as modern subjects is not easy. Comparably, ethnic groups that are not considered exotic, such as the Bai in Yunnan, engage in the celebration of difference under the pressure of tourism development even when their ethno-cultural identity is relatively less available as a resource for commodification (Blum 2001; McCarthy 2009). With a relatively higher degree of acculturation brought about by the influence of Chinese ideals and national values, these minority groups must carefully build upon selective aspects for ethnic branding to function both as an expression of unique identity and as citizenship practice.

This double bind resembles what anthropologists have examined in Native American and indigenous studies as no-win situations in which indigenous peoples face the contradictions and limitations of the concept of indigeneity in development and conservation projects (Ludlow et al. 2016). Local societies often risk government intervention however they present themselves because the indigenous slot is a narrow target that is easily over- or undershot (Tania Li 2000). While the notion of indigenous peoples is not officially recognized in China, scholars have acknowledged the emergence of an indigenous space in which the concept could be relevant and may foster particular social worlds (Hathaway 2010, 2016; Yeh 2007; Yanshuo Zhang 2021). Ethnic branding involves tactics to articulate a positive presence of minority peoples and indigenous knowledge through state-endorsed means. Thus, for those engaged in ethnic branding, they can present themselves neither as too different nor as not different enough because, as Beth Conklin (1997, 723) notices in situations like this, there is a fine line "between differences that attract and differences that offend, unnerve, or threaten." Though the Buyi are not usually deemed different from the rest of the Chinese society in the latter sense, they have a hard time demonstrating the former. This predicament ensues not only from the failure to be different enough but also from the unrecognizability of their difference (Cattelino 2010), whether it is rooted in the fluid and ambivalent nature of identity or the irreconcilability between preconceived expectations about indigenous populations and their lived realities (Bunten 2018).[22]

This book thus captures a critical juncture wherein trying to be different in fact may involve similar means, and even efforts to demarcate and articulate cultural difference tend to have surprisingly generic outcomes, as locals' lived experiences are becoming increasingly similar. In the pursuit of *gexing*, the Buyi refer to modes of cultural promotion and socioeconomic development from other groups, just as they have historically thrived on cultural borrowing for their own needs. As such, processes of symbol making and identity branding for cultural promotion reveal tremendous borrowing from and mimicking of others (Tenzin 2017, 559), which indeed resemble the ways ethnic groups have interacted with each other throughout history.

Going beyond the convention of analyzing China's ethnic minorities in opposition to a Han or state counterpart, my focus on ethnic branding advances modes of thinking about ethnic cultural politics as more triangulated (Sum et al. 2022) through detailed ethnography. The construction of cultural difference entails, on the one hand, efforts to distinguish oneself from others using multifaceted reference points for contrast and, on the other hand, cross-reference and even imitation. In other words, ethnic branding is not necessarily about essence but frequently about relative difference, often by gradation—something bigger in terms of size or scale, older in terms of the historical origin claimed, or more appealing to the public gaze. Making ethnic subjects recognizable in turn means crafting *gexing* by actively assuming arbitrarily distinctive characteristics. As efforts at differentiation indeed tend to follow one of the few available paths, scholars working on other ethnic communities in China may find resonance in my depiction of the Buyi and Wuyang Village.

FIELDWORK AND ETHNOGRAPHY

Engaging with the historical experiences and contemporary lives of the Buyi, this ethnography narrates a story that is also deeply personal. My ethnic background as a Buyi, though not quite one in the eyes of villagers, offered me a particular angle from which to discuss what it means to be Buyi. At once an insider and an outsider, I myself was caught at the intersection of multiple systems of difference. In everyday practice, being Buyi is not just about how an ethnicity is branded for outsiders, but how it is negotiated in real terms — body, language, manners, and levels of familiarity or distance. Being Buyi intersects with rural-urban differentiation and other variable ways of belonging, such as gender, class, and generation. As a female researcher, I navigated a somewhat ambiguous gender role: having the ability to access male circles through a formal way of socialization, while seeking to gain a more intimate view of women, who initially tended to keep their distance.[23] As someone with an urban upbringing and higher education, I had to come to terms with my privilege and acknowledged the different lived realities separating myself from many villagers. My quest to trace my own cultural roots thus often left me in an intriguing position. My persona as a Han-mixed-with-Buyi girl (mei^1 ha^5 de^2 $?i^3$), as Buyi villagers in Wuyang referred to me, epitomizes the process of sinicization in a long history of change and continuation. Not unlike Buyi fluidity and adaptability over history, some Buyi retain connections to an increasingly distant past even as they intermarry with other local populations, move to an urban setting, and receive a state-run public education.

This book intends therefore to present not a comprehensive portrait of the Buyi but rather a particular portrayal of a Buyi village at the critical juncture of early twenty-first-century China. I am aware of how, depending on the target audience, ethnic branding simultaneously takes place on different scales in Guizhou: on village, county, and provincial levels. Hence, while my ethnographic focus is Wuyang Village, I also interweave findings from long-term research in various parts of Guizhou, both to offer a diachronic perspective on the Buyi and to situate Wuyang in a larger regional context. My use of the village (*ʔdə ʔbɐn³*) as an analytical scale is intended to reflect how villagers themselves, and even Buyi elites originally from the countryside, use it as a key reference point to make sense of their life-world (figure 1). Being mindful of the porosity and elasticity of village boundaries that are contingent on rural-urban and administrative conditions, my discussion nevertheless lends the village a conceptual consistency as an entity toward which locals' sense of belonging and affiliation remains strong. Moreover, the village is an economic-political category—similar to ethnicity—that has been objectified in the branding process.

Situated about twelve kilometers from the jurisdictional county seat of the Zhenning Buyi-Miao Autonomous County in central-western Guizhou, Wuyang Village has been foregrounded as a new cultural destination since 2010. With about two hundred households primarily consisting of eight to nine hundred Buyi, the village spreads across roughly 7.5 square kilometers, 5 percent of which is arable land. Local officials suggested that Wuyang Village used to be "a dark point under the light" (*deng xia hei*), despite its proximity to the county center—especially because the road to the village had not been properly built until recent years. But the relatively late arrival of modernization granted the newly discovered village its uniqueness. Surrounded by karst limestone hills, the village owns plots of rice paddies and sits by a meandering, crystal river. As depicted in its Buyi name, the village's terrain is like "the bottom of a pan" (figure 2). Two stone bastions on the hilltops and a stone bridge built in the late imperial period, along with old stone residences passed down by generations, have become valuable resources, according to local elites.

Wuyang Village has been attracting growing attention from provincial- and municipal-level government authorities with assistance from many well-educated villagers who have left to work as civil servants at the county level and above, and yet still express local and ethnic pride in developing their hometown. It was in this context that I met through acquaintances a Buyi intellectual from the respectable Wu lineage in Wuyang, who encouraged me to visit his natal village to conduct preliminary fieldwork in 2011. As many Wu family members were both knowledgeable and hospitable,

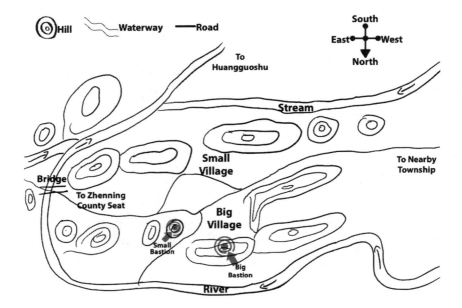

FIGURE 1. A map of Wuyang Village drawn by a male villager who had returned to Wuyang from migrant labor in August 2011, showing his perspective of the village facing south and the major sites.

I decided to return for my eighteen-month fieldwork in 2012–13, having found a host family where I could learn the Buyi language and culture and where I could help out as a fictive daughter when they cooked for occasional visitors.

Starting off as a base for the Painting and Calligraphy Academy under the provincial CPPCC (Chinese People's Political Consultative Conference), Wuyang Village has received a few awards, such as "Top 30 Charismatic Villages of Guizhou" in 2011 and a national-level "Traditional Chinese Village" in 2013.[24] While increasingly bringing in writers, artists, and photographers who seek to draw inspiration from the local natural and cultural landscapes for their works, such designations were intended to help rural communities attract funding for (agri)cultural heritage preservation, "so as to slow down the pace of destruction in the drive towards urbanization and industrialization" (China News Service 2013).

INTRODUCTION 23

FIGURE 2. Bird's-eye view of Wuyang Village taken from the Big Bastion, overlooking the Small Bastion, rows of houses, and rice fields amid karst limestone hills (2013).

Branded as the "thousand-year-old Buyi village" (*qiannian Buyi guzhai*), Wuyang was to be incorporated into the bigger picture of the county's tourism industry, connected to the nearby Huangguoshu Waterfall (about ten kilometers away), China's largest waterfall and one of the earliest tourist destinations in Guizhou. Interestingly, compared to Guizhou's eastern tourism circuit, which saw comparatively low numbers of early visitors, the western circuit, which spotlighted the Huangguoshu Waterfall, was flourishing in the mid-1980s. However, as the eastern tourism circuit became more accessible with new road networks and more known for the Miao and Dong cultures through the past couple of decades, earlier destinations on the western circuit, such as Stone Village near Huangguoshu Waterfall, were considered overcommodified and no longer attracted a great volume of tourists. Driven by the need to replenish originality, local government believed that Wuyang Village, once unknown to outsiders, could be a new highlight. As Zhenning is reportedly the only county in Guizhou inhabited by all three Buyi subdialect groups (as classified by ethnologists and linguists), some Buyi elites sought to craft Wuyang into a "capital of the Buyi" (*Buyi zhi du*), for instance, by inviting members from other subdialect groups to festive events and exhibiting their artifacts in its village museum.

While local cultural experts and media workers touted Wuyang Village as "an exemplar of Buyi culture" (*Buyi wenhua de yangben*), elites from Wuyang paradoxically referred to it as a "village of Confucian scholars" (*rulin cun*). This resulted from generations of Buyi male villagers seeking to gain upward mobility by adopting Confucian ideals, taking imperial examinations, and receiving state educations. The branding of Wuyang thus exemplifies the need to showcase the distinctiveness of Buyi culture, while it cannot avoid the relatively sinicized aspects of the historical experience of Buyi and even in locals' self-perception.

The designation of a Buyi historical village thus pinpoints the fundamental paradox of Chinese history and local development examined in previous sections. Walking a delicate line between preserving cultural purity and striving for socioeconomic progress, the village development projects seemed to hesitate over which direction to pursue. This book hence captures what local Buyi themselves perceived as their ethnic identity and cultural difference and illustrates how everyday activities and living spaces were organized or themed around ethnic branding.

In chapter 1, I offer a historical perspective to contextualize the Buyi's ethnic self-consciousness as they maintained dynamic interrelations with other groups and the powerful Han Chinese state center. Subsequent chapters turn to the various means by which local Buyi invested in ethnic branding and place branding. Chapter 2 analyzes how educated male elites sought Buyi distinctiveness by interpreting history based on Mo rituals, while the spiritual aspect is materialized into viewable artifacts—including written scripts, objects, and staged events—to demonstrate cultural difference. My focus turns in chapter 3 to female villagers as emblematic heritage bearers and targets of modernizing forces, examining how they actively engage with the domestic sphere and the public spectacles of Buyiness in the branding process. Unpacking villagers' responses to the local elite's efforts in setting up a village-based Buyi museum and museumifying the village, chapter 4 considers how the museum played both a formative and a reflexive role in collective memory and belonging, while serving as a site to welcome visitors as part of Wuyang Village's "impression management." Chapter 5 discusses infrastructure construction that affected the appearance of the village community and local landscape and unravels the paradox of developing and branding a historical village, which needed to be presented as ethnic and traditional and yet modernized all at once.

The chapters of this book piece together the tangible and intangible aspects of local Buyi cultural life, which are fashioned for image making and identity construction. In search of markers of cultural difference, local Buyi also strive to secure economic means and make sense of themselves. As ethnic branding becomes an affective anchor for identity, Wuyang Village may not be a unique case. The bittersweet story of the Buyi in contemporary China illustrates the aspirations, and challenges, of ethnic populations that have been caught in a double bind.

CHAPTER ONE

BECOMING BUYI IN A MULTIETHNIC HINTERLAND

UNCLE KUAN STRODE INTO the courtyard of my host family, whose Wu lineage he shares. Held in his hand was a piece of paper printed with the lyrics for the 1982 song "Inter-Ethnic Unity as Hundred Blossoms":

Socialism is as exuberant as a flower in blossom. . . .
Thanks to the Communist Party's leadership,
the Buyi and the Miao and the Han all enjoy our blissful lives.
. . . Especially as the state has recently opened up,
everyone becomes friends and family, just like blossoming flowers. . . .
The Han and the Miao open hearts to each other,
while we Buyi are among the first who build homes to settle down, before working and earning money.
. . . The Miao watch TV and learn skills; we Buyi understand new technologies even earlier through reading books, watching news and videos. . . .
The Han and the Buyi side by side, foreign tourists are amazed by such harmony. . . .
Vines and branches intertwine, fifty-six *minzu* [ethnic groups] of our whole nation unite to be strong, fifty-six flowers blooming across the whole world.
Generations of descendants from the Yellow Emperor live happily ever after as brothers and sisters.[1]

For the three weeks since I had first settled in Wuyang Village, he had regularly shared with me songs that, he thought, captured well the Buyi lifestyle and mindset. My presence, especially during those initial days of fieldwork, intrigued villagers like Uncle Kuan, who had been willing to help me learn the Buyi language and culture. Other than words like "socialism" or "TV news," most of the Chinese characters printed on this piece of paper did not make sense to me. Later on, I learned that it is a common practice among the literate Buyi to borrow Han characters with similar phonetics to record the Buyi language, which lacks a writing system but is a fundamental vehicle for rituals, singing, and everyday practices.

As I invited him to sit down in the central room of the old stone house, Uncle Kuan explained the origin of the song before translating it into standard Chinese. Reprinted in 2012 on the piece of paper he brought me, the song was composed in the early 1980s to celebrate the twentieth anniversary of the establishment of the Zhenning Buyi-Miao Autonomous County with jurisdiction over Wuyang Village. Uncle Kuan said that the survey team under the County Minzu Affairs Committee consulted him at the time, as he had some experience assisting itinerant art troupes. The year 1982 was also significant for *minzu* affairs and cultural revivals in Guizhou, at the dawn of China's Reform and Opening Up after Mao's demise.[2] Governmental offices were established to survey minority languages and literature and produce sociohistorical profiles of minority regions, while sports events and cultural performances, by a conglomerate of minority groups, were first held at the provincial level.[3] The metaphor of blooming flowers in the song, which still appears in official rhetoric today, not only signifies a time of post-Mao cultural revival but also arguably carries a trace of Mao's Hundred Flowers campaign (1956–57), which brought a brief period of liberalization, encouraging open expression of public opinion as well as new forms of art and cultural institutions to promote socialism.[4]

The explanation of this song Uncle Kuan subsequently offered was, however, more than a narrative of state building and nationalism. He specifically stressed what could be roughly translated as the "ethnocentrism" (*benwei zhuyi*) of the Buyi.[5] Despite the premise of unity and equality among all *minzu*, he pointed out that the Buyi composer, with an "egocentric motive," failed to elevate the status of other ethnic groups. "We have to demonstrate the awareness, heroism, and pride of the Buyi. But it is also a fact!" The Buyi, in Uncle Kuan's description, had been ahead of others and more advanced in "evolutionistic" terms. "We Buyi are good at learning new agricultural technologies and machineries, at accepting new crop species and manures. The Buyi were among the first who became friends with the Han, even before the Maoist era. We are always ahead of the Miao and able to understand the intentions of the central authority in advance. We have strong adaptability, often deploying new skills for our own use."[6]

This song, as Uncle Kuan implied, reveals the Buyi's self-perception and subjectivity to a certain extent. As one "blooming flower" among many, the Buyi have grown out of a multiplicity of identities and cultures, and yet their "vines and branches" are wrapped around a solid core: the dominant Chinese state. While marching forward with the rest of the nation, many Buyi see themselves as more advanced than other ethnic groups and on good terms with the majority Han. However, being advanced and being able to catch up with the times might be a conundrum for the Buyi in an age of ethnic branding that favors distinctive cultural character.

To understand ethnic branding that turns local lives into something discernible for their own benefit and for others' consumption, we first need to unravel ethnic formation that is not about the true essence of identity but is rather a situational paradigm intersecting with a variety of regional and local identities (Joniak-Lüthi 2013). The ways local actors navigate sociopolitical conditions over time have been fundamental in molding the consciousness and subjectivity of contemporary Chinese ethnic groups. This chapter offers a historical perspective about how ethnicity in China took place through different time periods based on the Buyi case, closely engaging with locally produced Chinese scholarship and literature, especially Buyi scholars' interpretations and oral history.

First, as the lyrics that Uncle Kuan shared with me suggest, the *minzu* scheme of which the label Buyi is a part has profoundly influenced various domains of everyday life. As the product of a Soviet-style classification project, these arbitrary identity categories "have entered not only into scholarship and tourism promotion, . . . but also into school curricula and ordinary journalistic discourse," and this kind of social construction is nevertheless "real for most of the participants, though they may disagree about the details" (Harrell 2001a, 153). In this sense, ethnicity is a process of becoming that is neither evanescent nor permanent and that is neither entirely political nor purely economic (Chua 2007). Buyi, like many other minority groups in China, have experienced and perceived the continuity and change from the socialist-era *minzu* scheme that set the tone for ethnic categories to the post-Mao reforms, which accentuate cultural difference.

Ethnicity in the longue durée, moreover, involves both incorporation and exclusion, in a context where various local populations have interacted with each other within one group (those identified as Buyi) and between ethnic groups (such as with Han and Miao). Through cross-ethnic engagement and intercultural interaction in contemporary China, ethnic othering is made even less determinate as boundaries continue to be erected, transgressed, and eroded (Schein and Luo 2016). The Buyi's self-perception and positioning in a multiethnic landscape keep shaping their ethnic branding in a way that suggests China's ethnic minorities do not exist in simple opposition to a Han or state counterpart but in a complex of historical, spatial, and linguistic interactions among intersecting social groups.

A LAND OF INTRICACY AND OPENNESS

China's southwestern borderland, which neighbors Southeast Asia, is known as an area where dense mountains and deep valleys overlap with the shared borders of administrative units at multiple levels. The Buyi people, spreading across southwest China and northwest Vietnam today, mostly inhabit regions near the Beipan (North Pan) and Nanpan (South Pan) Rivers, which are branches of the West River, itself the western tributary of the Pearl River. The Beipan and Nanpan Rivers flow along part of the southern border of Guizhou, first established as a provincial unit under the Ming regime in 1413. This region occupies the heavily eroded limestone highlands of the eastern Yun-Gui Plateau, which separates the fertile Sichuan basin to the north from the low plains of Guangxi to the south.[7] The heartland of the Buyi people, Guizhou is a landlocked region without any international border, and it has been notably considered more socially and economically remote than its contiguous provinces, given its impoverished agrarian sector combined with recalcitrant topography and limited accessibility (Schein 2014; Luo, Oakes, and Schein 2019).

Its challenging landscape, however, did not prevent Guizhou from becoming one of the dynamic contact zones on late imperial China's frontier (Giersch 2006). Despite its perceived remoteness, Guizhou became the thoroughfare and passageway that functioned as a switching point connecting the interior heartland to farther reaches of southwest China (Luo, Oakes, and Schein 2019, 271–72). Zhenning County in central-western Guizhou, my location of focus, is situated along a key passage zone with relatively easy accessibility. Here, coiled rivers open up into small basins amid clusters of limestone hills; this is where military and civilian troops were first dispatched by the imperial courts to pacify and incorporate the borderlands.[8] Hence, these areas have historically linked parts of southwest China through courier routes, as well as trade and migration, which have more recently witnessed rapid transformations brought about by urbanization and road-railway networks.

Mosaic geographical regions as such—where continual formation, disruption, and remaking of ethnic boundaries take place and where a number of intermingled non-Han inhabitants still remain unidentifiable—contributed to the ambiguity and fluidity of many local populations. First, ethnic identities of various local peoples, including those who later took on *minzu* labels, such as the Miao and the Buyi, have been complicated by constant interactions, migrations, intermarriages, and insurgencies for centuries.[9] Second, according to major scholarly discourse (Holm 2003; Weinstein 2014), the forebears of present-day Buyi—far from being a monolithic group—belonged to the proto-Tai peoples and originated from the ancient Hundred Yue (*Baiyue*) tribes, who were regarded as the indigenes of southern China. Even the ethnonym "Buyi" (*pu³ ʔi³*), which is

TABLE 1. Ethnohistorical terminology for local populations related to the Buyi

Groups considered as precedent to the Buyi[1]	Groups recorded in Buyi ritual scripts[2]	Groups described in local oral history (in Pinyin)
Zhongjia	$pu^3 ?i^3$ (autonym)	Buna
Bunayi	$pu^3 ha^5$ (modern-day Han)	Bunong
Bunongyi	$pu^3 jiu^2$ (modern-day Miao)	Buyai
Shuijia	$pu^3 zu\eta^2$ (modern-day Gelao)	Buman
Zhuang	$pu^3 mia\eta^2$ (modern-day Yi)	Buguang

Notes: 1. Chen (1942) 2004a, 79–80. 2. Wu Zhonggang and Wu Kaifeng 2014.

both an endonym used by the Buyi to refer to themselves and an exonym coined by ethnolinguists based on self-appellations in 1953 for the official *minzu* category, exemplifies the intricacy of this ethnicity. While "Bu" (pu^3) is a prefix used for most human-denominating vocabularies in the Buyi language, the second syllable, "yi" ($?i^3$)—which has more internal variations in pronunciation among subdialect groups—might correspond to a general signifier of numerous "barbaric" others at the peripheries in standard Chinese.[10] Other categorizations of the Buyi's supposed forebears during various periods of imperial China, like *Bafan* or *Zhongjia* (Li Hanlin 2001; Yang Tingshuo and Pan Shengzhi 2004), make the case even more perplexing. Table 1, for instance, offers a nonexhaustive list of ethnonyms related to Buyi and their adjacent groups that I found in pre-socialist archives, Buyi ritual scripts, and local oral histories. It demonstrates a complex set of ethnohistoric terminologies that related and differentiated local identities.

Most accounts of the Buyi's forebears (named Zhongjia in late imperial China, between the seventeenth and nineteenth centuries) appeared in official archives either in relation to criminal activities or uprisings (Weinstein 2014) or in the "Miao Albums," a set of illustrations that included them as classified natives (Hostetler 2001).[11] Few existing records were written and maintained by the ethnic populations themselves. To discover their own voices, local Buyi intellectuals have been paying great attention to one

32 CHAPTER ONE

key genre in recent decades: Mo ritual scriptures recorded with borrowed and modified Chinese characters in accordance with oral mantras at Buyi life-cycle ceremonies, especially during burials to guide the lost souls home (see chapter 2).[12] Through members of the elite Wu family from Wuyang Village who worked for the county government, I was introduced to a Wu brother who was revising his book manuscript about the Buyi people in Zhenning County, which had been published in 2014.

He summarized the text "Ritual Ceremony for the Dead" (*Gu xie jing* in Chinese), which sheds light on the context of the history of the present-day Buyi through coexistence with others as "ethnic harmony and fusion [*minzu ronghe*] rather than conflict."[13] The ritual script includes records of how the Buyi's early ancestors befriended other ethnicities through reciprocal exchanges: for instance, using bamboo rain hats that the Buyi ancestors were skilled at weaving as gifts (Wu Zhonggang and Wu Kaifeng 2014). These gifts were given to groups that may correspond to the present-day Han ($pu^3 ha^5$) and the Yi ($pu^3 miaŋ^2$), who returned gifts of sunflower stems used to start fires. When Buyi ancestors handed over the rain hats, the forebears of the Miao ($pu^3 jiu^2$) reciprocated with musk. Mutual borrowing and exchange also appeared in home-making skills (perhaps the "blueprint of house building"). The Buyi's ancestors learned these skills from others, which allowed them to move from natural caves and crude huts made from banana leaves, reeds, and straw to improved accommodations. They also passed these skills on to the Miao and other groups.[14]

The specific ecological niches inhabited by local populations ultimately underlie such cultural interactions and resulting relational contexts, forging "an economic integration driven by complementarity" (Scott 2009, 99). Centuries of coexistence in this multiethnic mosaic gave rise to a variety of ethnicities, who were stereotyped as rice planters, herders, swidden farmers, hunters, and gatherers who, in turn, benefited from various cyclical markets and trade gatherings (Yang Tingshuo 1995). The metaphoric growth of the flower in Uncle Kuan's song captures the interwoven stems and roots from which the Buyi, like many others, emerge and flourish. This constant process of shaping and becoming has thus allowed the possibility of hybrid livelihood strategies and permeable boundaries that bridge ethnicities.

Situated in a dynamic multiethnic context, the stereotype of the waterside Buyi historically characterized and continually affects the Buyi's group identity. This image derived from the group's tendency to reside near rivers and its long-term practice of rice paddy cultivation, resembling that of many Tai-speaking populations. Often situated in flat valleys and small basins with fertile soils and adequate water sources, many villages of the Buyi's forebears were perhaps more accessible and closer than other hill tribes to the newly arrived Han settlements dispatched by late imperial authorities aiming to reclaim land (*tuntian*) and civilize non-Han populations.[15] From the perspective of the imperial state, such sedentarized agriculture and livelihoods were ideal for population control and taxation.[16] According to both oral and written history, local ethnic populations like the Buyi's forebears actually assisted the Han migrants in settling down by teaching them how to farm the precious soils, deploying their accumulated skills and local experience (Aibida [1752] 2006, 4).

Somewhat different from the independent kingdom-making Tai groups at the Sino–Southeast Asian borderlands, the more scattered forebears of the present-day Buyi maintained a smattering of micro-regimes, or what historian Jodi Weinstein calls "semi-state spaces" (2014, 40), which had a less centralized power structure. Semi-state spaces differed from state spaces, which were lowland areas with an established state administration, and from non-state spaces in upland areas with no centralized polities at all (such as the Miao heartlands of southeastern Guizhou). In semi-state spaces, there were native officials and some regular administrative units, which were nonetheless targeted for standardization and centralization by increasing demand of the late imperial authority.[17]

Intensive cultural borrowing between various groups and strategic interactions with the imperial regimes thus produced a range of in-between or intermediary non-Han groups along the spectrum from uncivilized to civilized (Blum 2001; Hostetler 2001; Tenzin 2017). The forebears of the Buyi are believed to have maintained social structures and cultural practices similar

34   CHAPTER ONE

to the Han. In official writings dating from the mid-eighteenth century, the attire and customs of male Buyi forebears were almost no different from those of ordinary Han.[18] These changes may have also helped the Buyi's forebears to protect themselves from violent extermination, like that which had taken place in some parts of the "Miao" frontier (as a generic metonym for "barbarians," historical usage of "Miao" in popular and official discourse was closely associated to "*man*," denoting the southern tribes). By learning and borrowing Han words and characters, the forebears of the Buyi, who did not have their own script, were able to record their ritual texts and genealogies.[19] As bilingual peoples, some males also benefited from commercial exchanges and encounters with imperial elite. The oral history of the elite Wu family in Wuyang Village suggests that the family's ancestors had actively improved their Chinese language and Confucian learning for generations, and that, through this improvement, they became local gentry and achieved higher ranks in military and civil examinations.[20] By the early half of the twentieth century, scholars had observed such hybridization in Guizhou: "The Yi (夷) [present-day Buyi] are indeed more affluent than the Miao, and their education level is slightly higher than other natives; furthermore, many Han residing on riverside plains have intermarried with the Yi [Buyi]. Such hybridization naturally resulted in the increasing phenomenon of Han becoming Yi [Buyi; *hanren yihua*] and Yi [Buyi] becoming Han [*yiren hanhua*]" (Chen [1942] 2004b, 77).[21]

Starting out as "treacherous barbarians" who often carried sharp weapons, the Buyi's forebears had gradually "advanced toward culture" (*xianghua*) by adopting Han customs and respecting the law in the eyes of the central authorities (Aibida [1752] 2006, 223; see also Hostetler 2001, 151). In turn, the Buyi's forebears were historically more proactive in, rather than resistant to, the ways they interacted with and attached to the center. They tended to follow sociopolitical currents on their own terms, "always ahead of others," as proclaimed in the lyrics Uncle Kuan showed me. Such historical fluidity and hybridity, of which local ethnic populations had taken advantage, underwent transformations brought about by the socialist state.

COMING TO TERMS WITH SOCIALIST TRANSFORMATIONS AS BUYIZU

During the turbulent years of the early twentieth century, the political economies of Zhenning County and its neighboring regions were affected by various warlord and rebel forces, many of which took advantage of either the affluence brought by constant trade and transportation by horse and barge or the rugged terrain, which was easier to defend than to conquer. The Red Army of the Communist Party reached the county's dense mountainous regions, mostly inhabited by non-Han populations, during the Long March in 1935. Over the subsequent decade, the Red Army consolidated power by persuasively cooperating with local military groups who had had unfortunate encounters with the Nationalist forces and also by establishing underground guerrillas (Chen, Yan, and Ma 2008, 17; Wu Zhongshi 2014). Leaders of local ethnic groups who adopted revolutionary ideology and assisted the Communist regime have been closely linked to glorious depictions of Zhenning's history ever since.

After the People's Liberation Army (PLA) took over Zhenning in November 1949, ethnic minority issues were immediately brought into focus to facilitate the consolidation of political power. The coming to terms of local populations hence transpired during the socialist-era *minzu* classification in the early 1950s, which was the most sweeping attempt to ethnologically sort out the enormous population of the nascent People's Republic by drawing on earlier Republican-era scholarship and using the Soviet model for reference (Mullaney 2010). The Soviet model, based on Joseph Stalin's (1913) considerations of the nation and the USSR's ensuing policies, served as a template for the strategies of alliance during the 1930s between the Communist Party and minority groups whose support was essential to ensure victory over Nationalist forces (Michaud 2013). To continue fulfilling the agenda of letting the minority peoples "be their own masters" (*zuo ziji de zhuren*), which was meant to attract local revolutionary forces before the establishment of the People's Republic, more than two hundred non-Han

36   CHAPTER ONE

representatives were asked to attend a conference in Zhenning to endorse the new regime in January 1950 (Chen, Yan, and Ma 2008, 21). Between 1950 and 1953, besides implementing provisional plans such as brigand cleansing and land reform, a series of efforts were made to identify ethnic categories and promote training of select minority cadres (Zhenning Buyizu Miaozu Zizhixianzhi Bianzuan Weiyuanhui 2009, 160–63).

Notably, interactions between the national and the local formed an important part of the intellectual history of Zhenning. In November and December of 1950, the renowned scholar Fei Xiaotong led the third team of the Central Nationality Delegation's Southwest China Visiting Mission (Zhongyang Minzu Fangwen Tuan Xinan Fangwentuan Disan Fentuan) to Guizhou, with an underlying agenda to enhance the unity and equality of all ethnicities (Zhenning Buyizu Miaozu Zizhixian Gaikuang Bianxiezu 1985). The delegation, first and foremost, consulted with minority elites who possessed local knowledge and were familiar with sociopolitical networks on the ground, before holding symposia and gatherings to convey greetings to local minorities. The Wu brothers from Wuyang Village remembered that their mother, a respected teacher in Zhenning at the time, was consulted by Tian Shulan. Tian was an ethnologist in the delegation that visited the Biandanshan (Biandan Mountain) area near the Zhenning county seat, who was knowledgeable about southern China's ethnicities, including the Zhuang and the Li (Wu Zhonggang and Wu Kaifeng 2014).[22] The visiting mission also organized exhibitions, film screenings, and art performances, inviting minority peoples to sing and dance together, as ways of harmonizing the multiethnic relations that had lasted to the present day.

A pressing concern for the central government at the time was to reach a consensus on the identification and categorization of various ethnic groups, using the Stalinist model of defining nationalities (*minzu*) based on four common criteria—territory, language, economy, and psychological nature (Gros 2004; Mullaney 2010). Until the early 1950s, minorities around the Zhenning area were vaguely referred to as the Miao, the Hui, and the Yi; according to Fei Xiaotong (1951), the Yi (夷) was a confused mix of the Zhongjia (the Buyi's antecedents) and other groups. In Republican-era surveys written by fieldworkers in ethnology and sociology, groups related to the present-day Buyi included what were called Bunayi, Bunongyi, Zhongjia, Shuijia, and Zhuang at the time, and several of these groups appeared to live in proximity to one another in Zhenning (Chen [1942] 2004a, 79–80).

After a couple of years of ethnolinguistic and social survey, data collection, and interactive negotiation, a special meeting of the Guizhou Nationalities Affairs Commission convened and decided to use the autonym "Buyi" for the group's name after considering at least twenty other names (Mullaney 2010, 111–12). In 1953, the Buyizu became one of the first thirty-eight minority nationality groups identified by the socialist state. Meanwhile, encompassing the Buyi, Han, Miao, and Gelao populations (Wu Zhongshi 2014, 78), the Biandanshan Yi (夷) Autonomous District—Zhenning's first minority autonomous administrative unit—changed its name to the Biandanshan Buyi Autonomous District. The Biandanshan area in which Wuyang Village is located became a prototype for researching the Buyi (or more precisely, one particular subgroup of the Buyi), which made up over 60 percent of the local population (Guizhou Liushan Liushui Buyizu Juan et al. 2008).

In the following decade, after the local administration shifted between different prefectural and municipal jurisdictions, Zhenning was eventually established as a Buyi-Miao autonomous county in 1963, designating these two groups as the predominant non-Han populations.[23] In Guizhou and across China's ethnic peripheries, a number of autonomous units were established on multiple administrative levels from prefecture to township starting in the 1950s and 1960s, in order to fulfill the state's promise to guarantee cultural freedom and rights to minorities and provide them with economic aid.[24] New dispensations, preferential benefits, and substantial advantages were given to ethnic minorities under the new *minzu* policy, including new political and administrative posts as well as preferential access to technical schools and higher education (Kaup 2000). Thus, an increasing number of minority cadres were trained in government-organized sessions, and public education in minority areas was promoted through both elementary and middle schools during the early 1950s (Chen, Yan, and Ma 2008, 327; Wu Zhongshi 2014, 80). A few families from Wuyang Village recalled how their earlier generations had greatly benefited from such policies as they received education and promotion in the local bureaucracy. These schemes, intending to make local populations legible (Scott 1998), entailed labeling these *minzu* categories — "blossoming flowers" under socialism — as an inherently politicized project in relation to Chinese nation building.

It is noteworthy that, even though "Buyi" is the only state-recognized and most commonly used ethnonym, the internal differentiation among the Buyi still remains. Despite their depiction as a riverside ethnicity in popular discourse, scholars have discussed how the Buyi historically classified themselves according to the quality and elevation of the land they farmed (Weinstein 2014, 22), similar to the ecological and ethnic stratifications described in Edmund Leach's (1954) classic study of mainland Southeast Asia. Lowland dwellers among the Buyi (also transcribed as Bouyeix) were often called "people of the rice paddies" (Bouxnaz), a name that differentiated them from "people beyond the rice paddies" (Bouxnongz) and "people of the hills" (Bouxloeh) (Holm 2003, 9; see also Zhou Guoyan 1996).[25] These autonyms were relational terms that reflected how people conceived of themselves in contradistinction to other nearby groups. Terms such as these might provide "badges of self-identity" (Holm 2003, 9), but they do not necessarily imply any real sense of primordial or monolithic ethnic solidarity.

In Zhenning, ethnonyms such as "Buna" (Bouxnaz) and "Bunong" (Bouxnongz) are still used by local Buyi to differentiate among themselves according to variance in geographical location and language.[26] A local saying goes, "those living farther up are Buna, those farther down are Bunong." Besides the conception of altitude in the interior of hilly regions, up ($kən^2$) and down (la^3) are also correlated to north and south in Zhenning. The altitude indeed follows a descending pattern from the north down to the south, though the terrain in the south is more rugged with denser mountains. As a rule of thumb, Buna inhabit the upper region (*shangmian*), whereas Bunong are people living downward (*xiamian*), but these are inherently relative terms (map 2). One could be a Bunong as opposed to those living farther up and also a Buna to those even farther down.

Linguistically, the Bunong's pronunciation is thought to be duller and murkier compared to the Buna's clearer pronunciation. Someone "talking like a Bunong" would sound unclear or inarticulate for some Buna. Based on distinctions drawn by linguists, the Buyi residing in the area near the Zhenning county seat—that is, the upper mountain region (*shang shanqu*)—belong to the third subdialect zone (*di san tuyuqu*). The area immediately to its south is referred to as the central mountain region (*zhongbu shanqu*) and the second subdialect zone (*di'er tuyuqu*) of Buyi. And the southernmost part of Zhenning is the lower mountain region (*xia shanqu*) closest to the Buyi hinterland, which is the first subdialect zone (*di yi tuyuqu*) (Zhenning Buyizu Miaozu Zizhixian Gaikuang Bianxiezu 1985, 9–10).

For Wuyang villagers who reside close to the county seat, an unfamiliarity with Bunong is evident in stories told by older generations about how the Bunong were—and even are still—capable of poisoning people without notice. Narratives concerning poison in the minority regions of Guizhou have been common, deriving from climatic, sanitary, and psychological factors (Chen [1938] 2004; Guang [1940] 2004; Li Zhiren [1941] 2004); the discourse of poison has a powerfully othering effect and signifies interethnic relations in the Chinese borderlands (Diamond 1988; Wang Ming-ke 2003).[27] The area surrounding the current Zhenning county seat has benefited from contiguous land allowing wet-rice cultivation amid hills.[28] But farther south, where the terrain is more crisscrossed by mountains and humidity envelops river valleys, malaria and miasma were once prevalent—a likely origin of the poison narratives. For those in Wuyang Village, the Bunong live in unfamiliar (and possibly more primitive) environments and farther from the cultural, economic, and political center of the administrative county. The Buyi thus envision remoteness among themselves not only in spatiotemporal terms but also as relational categories to differentiate groups.

As various local groups were unified into one *minzu* category—the Buyizu—based on similar ethnolinguistic and socioeconomic traits through the

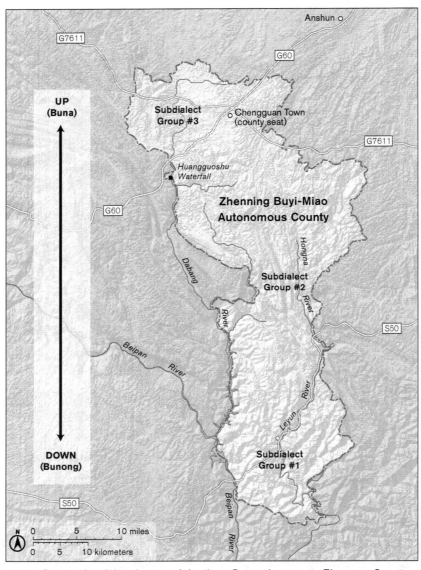

MAP 2. Geographical distribution of the three Buyi subgroups in Zhenning County.

Mao-era survey and census described earlier, local government attempted to standardize the Buyi language and even provide a written script, which was nonexistent before (Zhou Guoyan 2008, 144). A retired governmental staff member from the Wu lineage who returned to Wuyang Village, described his experience:

> When I was working for the Zhenning County Bureau of Education, I was dispatched to Guiyang [the provincial capital] and Duyun [the prefectural capital of Qiannan in southern Guizhou] for Buyi language and script training. It was during the late 1950s, when the provincial authority was trying to popularize the newly invented script based on the Latin alphabet.[29] They even edited a dictionary with Chinese vocabulary and Buyi pronunciations.
>
> It was at that time *when I realized that there was only one united group named the Buyi.* Some of my colleagues during the training came from Wangmo and Luodian [two counties in southern Guizhou]. At first, I could not understand a word they were saying. But later, through training, I have grown to realize that there were merely some differences in pronunciation and intonation between various Buyi subgroups. The Bunong just speak more softly than us Buna. I also knew that there was some mention of uniting the Buyi and the Zhuang, since some Zhuang speak and live the same way as we Buyi do.[30]

As recounted by this Wuyang resident, the state has worked toward clarifying groupness, despite nuanced differences, and consolidating ethnic boundaries over the socialist era, which in turn was internalized by local minorities. A crucial component for the local government has thus always been to identify and promote educational and cultural works by studying minority languages and scripts, collecting folkloric literature and storytelling, and developing sports activities in accordance with the *minzu* categories (Zhenning Buyizu Miaozu Zizhixianzhi Bianzuan Weiyuanhui 2009, 160–63).

Paradoxically, the alliances between the Buyi and the Zhuang (*Bu Zhuang lianmeng*) mentioned by the informant above — which lasted from 1956

42 CHAPTER ONE

to 1981, when uniform romanized scripts using the Latin alphabet were created for the two highly similar languages—implicitly undermine the effectiveness and authority of clear-cut *minzu* categories. As a northern geographical and linguistic extension of the Zhuang in Guangxi, the Buyi are historically inseparable and frequently difficult to differentiate from the Zhuang, the largest non-Han (and Tai-speaking) population in China today (Kaup 2000; Michaud, Barkataki-Ruscheweyh, and Swain 2016). Local and central authorities decided in the early 1950s that the Tai-speaking peoples of northern and southern Guangxi would all be identified as Zhuangzu, despite the apparent lack of internal cohesion and the known connections of those in northern Guangxi to the Buyi.[31] Katherine Kaup (2000) explains that the division between the Zhuang and the Buyi was largely determined by Guangxi-Guizhou boundaries, as *minzu* classification took place in strict accordance with provincial jurisdictions. Immediate family members in some cases were identified as two separate *minzu* if they straddled the provincial border, while Buyi and Zhuang intellectuals may stress the reified ethnic groups as distinct even though they know about the similarities in language and culture (Kaup 2000; Weinstein 2014).

In a nutshell, the case of the Buyi exemplifies how the socialist state of the Mao era hoped to label populations into their respective niches in relation to a centralized political economy administered by a party bureaucracy. Local Buyi continue to subtly negotiate their identities based on the Buna-Bunong differentiation, even though they share certain commonalities in cultural tradition and have had increasing interactions through employment and intermarriage. Zhenning's Buyi officials, in fact, proudly acclaim that it is the only county in Guizhou with populations from all three Buyi subdialect groups. However, at public spectacles that project the state's rhetoric of "unity in diversity" onto a localized setting, either all the Buyi subgroups mingle into one or members of different subgroups take part in showcasing different dimensions that are deemed integral to the Buyi culture. The *minzu* categories, as part of a political apparatus that has established the foundation for shaping the social landscape and cultural

BECOMING BUYI   43

life of modern-day China, were thus naturalized to administratively and ideologically define local societies and populations.[32]

LANGUAGE OF CHANGE AND LOSS

In rural communities, the establishment of the *minzu* scheme was accompanied by a series of socialist transformations through which the Chinese state sought to secure control over local populations. Fei Xiaotong (1951, 37–48) notes that, rather than being egalitarian, there was evident social stratification according to landed property and production relations among the Buyi before socialist reforms. As the Buyi had resided by fertile, irrigated fields, a landlord-tenant system was commonly practiced in agricultural production throughout Zhenning. To carry out the nationwide campaign to introduce collective land ownership, representatives of landlords and tenants were hence invited to a people's representative conference at the county level in the early 1950s (Wu Zhongshi 2014, 78). They subsequently became subject to the 1950–51 land reform and ensuing collectivization (Zhenning Buyizu Miaozu Zizhixianzhi Bianzuan Weiyuanhui 2009), along with other members of agrarian communities.

The elite Wu family's experience during the socialist years epitomized local maneuvers and struggles intertwined with the powerful state-making process. Earlier generations of the Wu family pursued Confucian learning and attempted the civil service examinations, sometimes earning prestige as literati, which was closely linked to imperial power and the formation of a local elite over time.[33] In the late imperial and Republican eras, elder members of the family had assumed critical roles as the headmen of the patriarchal system and as prominent figures in local ritual and political domains. The great-grandfather of the Wu brothers was a renowned member of the local gentry who was often invited by imperial officials and literati to nearby townships as a prestigious guest. Their father started his teaching career in the county's elementary schools after graduating from an educational institution established during the Republican era at the Zhenning county seat. The family in turn inherited a large amount of arable land and hired farmers to tend to their agricultural production.

During the land reform under Mao, land confiscated from former landlords and rich peasants was redistributed to tenants and smallholders. While the Wu family could have easily been categorized as landlords and become a target of the socialist reforms, they escaped the otherwise brutal fate thanks to a local district chief who designated the Wu family as rich peasants because the Wu father was a full-time teacher and the family maintained cordial relationships with various Wuyang villagers. A few years later, as collectivization began, residents of Wuyang Village were divided into four agricultural production teams on the basis of kinship relations of the Wu and the Yang lineages. Elder males of the clans were assigned to be heads of the production teams. This division is still used during village meetings for mobilization purposes in contemporary times.

The Wu family, however, was not able to avoid the turmoil of the Cultural Revolution (1966–76). When the Destroy the Four Olds and Establish the Four New campaign (Po Sijiu, Li Sixin)—which targeted ideas, cultures, customs, and habits—swept the country in 1966, intense surveillance and destruction alarmed the father of the Wu brothers, who immediately returned to the family's old house in Wuyang Village. The family either burned or buried anything suggestive of aristocratic and superstitious manners, from literati outfits to ritual scripts. Among countless old relics, an ancestral altar and delicate woodcarvings from their roof were destroyed for the sake of self-protection. As much entrenched as the still visible "Quotations from Chairman Mao" painted on the outer walls of Wuyang's old stone houses, a sense of guilt for these actions has been rooted in the Wu family's hearts ever since. This traumatic experience later motivated many local elites to revive traditional Buyi culture and to invest in salvaging and reinventing traditions, especially rituals and artifacts, in the post-Mao reform era.

The drive to revive ethnic traditions was also spurred on by national-level policy changes and attempts by the then leadership to take *minzu* issues seriously. In the late 1970s and early 1980s, the socialist state turned to

Reform and Opening Up policies and encouraged cultural revivals. The post-Mao era in turn witnessed the confluence of an (un)self-conscious resurgence of cultural practices among local peoples and deliberate promotion of such practices by state organs, along with economic reform and cultural liberalization (Schein 1989, 199). In propaganda brochures and at public spectacles, images of the Buyi have thus been integral to demonstrating the Zhenning county government's efforts to develop local *minzu* industries such as handicrafts and specialty liquor, as well as valorizing cultural traditions. At minority festivals, such as the annual Buyi event on the sixth day of the sixth month of the lunar calendar (Liuyueliu) in 1984, the advantages of *minzu* policies and autonomous regions were showcased through symposia and performances (Chen, Yan, and Ma 2008, 330).

Provincial to county-level governments also set up professional and academic organizations, such as *minzu xuehui* or associations for *minzu* studies, for each officially designated *minzu* category. In 1988, the same year that members of the Miao intelligentsia convened the inaugural meeting of the Guizhou Miao Studies Association (Schein 2000, 229), the Guizhou Buyi Studies Association was established. Many members of this semigovernmental association were officials, scholars, and journalists who were trained as minority cadres and intellectuals during the socialist era. The process of knowledge production regarding minority groups and their cultures, therefore, has strong associations with China's political structure and agenda.

The idea that attachment to the center and to mainstream culture has historically improved the Buyi's social, economic, and political status has had a contemporary reincarnation. The Buyi have kept pace with large-scale processes of change, shown by, for example, the relatively high level of literacy among the Buyi nowadays and the large proportion of Buyi migrants who increasingly stay in coastal provinces. However, times of change and uncertainty have also brought forth a discourse and sentiment concerning sinicization (*hanhua*)—becoming more like Han—which is prevalent among the Buyi today. Triggered by an identity crisis resulting from Western imperialism in the early twentieth century, sinicization was

46   CHAPTER ONE

a nationalist attempt to reinforce Chinese culturalism and state integration wrapped around a solid Han core (Leibold 2007, 5, 21–22). But in China's southwestern peripheries, the term was closely associated with historical memories of imperial expansion and moral transformation with the aim of acculturation to Han Chinese culture or assimilation by it. This induced a widespread concern over cultural change and identity loss among the Buyi in the seemingly inevitable process of becoming Han and progress toward modernity. The historical description of the Buyi in archives that they had "adhered to Han customs and gradually changed their original Buyi habits" (Zhongguo Difangzhi Jicheng Bianji Gongzuo Weiyuanhui [1948] 2006, 13502) may have delighted the state because of its civilizing mission, but may not hold the same meaning for the Buyi, especially in the contemporary context.

In a discussion I had in November 2013 with several male villagers about whether the Buyi would become sinicized, a retired elementary school teacher in his sixties who had returned to Wuyang Village to monitor the construction of his family's new concrete house expressed his idea in a teleological way: "Buyi culture will gradually disappear, though it is hard to estimate when that happens. Maybe several centuries from now, but within the next one hundred years it will be okay."

"Well, not only us, but the Miao will also face the same situation," another elderly male villager added. Sitting next to us and watching television news, he had overheard our conversation in the semipublic space of the sole store in Wuyang Village, owned by a family that left its door open, beckoning passersby inside. "We have lots of new vocabulary words, like 'socialism,' 'television,' 'refrigerator,' etc. These are all in standard Chinese. These words do not contain Buyi culture."

Slightly disagreeing, the retired schoolteacher then attempted a justification: "It is not really an issue of whether Han vocabulary has replaced [Buyi] and taken over [*zhanyong*]. It is social development [*shehui fazhan*] that has [taken over]."

"Social development" here refers to contemporary socioeconomic transformations with lasting effects in which local communities have been engaging—schooling, intermarriage, and migrant labor, to name a few. These interconnected factors have contributed to the loss of Buyi culture and perhaps a perception that "the minorities are becoming fewer and fewer" (*shao*, as in *shaoshu minzu* or minority nationalities, also means "few" and "less"). Moreover, the hollowing countryside in contemporary China due to labor outflow and farmland loss, as well as fading traditional values and social order, engenders a sense of crisis of rural identity on a general scale, which converges with the crisis of a gradually disappearing or assimilated ethnic minority identity.[34]

Local Buyi were concerned about language shift or language loss, as shown in the conversation above, which manifests as a major change from the habitual use of Buyi to use of local Han dialect and standard Chinese (the latter in more official settings).[35] Bilingualism in Buyi and Chinese is quite prevalent in the Buyi population (He 1998, 8; Wu, Snyder, and Liang 2007, xvi), as many Buyi people use the Buyi language for initial education at home and later switch to the national language for more advanced education.[36] As the Buyi intermarry more with Han they encounter at school or during migrant work, there is a fear that future generations will become more Chinese-speaking. The use of Chinese language is expanding with increased access to mass media and other modern communicative channels like cell phones.

Wuyang Village and the surrounding area have remained a stronghold of Buyi language and culture, where Buyi make up the majority of the local population. Children in most families are not allowed to speak Han after returning from school, where they receive Chinese lessons, and could otherwise be scolded by their parents or grandparents. Young men who do migrant work in the coastal provinces and return with fashionably dyed hairstyles during the Lunar New Year still converse in Buyi, which confers on them an exclusive membership status in their community. However, in areas with rapid urbanization (such as the outskirts of the provincial capital, Guiyang, where my relatives reside), a three-generational pattern of language shift has begun to emerge where the grandparents still speak Buyi, the parents understand Buyi but do not speak, and the grandchildren

48   CHAPTER ONE

do not understand Buyi at all. Similar changes in other key dimensions of traditional values and cultural practices, including clothing, singing, and rituals, are perceived as occurring.

"What if the Buyi culture no longer exists later on?" A question that I have heard my paternal family lament over, which seems to hint at a possible expiration date for Buyi culture, finds emotional resonance among my Buyi interlocutors. Many Buyi elites feel the need to rescue the "disappearing Buyi" (at least selective aspects of culture and language within the allowable parameter) from the onslaught of modern development. This concern is intensified when the Buyi are pitted against ethnic groups like the Miao in the burgeoning cultural markets looking to tap into signature artifacts and practices of minority peoples.

THE POLITICS OF (IN)VISIBILITY

As the Buyi actively marched forward with the socialist nation, their self-perception as a unified *Buyizu* solidified by reproducing the *minzu* marker for themselves, especially in relation to how they differentiate themselves from others. For instance, some Buyi have continued to "other" the adjacent Miao ethnic group. The state has historically regarded the *Miaozu*, also forged from a diverse assemblage of local populations (Diamond 1995; Yang Zhiqiang 2009), as harder to control and more backward in an ethnically based hierarchy. The Buyi have distanced themselves from the Miao, who were indirectly pushed or even forcefully chased into mountains and higher-altitude areas. Many legends attached to the limestone hills and caves around Wuyang Village involve conflicts and disputes with the Miao as well as ancient treasures hidden in haste by the Miao before they fled. The Miao were stigmatized to the extent that Buyi, if mistakenly referred to as Miao, would react as if insulted (Zhongguo Difangzhi Jicheng Bianji Gongzuo Weiyuanhui [1948] 2006, 13503).[37] In many areas that the Buyi and the Miao have cohabited, marrying a Miao was once taboo for the Buyi. And if a Miao woman married into a Buyi household, the daughter-in-law would be restricted from preparing or participating in burial rituals and ceremonies for ancestral worship; otherwise, the Buyi would fear an inefficacy of ritualistic procedures and a disruption of prosperity for future generations.

In the eyes of many Buyi, the Miao "could not catch up with the times" (*ganbushang shidai*). Whether among Buyi rural migrant laborers who live close to Miao migrant laborers in the coastal areas of southeastern China or Buyi cadres who work with Miao cadres in government offices, this bias has persisted. Following the analysis of the Sino-Tibetan borderland by Taiwanese historical anthropologist Wang Ming-ke (2003, 69), a relational and perhaps segmentary mode of thinking could apply to such geo-cultural configurations. The Han look down on Buyi communities, who live by mountain rivers, whereas the Buyi look down on the Miao, who live high on the rugged hills. The connotation of "rustic, wild, and uncouth" attached to those up in the mountains (Scott 2009, 100–103) resulted from the fact that civilization was gauged by geography and elevation.

This relational dynamic produced an asymmetrical pattern of interaction—linguistically and materially—among the Han, the Buyi, and the Miao.[38] While my paternal grandaunt once told me that anyone fluent in all three languages would not fear to go around the world, a nonreciprocal linguistic pattern has also existed. Most Buyi know how to speak Chinese but not Miao, which they regard as utterly unintelligible and perplexing, given its considerable number of local and regional variations. Buyi villagers often refer to any language they do not understand as Miao ($k'a\eta^3$ jiu^2), believing that the Miao language is the hardest to learn and Chinese the easiest (this certainly holds true with the more recent help of mass media, state education, and labor migration). Some Wuyang villagers also suggested that the reason for the linguistic disparity might be that the Buyi have interacted less with the Miao than with the Han.

Historically, some Miao (and Yao) have learned to speak Buyi in order to gain access to information and necessities such as rice, salt, cotton, and tung oil. Insofar as language plays a part in cultural contact and social mobility, local material and social practices in turn manifest the intermediate role of the Buyi. Taking into account that uncivilized and civilized in Chinese political and popular discourses were conceptualized as processual categories (Hostetler 2001; Teng 2004), the Buyi straddled the two presumed spheres as an intermediary and maintained interconnection with other ethnicities in the region.

The relational dynamics among the Buyi, the Miao, and the Han also project onto the local political arena. In Zhenning Buyi-Miao Autonomous County, a certain quota of educated elites from the Buyi and the Miao hold office (Zhenning Buyizu Miaozu Zizhixianzhi Bianzuan Weiyuanhui 2009), even though these positions, which represent the state and embody centralized power, are still oftentimes associated with the Han. At a Miao annual festival event at the county seat in 2013, for instance, a Miao spokesperson announced in the introductory speech that the celebration was shared between the "big brother Han" (*Hanzu laodage*) and the "cousin Buyi" (*Buyi laobiao*). The Han are hence depicted as powerfully and decisively leading at the forefront (as a brother with seniority), whereas the Buyi are interestingly not quite as intimate as a brother but instead a cousin to the Miao (with no indication of seniority).[39]

Through a simultaneous process of inclusion and exclusion, the boundary of the Buyi as a unified group vis-à-vis ethnicities such as the Han and the Miao has become relatively clear. Such interethnic relations, to some extent, further consolidated the Buyi's self-awareness, or "ethnocentrism" in Uncle Kuan's term—even though all *minzu* are supposed to be equal and unified under the socialist state. The Buyi felt that they had been ahead of other minority groups, especially having endeavored over time to achieve socioeconomic progress, but now this interethnic dynamic comes with a twist.

Although historically the Miao ranked beneath the Buyi in official and popular perceptions of non-Han groups, the desire for ethnically unique and exotic features has resulted in a reversal of the old hierarchy. Now that the context has shifted, neighboring groups, such as the Miao, are consequently far ahead in this new game. For instance, the traditional Buyi women's costume for life-cycle rituals (such as marriage and burial) and public performances may represent a visual element that distinguishes the

Buyi from other groups and evokes local pride. And yet, displaying these costumes and ornaments in the village museum of Wuyang reminds some Buyi elites and villagers that they have not inherited—and are thus not able to display—as many silver ornaments as the Miao people. In addition, at various county-level cultural events, Buyi villagers from Wuyang noticed that the Miao groups were able to stage a unique form of dance using *lusheng* (the bamboo reed pipe that is the emblematic musical instrument of the Miao), whereas the Buyi choreography relies on simple movements recently created.

The sense of change and loss I discussed earlier contributes to the Buyi's perception of their relative invisibility in public culture. Intriguingly, one way of understanding such invisibility elaborates on the water-like features of Buyi ethnicity, or a culture of water (*shui de wenhua*). Uncle Wu, who continued to study Buyi rituals and cultural history after leaving his natal village Wuyang to receive higher education and work for a state-owned enterprise, reiterated the idea of water as the metaphorical psyche of the Buyi during my interviews with him in June 2013:

> Because our ancestors have historically occupied fertile soils with sufficient irrigation in a region with limited availability of farmable land, we have inhabited advantageous terrains in southern China. There was no need to compete with others like the Miao or those in the north. We have been rather content with the status quo and go with the flow. Just like the water, we Buyi are too soft and gentle [*rouhe*], not tough; we are very friendly and adaptable to others. We don't fight for ourselves at the forefront, and thus we are less visible and less united.

As elaborated upon by some Buyi educated elites seeking to offer an explanation for the invisibility of the Buyi in local cultural politics, a waterlike character may not be desirable at present, because it is too fluid and adaptable, without unique qualities of its own. The flip side, as suggested, was intragroup competition within the Buyi, as compared to the relative lack thereof within the Miao. Despite huge variance among those identified as Miao, some Buyi elites still regard them as more united. They believe that the Miao's core identity and solidarity, derived from having withstood a long history of warfare and constant attack from powerful opponents (especially the central authorities), is what has caused Miao representatives and political elites to engage in mutual aid and collegial support on the regional level. By contrast, in the words of a Buyi official I interviewed in May 2013, for many Buyi "it is always about me and you, even within the same ethnic group. It is fine to maintain deeply rooted ethnocentric awareness [*minzu yishi*], but why compete against each other in the spirit of localism? Each of the Buyi areas is eager to be the first or the best, now that they are constructing cultural attractions. It is just a means of packaging/branding [*baozhuang*] anyway."

According to these reckonings, the Buyi—a waterlike ethnicity that has always adapted its mode of being to thrive—has been reduced to a collection of self-interested fragments, united only by the *minzu* label they share. The Buyi's flexibility and malleability throughout history have become liabilities, undermining the Buyi's ability to be distinctive in the contemporary context. The case of the Buyi hence speaks to the plight of many interstitial ethnicities, who are neither integrated into the power center nor oppositional to or obviously distinct from the mainstream. Lacking adequately distinguishable features, the Buyi are somehow turned into the weaponless weak, because they lack the "weapons of the weak" (cf. Scott 1985)—in this case, the resistant, exoticized attributes possessed by more marginalized ethnicities.

In a geopolitical context as well, Buyi elites perceive themselves to be at a relative disadvantage. As a group, the Miao—one of whose divisions is the internationally known Hmong—have many subvariations and are thus transregional and even transnational. The Buyi, on the other hand, with nearly 90 percent of the population resident in Guizhou, are largely constrained to one province. Guizhou, furthermore, is a hinterland province without international borders and has been described as a chronically "disadvantaged interior region" (Oakes 2000, 669). This leaves the Buyi in an undesirable situation and results in Buyi intellectuals feeling unable to reach out to translocal arenas.

According to a Han township cadre in charge of Wuyang Village, most people have heard of Miao culture, whereas there is no well-known Buyi place. "You see, the Buyi inheritance is gradually disappearing. And compared to that of other groups in Guizhou, the promotion and development of the Buyi culture is already lagging behind [*luohou*]." As he put it, without a well-crafted brand to bring publicity, tourism development and cultural promotion cannot be converted into material benefits for the local population. "Lagging behind" here was not referring to the timing by which the Buyi joined the wave of tourism and cultural promotion, nor did it correspond to the long-standing discourse about the backwardness of minority populations. It cautioned that Buyi culture had not achieved effective branding, publicity, or cultural commodification, while those historically more distant from the mainstream and from modernization had gained the economic upper hand through their uniqueness.

"A CULTURE OF WATER"

Within China's multiethnic borderlands, identities newly classified under Mao's socialism were carved out of a formerly shifting set of cultural practices through which people had cultivated multiple axes of relatedness. Spatio-cultural configuration and political transformation underlie how the Buyi have juggled their positioning over time. In a mosaic context in which ecology, geography, and elevation have each made a difference, the Buyi persisted and flourished based on interactions with other ethnicities. Simultaneously, the Buyi's historical memories have been attached to one powerful center, a Han Chinese core. The Buyi have thus historically made sense of their existence through a relational framework, which I have unraveled from an emic perspective combined with the etic construction.

In the self-perception and reflection of Buyi identity, water is related to the elastic, fluid nature of ethnicity, because it has been central to Buyi livelihood and subjectivity as an intermediary between the polarized spheres of the Han and the non-Han. Over time, the Buyi have been positioned as "almost Han" or "on-their-way-to-being Han" (Scott 2009, 103), but they can never become Han, nor do they want to become Han. The predicament of groups like the Buyi in contemporary China and perhaps elsewhere in the world is that they may have to comply with national needs but are not full-status participants in the nation's development (Tania Li 2000; Siu 2007). The persistence of stereotypical categories and images like the sinicized minority, which may have been internalized by the Buyi themselves, could result in compromised understandings that overlook the complicated circumstances local populations, especially less visible ones, face in reality.

At the forefront of fast-changing sociopolitical currents, the Buyi have gained certain prospects but have also faced precarities associated with transformative effects on local communities. In the current age of ethnic branding, the Buyi's inward search for uniqueness in their grassroots beliefs and practices is still entangled with the language of the state and cultural politics in the larger regional sphere. Yet, despite the urge to highlight essentialized ethnic identity, the Buyi's historical experience of being fluid and flexible continues to inform their delicate positioning. The Buyi—with a persona described as a culture of water—are always engaging with the continuous flux of potentiality and unpredictability, that is, of openness and of becoming. But the extent to which they can negotiate and maneuver is closely dependent on the parameters of the political and social systems in which they are embedded. The rest of the book delineates the becoming of the Buyi through its contemporary branding in the case of Wuyang Village; as "highly subjective, resilient, and situationally constructed" (Leibold 2007, 21), Buyiness exemplifies a continual process of existence that is historically contextualized and ever unfinished.

CHAPTER TWO

MO RITUALS, BUYI EXPERTS, AND POST-MAO CULTURAL REVIVALS

IN JULY 2013, WUYANG VILLAGE put on a boisterous celebration for the sixth day of the sixth lunar month (Liuyueliu), an important festival originally held to pray for a good harvest in most Buyi regions.[1] The village was the primary site assigned by the county government that year to host a full day of events for officials and tourists from afar. After a series of song-and-dance performances staged as typical festive activities for Liuyueliu, hundreds of spectators moved to the communal playground in Wuyang Village to witness a new highlight of this ceremonial day. Earlier that morning, the exterior of the village committee building—the main official building that marked the village's communal space—had had a makeover. The banner from the 2012 Lunar New Year celebration emblazoned with the phrase "The Thousand-Year Buyi Village in Everyday Life," which had been draped from the building's balcony, had been replaced by a huge signboard of a mythical figure. It was a reconstructed portrait of Baolutuo ($pau^5 lo^3 tuə^6$), the creator of the "Mo ($muə^1$) rituals" conceived by Chairman Yang, a retired chairperson of the county CPPCC (Chinese People's Political Consultative Conference).

Director Wu, a key organizer of that day's event who headed the County Gazetteer Office at the time, is a male descendant of the elite Wu family originally from Wuyang Village, whose many members received a formal education and official ranks. Director Wu and his brothers, along with their

56 CHAPTER TWO

brother-in-law Chairman Yang, had been collecting and interpreting the Mo ritual scripts, many of which had not been handed down or were unfortunately ruined during the Cultural Revolution. The day of the festival, Director Wu briefly presented some background on the subsequent ritual ceremony to be conducted for the benefit of the audience. After describing the festive meaning of Liuyueliu, including its original prayer for harvest and stability, he went on to introduce the Mo through a loudspeaker:

> The Mo culture is what distinguishes the Buyi from other *minzu*, specifically manifested through the Mo scripture [*Mojing*] and the set of Mo ritual practices. The scripture covers a wide range of ritual contents, but most important is the text on *gu xie* (*ku⁶ ɕie⁵*) [the ceremony for the dead]. The Mo scripture delineates the beliefs, worship, and taboos of the Buyi. It also records the origin and survival of the Buyi, such as how the Buyi ancestors learned to use fire and tools and became an ethnicity that is good at planting rice. Thus, the Mo scripture both presents an ancient history of the Buyi and is a literary classic that carries fundamental significance among the Buyi.
>
> The masters of Mo [*Moshi*, or *pu³ muə¹* in Buyi] are cultural workers and ritual specialists who carry down the Mo culture. Mo masters in different regions must make a ceremonial call on Baolutuo before becoming a Mo master or initiating a Mo ritual. Baolutuo is not only the founder of the Mo rituals but also the progenitor of humanities [*renwen shizu*] for Buyi society. There are variations on the Mo scripture as the texts have been copied and circulated among different regions. But as they are deemed to be passed down from the same Baolutuo, these texts are consistent in essence.
>
> Belief in Mo rituals and respect for Mo masters mark the distinctive *minzu* culture of the Buyi. To this day, the Mo culture contains values with positive connotations, such as reverence for nature as symbiotic with human society; this resembles the ideal of great harmony and unity [*hexie sixiang, datong yishi*] in Han Confucian philosophy. The County Association for Buyi Studies, a semigovernmental academic society con-

sisting of Buyi political elites and cultural workers, performs this ceremony to promote Mo culture.

Lu, a seventy-year-old Mo master, was one of the ritual specialists from the central part of the county invited by Chairman Yang to initiate the Baolutuo worship ceremony. Hailing from the same township, not only had Master Lu and Chairman Yang been acquainted for years, but Master Lu was among the local specialists who had helped Chairman Yang translate the Mo ritual texts into Chinese and reviewed his research manuscripts (Yang Zhibin 2011a). For the Liuyueliu celebration, Master Lu conducted an abridged version of the ritual in memory of Baolutuo. With at least seven flashing cameras documenting the scene at close range, Master Lu read a few lines from a script and let three drops of fresh chicken blood fall into rice alcohol, while a pig's head was presented in front of Master Lu and three sticks of incense and some paper money were burned. Director Wu then led all members of the County Association for Buyi Studies — whom he suggested were "representing all fellow Buyi siblings [*Buyi tongbao*]" — to bow three times in front of the fabricated portrait hanging from the committee building's balcony.

Unraveling this key event, which demonstrates the local Buyi elite's careful packaging of tradition, this chapter examines the ethnic branding of ritual elements that manifest in the post-Mao era of cultural revival in southwest China. The way Director Wu introduced the Mo rituals sheds light on how local ritual specialists and, in particular, the *minzu* elite, make sense of the rituals that supposedly constitute the ultimate cultural representation of Buyi identity. The Liuyueliu event also shows how local officials and cultural experts sought to formalize the worship of Baolutuo, a common mythical figure and symbol of Mo, through both institutional and informal networks. The preservation of related Mo texts, artifacts, and practices as key elements of the Buyi's cultural heritage thus derives from the salvaging efforts by local elites to brand Buyi uniqueness.

Paradoxically, while foregrounding Mo as what distinguishes the Buyi from others, Director Wu also compared it to Han Confucian ideals. A series of indigenous rituals inherent to ancestral worship, life cycle, and cosmology in the Buyi community, Mo beliefs and practices are, in fact, syncretic with Chinese Buddhism, Daoism, and Confucianism. Using borrowed or modified Chinese characters, the ritual texts are intended to record and correspond with the oral form of Mo rituals conducted in the Buyi language. The modified characters were recognized by the State Council in 2009 as the written script of Buyi, and thus the Buyi became a minority group with a writing system of their own. Buyi cadres and intellectuals also acknowledge Mo's connection to the beliefs and practices of other Tai-speaking groups. Well aware of the fact that Mo is a ritual and cosmogonic system shared by many Zhuang people as well (Holm 2003, 2004, 2013), Buyi elites have consciously striven to create a connection between Buyi cultural practices and a broader regional history within the Chinese state and, more broadly, with the Sino–Southeast Asian borderland.

Collaborations between local Mo practitioners and scholars have been essential throughout the process of ritual perception and interpretation, which is often not oriented toward a Buyi audience. Critically, the knowledge production process related to local Mo rituals highlights the significance of experts in local societies and their shifting roles—from ritual experts under classical anthropological inquiry to professional intellectuals in more recent reflexive engagement since the 1980s (Boyer 2008). These experts, equipped with ritual and cultural expertise, often come into coexistence and convergence, which is further complicated by the fact that some of these educated elites also work for local-level bureaucracies in ethnic minority regions. Like the Zhuang, who are standardizing Mo as a religion within the state's institutional framework (Kao 2014), the Buyi elites seek legitimacy and authority over local religion and culture. They take on a search for uniqueness on the basis of grassroots beliefs and practices while intricately aligning themselves with state language and *minzu* politics.

While minority cultural experts are busy assembling historical narratives and interpreting cultural symbols of their own ethnic groups for knowledge production and cultural promotion, they do so with an economically oriented purpose. Existing scholarship on religious revival and development in contemporary China situates religion within a state-based framework with increasing market influence (Ashiwa and Wank 2009; Chau 2006; Oakes and Sutton 2010; Yang and Tamney 2005). These contemporary ritual specialists and minority intellectuals have thus become "memory entrepreneurs," who both rely on their own memory of cultural traditions and search for new ways to restore lost traditions, actively attracting popular attention and developing commercial potential in an age of ethnic branding.[2] These key experts who document fading customs are not simply self-appointed scribes recording the cultural practices of their people but are themselves cultural producers (Schein 2000, 205; You 2020, 217). Forging both alliance and competition within and beyond the Buyi, Buyi experts have produced knowledge that shapes how both local Buyi people and outsiders perceive the Buyi's past and present, and perhaps knowledge that affects the future as well.

MO SPECIALISTS, BUYI ELITES, AND THE POWER OF EXPERTS

Local Chinese society has historically been a hotbed of creative cultural production and reconstruction, generating worlds of difference within local communal ritual events (Siu 1990a; Dean 1998). Ritual forms and specializations were invented or modified in an effort to capture and channel emergent social and political power at the local level, parallel to—or even overlapping with—other institutional domains and processes, including lineage formation or elite associations.[3] Embedded in a complex web of lineage and religious ties as the "cultural nexus of power" that linked rural society to the imperial state (Duara 1988; Faure 2007), key figures with their varied roles in ritual formation and innovation had derived authority and status from symbolic resources and shaped the exercise and negotiation of power in local communities. Most importantly, the religious sphere constituted a public domain through which the village elite sought to express its leadership aspirations and responsibilities (Duara 1988, 148).

Local leadership, along with traditional ritual-symbolic values, was nonetheless undermined by the epochal intrusion of the state during modernizing reforms and attacks against superstition, lasting from the Republican era to the decades under the Communist Party's rule (most evidently during the Cultural Revolution). With a relatively monolithic government apparatus that replaced a diversity of local powerholders, the socialist state penetrated local social-cultural landscapes, reinforcing its positioning as a legitimate authority over ritual and religious matters that subsequently underwent vast changes.[4] Generations of local residents have internalized the institutional and ideological power of the Chinese state while reproducing such power in everyday pursuits, not least in life-cycle rituals and community festivals. This process of "state involution" (Siu 1989a, 1989b) took place as the Maoist state bureaucracy and its socialist transformation has become a powerful ordering frame for local societies and subjects.[5]

Cultural revival by local elites in the post-Mao reform era was then "enacted as a reaction against the recent past, not against the contemporary state, which was perceived as similarly committed to the revival agenda and to the repudiation of the destructive past" (Schein 2000, 226–27). While the socialist past did not completely destroy cultural life, local minority intellectuals and cadres were eager to wrestle their own culture back from its previous symbolic impoverishment—regarded as backwardness or feudal superstition—by exploring new cultural and institutional spaces (Litzinger 2000). In the present day, local Buyi elites who are central to the kinship and ritual networks of rural communities may well be Communist Party cadres and are often those actively mobilizing economic and cultural resources for local development. In refashioning the Mo rituals, which are still important to many rural Buyi, local elites with higher levels of education have significant leverage in conducting, interpreting, and valorizing these beliefs and practices, which are not easily comprehensible to commoners.

When the youngest son of my hostess, Senior Grandma Wu, got married in March 2013, I was somewhat surprised to see Director Wu, then head of the County Gazetteer Office, acting as the ritual master who conducted the wedding ceremony for the couple. Well before the wedding, he determined the auspicious date and time for the ritual. When the wedding day dawned, he recited texts and guided the procedure as the bride entered the central room and kowtowed together with her husband in front of a table of family elders. It seemed odd at first that a county official would conduct a ritual for a rural family whose members occasionally resided in the county seat and were periodically involved in agricultural activity. Though they were only in their early fifties at the time, Senior Grandma Wu and her husband were part of the most senior generation of the Wu lineage, to which Director Wu belongs. As my fieldwork proceeded, it turned out that some Wu villagers in the same lineage had also invited Director Wu to conduct rituals for other occasions, such as praying for their family upon building a new house. Because Wuyang Village no longer has Mo specialists like Master Lu, who usually live in villages in more remote parts of the county, Director Wu, who learned the Mo practices from his father, remains important for local families that rely on Buyi life-cycle rituals. Many people referred to those who conduct these rituals as *xiansheng*, borrowing a Chinese word that denotes "local teacher" or "learned person."[6] Director Wu is not only a senior male member of the Wu lineage but also considered a well-educated authority in the community.

Traditionally, Mo ritual masters or practitioners have been referred to as *Bumo* (*pu³ muə¹*) or *Mogong/laomo* in the local Chinese language. They are the original owners of the ritual texts and perform the rituals themselves, reciting the scriptures for performing divinations and exorcisms, making sacrifices, or calling back lost souls.[7] In earlier historical records (Holm 2003; Weinstein 2014) and still in some areas nowadays, the Mo masters are called *baomo* or *baomu*, in which *bao* (*pau⁵*) is the Buyi word for grandfather or male elder, often used respectfully. While the accurate historical origin of the Mo is open to debate, David Holm (2003) conjectured that, in centuries past, important lineages of Mo practitioners were probably attached to native chieftains or chiefly clans.

Similar to the more systematic and extensive Zhuang scriptures (Holm 2013), the Buyi Mo scripts were created by borrowing, and at times modifying, Chinese characters.[8] Largely imitating the way Chinese characters are composed of radicals (graphical components), the recombination of

62   CHAPTER TWO

TABLE 2. Examples of modified Chinese characters used in Mo rituals

Modified character	Pronunciation (International Phonetic Alphabet)	Meaning	Explanation
那田	na^2	rice field	The upper part of the character is pronounced "na(4)" in Chinese, which phonetically resembles the Buyi term for "rice field." The bottom part of the character is the Chinese character that denotes "rice field."
盖鸟	kai^5	chicken	The left part of the character is pronounced "gai(4)" in Chinese, which phonetically resembles the Buyi term for "chicken." The right part of the character is the Chinese character used for categories of bird species.

radicals in the Buyi Mo scripts was intended to correspond with the phonetic and semantic features of the Buyi language (see table 2 for examples of such characters learned from Master Mo in southern Guizhou's Libo County during summer 2010).[9]

The ritual texts were hence incomprehensible to many Buyi villagers, let alone outsiders—and perhaps deliberately so (see also Weinstein 2007). Moreover, Chinese Daoism and Buddhism have been incorporated into the Mo ritual complex through long-term interactions with the Han and other ethnicities (Zhou Guomao 2006). Many Mo masters have presumably received education (*you wenhua*) and subsequently used (Han) Chinese cultural elements to record their knowledge. As the Buyi have been highly adaptable and willing to borrow ideas and terminology from their neighbors, some suggest that this in part leads to the prevalent conception of the Buyi as being more advanced or sinicized than certain other ethnic minority groups.[10]

As is typical of knowledge transmission among religious groups (Chau 2011, 17–19), the Mo rituals have been mostly passed down over many years through a familial apprenticeship system that aims to cater to the ritual demands of a local clientele. New learners are taught skills from their fathers, grandfathers, and closely related masters, often relying on a fixed repertoire of ritual knowledge and scripts exclusive to the group. The Mo masters have exclusively been male heirs with qualified prestige and authority among local communities who were capable of—and interested in—learning the Mo scripts and the value systems therein.

The Wu ancestors (particularly Director Wu's great-great-grandfather, great-grandfather, and father) had great skill in practicing the Mo rituals and were also well known in the region as gentry (in the late imperial period) and as intellectuals (in the 1950s).[11] The father of Director Wu, whom one of the Wu brothers referred to as a "Buyi high-level intellectual" (*gaoceng zhishifenzi*), was a Chinese teacher in primary schools in nearby regions after the establishment of the People's Republic. While the Wu brothers lived away from their original home, Wuyang Village, they were nurtured and edified by parents who shared many Buyi traditions, including Mo beliefs. When the Cultural Revolution targeted folk beliefs and rituals as the "four olds" (old ideas, old culture, old customs, and old habits), however, the Wu brothers were forced to destroy many heirlooms and archives back in the village for self-protection. Among the relics they burned were the ritual costumes their great-great-grandfather wore, which the Wu brothers repeatedly recalled in writings (Wu Zhonggang and Wu Zhongshi 2012, 70) and in interviews with me. They also attempted to hide old ritual scripts underneath haystacks in their cattle pen; unfortunately, all of these were dampened and decayed after a downpour.

Members of the Wu family, driven by a deep sense of guilt and crisis about this fractured historical memory, have endeavored since the 1980s to document the historical narrative and legacy they inherited from their ancestors, mostly based on oral history and depicting everyday experience from an *insider* perspective. Many family members working as teachers, staff at working units, and county officials have continued to decipher and practice ritual traditions. In 2014, a book coauthored by a few members of the Wu family was published by the County Association for Buyi Studies.

64   CHAPTER TWO

Titled *The Buyi Ethnicity in Zhenning County* (Zhenning Buyizu), the book seeks to generate new discourse and interpret a wide range of cultural aspects, from Buyi cosmology and rituals to the patterns on local costumes (Wu Zhonggang and Wu Kaifeng 2014).

The elite members of the Wu family by no means represent the entire range of the Buyi people, but there are similar cases across Guizhou in which relatively renowned Buyi experts and intellectuals come from prestigious family backgrounds with significant Mo influences and advanced education levels. For instance, two brothers named Zhou from another county in Guizhou, whom Chairman Yang deems to have made huge contributions to the study of Mo culture, were raised in a distinguished Mo master family (*Mogong shijia*). They are now university professors of ethnology and language and literature, one in Guiyang and the other in Beijing.

Precisely because only a select few could understand the Mo ritual texts and practices, translations have been highly dependent on the perspectives of those few. Due to the level of literacy and inherited teachings required, it is very challenging for outsiders to learn the Mo belief system. Not only does one have to be highly proficient in the Buyi language and capable of recognizing the modified Chinese characters, but guidance provided by the Mo masters is also vital. Even some local Buyi scholars with graduate degrees have found it difficult to understand the essence of the Mo ritual system.

For someone like Chairman Yang, who was not born to a Bumo family, however, the way to achieve in-depth understanding of the Mo system was to seek a collaboration with grassroots Mo masters. Beginning in the early 2000s, while he was still chairing the county CPPCC, he consulted and sometimes brought together Buyi experts and Mo masters from across the county to examine and discuss the meaning of specific ritual texts (Yang Zhibin 2011a, 248; 2012, 83). After observing the entire process of a kinsman's funeral or leading a team to collect the ritual scripts, Chairman Yang then organized ritual specialists, knowledgeable relatives, and colleagues, including the Wu brothers (his brothers-in-law) and Master Lu, to conduct research. He has since written research articles that were included in his autobiography, presented papers at symposiums, and published a 2011 monograph.

Educated and authoritative figures like these Buyi elite are not rare in any local mobilization and cultural revival. While they can no longer be classified as peasantry, they have emerged from the agrarian context and are still deeply rooted in local lineage and kinship networks. Though sociopolitical transformations in the twentieth century took a toll on all domains of life, not least the religious and cultural domains, contemporary *minzu* elite utilized the new institutional spaces and symbolic resources available to them to stay in power. Based on significant use of positional power derived from their education and office holdings, they perform directive, organizational, and educative functions, exercising powerful intellects and will at the local level. That some Buyi elite have taken on the roles of both traditional ritual experts and professional intellectuals today constitutes a specific form of *mētis* (à la Scott 1998) — a set of practical skills and experiential knowledge with which both grassroots community members and members of dominant social groups can engage.

Both the oral and written forms of the Mo rituals have granted greater legitimacy and authority to the ritual elite. The recitation of texts — poetic and meaningful words distinct from ordinary experience in the form of scriptures, mantras, or orally transmitted songs — is the most salient feature of these rituals (Holm 2003, 23).[12] Moreover, Mo rituals do not simply exert rhetorical power through the performance of ritual speech; importantly, the ritual texts, especially the borrowed or modified Chinese characters, assume a power of writing and literacy through their sheer presence.

Many Buyi elite and experts not only truly respect the Mo ritual system and believe in it but are keen to systematically record and interpret specific aspects, as well as the totality, of such traditional beliefs and ritual practices. Adam Yuet Chau's (2006) term "intellectual believers" — though it seems to be an ideal type — may describe these local figures within a certain kind of religious habitus.[13] Both their ingrained belief tradition (a structured structure) and the changing sociopolitical climate and their scholarly interpretations (a structuring structure) induce intellectual believers to base

66   CHAPTER TWO

their beliefs in part on intellectual coherence and the systematic relatedness of religious ideas and practices (Chau 2006, 67). But as the Buyi elite endow Mo rituals with intellectual credibility, they also distance themselves from the rituals, which have become their object of study.

ACADEMICIZING THE GODS AND REGIONAL POLITICS

The ways in which Buyi experts engage with Mo rituals are inevitably tied to state-society transformations over time. According to some Buyi scholars, conceptualizations of Mo rituals in Chinese scholarship have shifted over decades, corresponding to academic dynamics closely aligned with *minzu* politics.[14] In the Republican era, most scholarly discussions of the Mo were simply descriptive. Ethnologists at the time did not deviate significantly from earlier archives (including the "Miao Albums") that delineated customs of Guizhou's ethnic inhabitants, such as native burial phenomena, in imperial China. They conducted surveys in the minority—today's Miao and Buyi—regions in Guizhou and recorded funeral customs in a folkloric manner (see, for instance, Chen [1942] 2004c, 200).

Beginning in the 1950s, Mo was deemed a form of folklore literature based on text compilations and relevant analyses. Cultural workers at the local level assisted researchers who were sent by the central government with their sociohistorical surveys of minority regions. Partly because of the dominant Maoist ideology, which championed atheist socialism and viewed popular religions as superstitious or feudal, the ritualistic nature of the Mo scriptures was dismissed or underplayed (Zhou Guomao 2012, 3). Furthermore, due to copying and printing conditions at the time, the original Mo scriptures were not collected or presented in written form, but rather were documented as folk literature and chants and only circulated among government offices.[15] During the Cultural Revolution, Mo, as a superstition, was considered part of the "four olds" and was hence subjected to intense surveillance and destruction throughout the region—the source of the Wu brothers' past sin. Even so, in some areas, such ritual practices never really died out, as people continued to conduct them and pass them

RITUALS, EXPERTS, AND CULTURAL REVIVALS   67

down secretly, while local Buyi officials sometimes turned a blind eye to these activities.[16]

The 1980s saw a resurgence of compiling and editing Mo scriptures and chanted songs as folklore literature (see Huang and Hoff 2006). While making phonetic notations and translated collations based on previously compiled materials, Buyi researchers discovered more versions and copies of related scriptures from local communities.[17] Starting in the 1990s, scholars have increasingly treated Mo as a cultural system in order to explicate its constitutive elements, such as the meaning of certain ritual language or objects.

Chairman Yang, for instance, would be considered a major enthusiast of the Mo cultural system, based on his efforts to understand and explain it while working at the county level. After receiving three years of college training for select minority cadres at the Central University of Nationalities (Zhongyang Minzu Xueyuan) in Beijing, today's Minzu University of China (Yang Zhibin 2011b), Chairman Yang returned to Zhenning County. There, he worked for its government system for almost four decades and eventually retired from the chairperson position of the county CPPCC in 2011. His wife was also a county-level Buyi official, born and raised in Wuyang Village. As Chairman Yang had sufficient time after retirement and maintained a high sociopolitical status, he was in a position to serve as mediator between various local government agencies where he had worked and Wuyang Village, where his affinal relatives lived. Chairman Yang has aspired to develop Wuyang Village's heritage tourism both to help improve the living standard of his fellow villagers and to salvage the Buyi's lost past.

Chairman Yang's earlier research was based on the three-day funeral of one of his relatives in 2005 and an in-depth interview with a Buyi Mo master from his township in 2007 (Yang Zhibin 2012, 248, 260). In 2005, Mr. Lu decided to conduct a ceremonial burial for his mother. As one of Mr. Lu's kinsmen, Chairman Yang followed the whole event over the course of three days and then entreated the Mo master who conducted it to explain each and every procedure. Later, in 2007, another Mo master in his sixties, a retired teacher with a college degree, assisted Chairman

68   CHAPTER TWO

Yang with translating line by line the ritual scripture their family had inherited. These were all published in later sections of Chairman Yang's 2011 autobiography, including only the Chinese translations and not the original copies of the texts.

In 2009, a significant change in the recognition of Buyi at a much broader level resulted in increasing attention paid to Mo ritual texts, especially the modified Chinese characters. While considering scripts recorded by the Shui ethnic group for the National Rare Manuscript List in 2008, an official from the Libo County Archival Bureau noticed a similarity between the ancient Zhuang characters found in Guangxi and the ones seen in Buyi Mo scripts. Upon returning to Libo, he and other county officials began to collect and compile old Buyi scripts (Wang Yugui 2012, 22–23). While there are various Buyi areas across Guizhou that practice Mo rituals with similar characters, Buyi elite in Libo took the initiative to apply for official recognition.[18] As a result of their efforts, supported by the Guizhou Provincial Association for Buyi Studies, the State Council designated the Buyi in 2009 as China's eighteenth minority nationality group with a self-created script.

As some ritual experts explained to me, the Mo records found in Libo have the largest number of modified Chinese characters (interestingly, Libo is both geographically and historically more connected to the Zhuang regions in Guangxi than other Buyi-populated counties of Guizhou). To further compile Buyi scripts and identify Buyi characters, salvaging efforts have continued since 2009 with help from Buyi experts in Beijing, the head of the Association for Buyi Studies in Yunnan, and even the head of the Association for Zhuang Studies in Guangxi (Wang Yugui 2012, 29). Indicating the historically accumulated wisdom of the Buyi through interactions with other ethnicities, the scriptures have facilitated the shift of the Mo ritual system from literary classic to intangible heritage as designated by the state, especially as the wave of UNESCO intangible cultural heritage (*feiwuzhi wenhua yichan*) identification began to sweep across China in the early 2000s.

Upon state recognition in 2009 that drew attention to Buyi Mo rituals across the province, the Zhenning CPPCC committee held a meeting specifically on the theme of Mo culture in 2010. The county government established a research team to visit all the Buyi villages over a period of three months in order to survey existing Mo scriptures and ritual specialists (Yang Zhibin 2011a, 1–5). During the survey, the team collected and discovered a well-preserved, relatively complete scripture from a village in the township where Chairman Yang came from. The old Mo master who preserved this set of scriptures told the survey team:

> We Buyi simply believe in Mo. During the Cultural Revolution, somebody forced me to burn the scripts because conducting Mo *rituals* was superstition. We Bumo felt so bitterly disappointed and were afraid that our ancestral legacy would disappear from our generation. Now you came to study it, meaning that the party and the government pay attention to our minority customs and are willing to carry down the Mo. This is very good and very important. I am willing to give you the script as a gift to acknowledge your study, while my only request is that you help me make twelve copies so as to distribute them to the twelve Bumo [in our team/hall] as a souvenir. (Yang Zhibin 2011a, 2)

Based on the scripture provided by the old master, Chairman Yang and his Mo master helpers produced a monograph titled *The Study of the Buyi's Mo Culture* (Buyizu Mo wenhua yanjiu) in 2011 with a loose translation accompanied by further explanation and annotation. The monograph includes a photocopied version of the original scripture. Such processes of academicizing local rituals have intensified in recent years, as different groups compete, with the help of folklorists and other experts, to get their deity worship or ritual practice recognized and accredited by the state as intangible cultural heritage to be promoted and celebrated (see also Chau 2011). While examining a folk cult in southeastern China, Kenneth Dean (1998, 261–63) has noted an interesting phenomenon prevalent across the country—the "Conferences of the Gods." He observed that scholars are increasingly mobilized by temple committees and local governments to join efforts to legitimize a particular deity cult or religious festival by participating in sponsored academic conferences and lending their scholarly credentials to claims of antiquity or cultural significance.

To valorize the Mo as Buyi classics with symbolic significance, a landmark symposium titled "Mo Culture of the Buyizu" was held by the Guizhou Provincial Association for Buyi Studies in March 2012 in Guiyang, the provincial capital. This symposium was funded by the Japan Society for the Promotion of Science; one of the organizers, originally from Guizhou, was a postdoctoral researcher at a Japanese institute who applied for the funding as a scholarly exchange project at the time. Participants ranged from Buyi scholars at top academic institutions in the province to teachers at middle schools to researchers working for institutes specializing in *minzu* studies at the county level, from county officials in charge of ethnic and religious affairs to journalists and editors from the provincial newspaper and publishing house focusing on *minzu* issues, and from museum workers to local members of the Chinese Folk Literature and Art Society.[19] Chairman Yang and two brothers of the Wu family—Director Wu and the main editor of their new book, *The Buyi Ethnicity in Zhenning County*—were also invited.

Those who participated in the 2012 symposium exemplify the diverse members of the Association for Buyi Studies. With college and even advanced degrees, many of these participants straddle the boundaries between official, writer/literati, scholar, and media/cultural worker. While they actively engage in the production of specialized ritual knowledge, some are also trained as representatives from their particular minority group in schools with pedagogical approaches grounded in *minzu* studies within a socialist framework. Many have collaborated with local Mo masters in compiling and translating Mo scripts over decades, while some are local ritual specialists themselves. Some participating institutions, such as publishing services, have been continuously searching for, compiling, and publishing Mo scriptures, related translations, and academic analyses. Louisa Schein (2000, 206) has pointed out the dual character of such written accounts, which are little read by most local people: the use of written Chinese affiliated the minority scribes with the state-sponsored objective of preservation, while the content of their works valorized their ethnic distinction. These efforts would, in effect, continue to be encouraged and funded by state agencies emphasizing cultural construction (*wenhua jianshe*) (Zhou

Guomao 2012, 7) and the salvage of manuscript and relic alike in the service of restoring China's traditional culture.

ASSERTING HISTORICAL SIGNIFICANCE AND VALORIZING THE MO IN A MODERN CONTEXT

Around the turn of the twenty-first century, the political utility of *wenhua* (culture) seemed to be geared to shoring up the ideas of Chinese place and Chinese identity, as traditional culture was retrofitted to uphold state-recognized values (Schein 2018). Now that the contemporary Chinese state looks to act as a patron for activities involving popular beliefs acknowledged to have historical and cultural significance, many elites strive to frame and articulate rituals in ways that reference the party-state agenda. Though Mo does not fit into any category of the five officially recognized faiths (i.e., Buddhism, Taoism, Islam, Catholicism, and Protestantism) that meet China's definition of religion (*zongjiao*), it nevertheless showcases the return to tradition in minority regions, a practice recognized within the permissible parameters of national culture (Borchert 2005; Oakes and Sutton 2010). Thus, the Buyi elite are by no means simply local literati or intellectuals; they must also speak to a broader audience, from legitimizing the belief system as ethnic tradition and intangible heritage to repackaging certain elements for touristic displays. Many minority specialists crafted hybrid products that fused local material with contemporary modes of cultural representation (Schein 2000, 205). Reflecting sociopolitical climates over time, the ways in which Buyi elites have reclaimed the significant value of Mo ritual beliefs and practices also show that post-Mao cultural revivals are interlaced with state discourse and ideology as well as emerging market forces.

The definition of Mo in a modern context, whether as *minzu* religion or cultural system, remains unresolved. As shown above, the uses of "Mo" by Buyi experts, sometimes oscillating between religion (*Mojiao*), culture (*Mo wenhua*), and classics (*Mojing jingdian* or *dianji*), seem ambiguous and interchangeable (Zhou Guomao 1995). There are numerous beliefs and rituals as such that exist outside China's modern framing of religion and are enacted as public rituals of lineage or territorial identification of communities (Oakes and Sutton 2010, 13). At the 2012 symposium mentioned above, a leading Buyi scholar, Zhou Guomao (2012, 1), generally defined Mo culture as the set of "cultural phenomena oriented to the Mo beliefs that include material, institutional, behavioral and spiritual forms." In an earlier manuscript, he suggested that Mo could be regarded as a "*minzu* religion" or a "semi-religion" (*zhun zongjiao*).[20] His reasoning focused on the existence of specialized religious professionals, the Bumo, and the formation of a most divine deity—Baolutuo—worshipped by all Bumo; relatively systematic scriptures (*tə¹ muə¹*), especially those for funeral rituals calling for lost souls and others involved in exorcism and healing; regulated procedures and ritual etiquettes followed by generations of Bumo; and last but not least, basic doctrines that connect life-worlds with supernatural worlds (Zhou Guomao 2006, 69–71). Supplementing a point that Bumo are tied together as a structured organization, Chairman Yang (2011a, 278) suggests that Mo is the "religion of the Buyi."

Part of the challenge of historicizing Mo is evident in the process of interpreting these belief systems and cultural practices. Buyi experts have realized that they are engaged in difficult decisions to make their explanations clear. Importantly, due to the different language system used in the recitation and the scripture, Chairman Yang and his Mo master helpers often found it challenging to translate Mo texts into Chinese. Even if they could find an equivalent word in Chinese, its meanings and values would not necessarily match what the Buyi expression conveyed. Because much of the existing literature on the Buyi and other ethnic minority groups has centered on Marxist evolutionary stages or Han-centric historiography over dynasties, the Wu family believes that its intellectual efforts constitute a major breakthrough, differing from existing scholarship, which either adopts an outsider's perspective or presents analyses in an ungrounded, inadequate manner.

For instance, Buyi intellectuals were well aware of the complicated and often syncretic animistic beliefs local communities have held, which they sought to clarify to avoid simplification or misinterpretation. In the summer of 2013, while sharing with me his manuscript of what was later published as *The Buyi Ethnicity in Zhenning County* (Wu Zhonggang and Wu Kaifeng 2014), one of the Wu brothers explained that two belief systems—one oriented toward nature and the other toward ghosts—coexist in the Buyi communities. Bumo help local Buyi people make contact with both natural deities (such as the mountain god) and ghosts (dead ancestors). The Wu brother also suggested that there are distinctions between faith (*xinyang*), worship (*chongbai*), and awe or respect (*jingwei*) for the Buyi. Faith, directed toward heaven (*tian* in standard Chinese, *kən² ʔbən¹* in Buyi), makes it the highest ruling deity, equivalent to Allah for Islam and God for Christianity. Worship of ancestors derives from the belief that the ancestors are dispatched by heaven to take over the generations to come, whereas awe or respect is directed toward every object that can be regarded as a deity (*shenling*). In addition, the Wu family considered a breakthrough their attempt to identify Baogendei (*pau⁵ kən² tei⁶*) as different from the earth deity (*tudigong*) among the Han. "We believe in heaven above us. 'Tudigong' as a standardized denomination for the earth deity was merely borrowed from the nearby Han, and us Buyi also place a little shrine for Baogendei at our village entrance. But heaven has more authority than the usual land-based deity."

Buyi elites hope that, diverging from Han-centric historical narratives, Mo scripture could provide some historical narrative and memory from the Buyi's emic perspective, however fragmented it might be. While most of the preserved ritual books date only to the late imperial period, local experts claim that the Buyi Mo scripts were created no later than the Tang-Song period (roughly from the seventh to the thirteenth century).[21] One of the primary pieces of evidence involves the archaic place-names used in the recited texts for the purpose of guiding lost souls to their historical places of origin.[22] While tracing the places of origin of Buyi ancestors, some Mo texts described their historical interactions with other ethnic groups over the mosaic landscapes. Some Mo scripts also recorded animistic cosmologies inherently tied to water, land, and forests, as well as the Buyi's relationship to the environment, such as livelihoods based on rice planting and house building.

Mo rituals, according to local experts, essentially provided a channel for the Buyi to negotiate their orientations and articulate their aspirations for status and wealth historically. The death ritual examined by Chairman Yang (2011a) described the prayers therein: "We will ask the ritual master to come conduct burial ceremonies. In that case, along with our livestock and treasures, we would be blessed. Our descendants would continue to be wealthy. They would pass the imperial examination and become officials. They could take good care of Guizhou—whatever places it has—on behalf of the emperor."[23]

It is hard to refute the idea that the imperial state instrumentalized the Buyi—for example, by using Buyi native chieftains (*tusi*, or hereditary leaders recognized as imperial officials) to govern many multiethnic areas.[24] And yet, Buyi leaders and village headmen, as well as Mo masters, exercised their own form of power: they relied on their ritual literacy in the Buyi language and on other symbolic resources to serve as supravillage intermediaries, sustaining their status and authority while mediating with the central authorities.

While the Mo ritual system served in some areas to create transregional community networks that in turn created semiautonomous spheres to resist central authority in the late imperial period (Weinstein 2014), many Buyi elite I spoke with stressed that Mo beliefs and practices are not accompanied by a political agenda and do not pose a threat to state authority. Tim Oakes and Donald Sutton (2010, 13–14) rightly state that a key theme of the reform period in post-Mao China is the continuing state effort to co-opt and supervise religious activities, which has been a much longer-term project of governance and cultural authority. In turn, religious entities such as lineage temples and local deities that echo the ideology of the state are given room to maneuver provided they assist in maintaining harmony in society.

In Director Wu's discussion of Mo at the Liuyueliu event, he specifically mentioned the importance of such rituals based on their respect for nature and their alignment with Confucian philosophy. This view, according to the Buyi elite's interpretations of Mo, aligns closely with China's contemporary state ideology. The Chinese government, especially since the early 2000s, has been primarily concerned with building a harmonious society (*hexie shehui*) and harnessing traditional values, such as Confucian philosophical thought. Many folk rituals in China have been promoted as essential elements of Chinese culture. The party-state permits activities involving popular beliefs that are acknowledged as having historical and cultural value as long as they are defined as cultural rather than religious (Ashiwa 2009, 59). Insofar as local rituals are mobilized as an instrument in the state's campaign to promote a harmonious society and a socialist spiritual civilization (*shehuizhuyi jingshen wenming*) (Oakes and Sutton 2010, 4), local elites may accumulate folk, religious, and personal faith that is not necessarily antagonistic to their political faith.

While intellectual efforts to unpack Mo are ongoing, local elites have now harnessed them for cultural promotion, to serve as a form of tourist attraction and heritage preservation. Based on her fieldwork among the Zhuang, Ya-ning Kao (2014, 135) notes that the current standardization process of the Mo produces a single text that can be considered orthodox once the materials have been collected, studied, approved by scholars, recognized by the Chinese government, and listed as belonging to a cultural heritage. Similarly, Mo scripture has been listed at both the municipal and the provincial level as intangible cultural heritage in Anshun (with jurisdiction over Zhenning County) and Guizhou.[25] Still carrying its socialist-era categorization, it is categorized as folk literature consisting of ancient songs narrating the Buyi's origin and customs (Anshun Shi Wenhua Ju 2009, 322, 327). However, textual materials do not suffice to manifest it as a quintessential Buyi tradition. Visualization techniques that can craft something immediately to be seen are needed for ethnic branding.

VISUALIZING BAOLUTUO: FROM RITUAL TEXT TO SYMBOLIC FIGURE

While ritual scriptures and practices, and their corresponding interpretations, vary across time and space, Buyi intellectuals have valorized certain historical elements as super-symbols to demonstrate the common Mo

76 CHAPTER TWO

religiosity among the Buyi. To that end, Baolutuo has been framed as a central figure that can connect Mo beliefs across Buyi populations, perhaps even forging a pan-Tai phenomenon.[26] Reconstructing this figure thus leaves much space for local imagination and crafting based on Mo scriptures and ancestral worship, similar to what is seen among the Zhuang in Guangxi.

According to Holm (2004, 20–23), Baolutuo (Baeu Rodo in his transliteration) usually appears with Molujia (Mo Loekgyap in Holm's transliteration, $mie^6 lo^3 ka?^8$ in Buyi) as a male-female pair who are the founders of the sacrificial order and the apical ancestors of the Zhuang people. Found in the western part of Guangxi and some areas in southeastern Yunnan, texts and cults of Baolutuo and Molujia have also existed throughout the Buyi-speaking areas of southwestern, southern, and central Guizhou (Zhou Guomao 1995). While Molujia is credited as the ancestress who created humankind, stories about Baolutuo are far more plentiful. Though he put human beings and other creatures in order, Baolutuo was by no means a god; instead, he was treated as an ancestral figure (Holm 2004, 20–21). A scholar who had worked on the Zhuang scriptures since the mid-1980s suggested, when interviewed by Holm, that Baolutuo had no string of official titles and that there was no territorial aspect to his cult; rather, it was all a matter of blood relations.[27]

In Buyi-speaking areas, these two apical figures (primarily Baolutuo) are venerated as the ancestral masters of the Bumo — that is, as founders of the priestly lineage represented by the Bumo and the inventors of their rituals (Zhou Guomao 1995). Zhou Guomao (2006, 10) states that Baolutuo, with omnipotent talents and abilities, might have arisen from patriarchy. In some Bumo households, a spirit-place is set up for Baolutuo to one side of the domestic altar. Before performing lengthy and important rituals, such as funerals, Bumo conduct a special rite, "Inviting the Master," for protection. Some mythical tales about Baolutuo are transmitted by ancient songs (guge) sung on important festival days (Holm 2004, 21–22). Although the myths and texts about Baolutuo were circulated and handed down from generation to generation in a number of different forms, Buyi elites emphasize the common origin of the Mo system by quoting a line from

Mo scripture: "Twelve [disciples of] Baolutuo; the head is not the same, but the tail is [$ko\mathit{?}^7 mi^2 fu\vartheta^2 pe^l fu\vartheta^2$]."[28] Director Wu once explained to me: "The tail [branch] is not the same, but the head [root] is." Both connote the coherence of the Mo legacy.

Though various accounts of Baolutuo seem to blur the distinction between deity, ghost, and ancestor, Baolutuo has served as a bilateral agent between the local, existential present and the mythical, supernatural, and translocal past.[29] Valorizing Baolutuo rather than Molujia not only reinforces patriarchy (as opposed to matriarchy, which was considered to have deeper historical roots—and yet be backward—according to the Marxist-Leninist evolutionary narrative), but it also reflects how locals today (re)imagine their historical origin and ancestor worship in the context of a larger polity.[30] Baolutuo as a concept is vague enough to be reified as a symbolic figure who is commonly worshipped and venerated.

During the editing process of his 2011 monograph, Chairman Yang's crew had already started to propose establishing Baolutuo as the primogenitor of the Mo ritual system. "It doesn't matter who Baolutuo really was; what's important is that all the Buyi Bumo acknowledge him as the founder. As respect paid to all the Bumo who present offerings and prayers to Baolutuo on important festival days each year, we suggest choosing a date to make Baolutuo worship into a Buyi festival" (Yang Zhibin 2011a, 200). For the 2012 Guiyang symposium on Mo culture, Chairman Yang initially planned to team up with the Wu brothers to reflect on several questions concerning the Mo. But instead, Chairman Yang single-authored a short piece on Baolutuo (or Bao'ertuo) primarily drawn from his 2011 monograph and presented it at the symposium (Yang Zhibin 2012, 83–84). At the end of the piece, he asked the Provincial Association for Buyi Studies to consider his proposal to establish the divine status of Baolutuo among all the Buyi people and to worship Baolutuo through various activities to "enrich *minzu* culture and develop the tourism industry."

As no one currently residing in Wuyang Village could conduct the rituals, which are nonetheless still important to local people's lives, reintroducing Mo culture has been a key dimension of Chairman Yang's plan to

78 CHAPTER TWO

brand and promote the "thousand-year Buyi village."[31] Since Baolutuo is the "commonly acknowledged cultural element that is most concentrated with rich history and ethnic religious belief," Chairman Yang told me that it should be prioritized in establishing Mo culture in Wuyang Village. For him, scattered polytheist or animistic beliefs were not adequate for a scaled and systematic display. For instance, Baogendei, the deity of earth/heaven, represents a kind of nature worship but is not distinctive enough to be promoted. As far as he knew, not a single village or clan in Buyi areas had ever specifically worshipped Baolutuo, the Mo primogenitor. He did learn, however, that in certain Zhuang regions in Guangxi, a sacred site had been created to worship Baolutuo. On the fifteenth day of the first lunar month, over ten thousand people visited that site for ceremonial worship.[32]

In 2011, Chairman Yang acquired a stone resembling an old man's head from a Mo master in a small market town at the southern end of the county. The Mo master claimed that the stone, found in the middle of the Beipan River, was an incarnation of Baolutuo that appeared in his dream. According to a village elder I interviewed from the same town, who doubted the validity of the stone, the stone had been pulled up from the river with great effort and sold for ¥1,100 (a little more than $150). Since then, Chairman Yang has used it as an icon of stone worship and, moreover, of Mo beliefs. When the stone was brought to Wuyang for the opening of the village museum in 2013, which I participated in and observed, he said, "Let's worship it as the common *bao* [prestigious elderly male] of all the Buyi."

To make this symbolic figure more visible beyond its appearance in preserved scripts and the iconic stone exhibited in the village museum, Chairman Yang has sought to materialize Baolutuo in other concrete forms. Chairman Yang first published a proposed image of Baolutuo on the front page of his monograph (Yang Zhibin 2011a). According to Chairman Yang, that original portrait of Baolutuo was further revised to make the signboard (at least ten meters wide and three meters high) hanging in Wuyang Village for the 2013 Liuyueliu festival, so as to produce the propaganda effect he desired. Both of these Baolutuo images were drawn by Teacher Wei, who hailed from a Buyi village near the county seat and has worked at the county cultural center since graduating from the Art Department of Minzu University of China in Beijing. Chairman Yang often called Teacher Wei for assistance during the process of branding Wuyang Village due to his expertise in artistic design.

"To create [*chuangzao*] the Mo, we need to design [*cehua*] it in a *primitive* [*yuanshi*] way, so that it can be distinguished from other *minzu* worship, and in turn, demonstrate its uniqueness [*gexing*]." Over a meal with local Buyi officials and village cadres in Wuyang one day, during which I was present, Chairman Yang described a vision of his own devising. He critiqued worship of the Bamboo King, promoted by a Miao group in the central part of Zhenning County, pointing out that the appearance and attire of the Bamboo King they designed closely resembled that of the Qing emperor Kangxi. "Since Baolutuo was the founder of the Mo rituals and the primogenitor of the Buyi, he should be configured and presented as a premodern figure," Chairman Yang declared.

Baolutuo was therefore portrayed as a middle-aged man with long hair tied with paper mulberry fiber, sitting by a cliff with rivers and waterfalls roaring below. The figure in the big signboard, however, looks older than the one published in Chairman Yang's book, with grayer eyebrows, sideburns, and beard. Sitting under a pine tree, he holds a stone plate (or a banana leaf, as portrayed in the signboard) — this was before paged books came into existence — inscribed with the initial symbols of the Mo in his hands. Rather than the modified Chinese characters in Mo scriptures preserved up to the present day, the inscriptions Chairman Yang designed were twelve Chinese zodiac animals meant to represent the twelve disciples of Baolutuo. Chairman Yang suggested that Baolutuo, with the fingers of one hand pinched (a hand gesture similar to a Buddha), is contemplating the Mo ideals in relation to heaven and earth and the human world. Instead of tree fibers binding Baolutuo's arms and legs as designed in Chairman Yang's published monograph, the figure on the signboard is wearing a blue robe draped over one shoulder (figure 3).

With the intention of creating an antique and mystical feel, archaic characters were added on the signboard, which some villagers pointed out

FIGURE 3. The huge signboard featuring Baolutuo hung from the village committee building, under which a Buyi dance performance was staged (2013).

to me. A villager who used to teach elementary school at the county seat suggested that the inscription printed on the portrait resembles oracle bone script (*jiaguwen*), the earliest known form of ancient Chinese writing, and he made a wild guess that a character looked like "rice field." As Chairman Yang later confirmed, when he invited me to a hot pot gathering at the county seat to bid me farewell at the end of my fieldwork in November 2013, those archaic characters originated from the Red Cliff Inscriptions (*hongya tianshu*) found around the Buyi areas in Anshun City, which are "not that far from Wuyang Village." According to scholarly and official discourse, these inscriptions as engraved symbols on a huge light-red cliff are unlike any known ancient characters and, in fact, remain undeciphered. Chairman Yang suggested that the Red Cliff Inscriptions, dated much earlier than the modified Chinese characters recognized by the State Council in 2009, were indeed Buyi ancient scripts. According to him, "The well-known Red-Cliff Inscriptions were no doubt created by ancient Buyi ancestors. There is no need to debate who the creators were. We could never figure out what

RITUALS, EXPERTS, AND CULTURAL REVIVALS 81

ethnicity it was called back then, but for sure it was Bu-yi (pu^3 $2i^3$)." Here Chairman Yang was suggesting that, despite the changing appellations other groups have historically used to refer to the Buyi, the Buyi have always called themselves Buyi. A few Buyi cadres from Wuyang Village who were Chairman Yang's assistants in village development and joined us for the hot pot gathering echoed him in agreement.

By using valorized features of archaic scripts and a reinvented mythical figure, Chairman Yang sought to create a common deity for the Buyi people. As a somewhat self-appointed expert, Chairman Yang resembles many other local officials whose main concern is to repackage religion and display it to visitors, emphasizing the spectacular and the picturesque (Oakes and Sutton 2010, 16). They market what might be proximate to religion as folk customs and local culture, selecting portions suited for display and performance and augmenting them with artistic elements from other regions and provinces. Much like the Zhuang scholars and officials in Holm's (2004) discussion, Buyi elites take pride in this newly resurgent sense of ethnic identity based on a kind of historicized origin myth.

However, villagers did not necessarily know who the symbolic Baolutuo was, nor did the elaborately staged Mo ritual mean much to them. After the Liuyueliu events ended that day, I revisited the playground after supper and found a group of male villagers lingering and discussing the portrait of the ancestral figure on the huge signboard hung by Chairman Yang. "This old guy is quite ugly," a few of them groaned. Some were also trying to understand the artistic patterns of the portrait's background, which were intended to create an antique and mythical experience. A couple of men who were relatively more educated, retired from teaching primary school at the county seat, pondered the origin of the figure. They assumed he had passed away on the sixth day of the sixth lunar month (given the withering trees behind him) and, as such, that the ceremony was conducted in his memory. Some thought he might be a buddha at first, although a buddha would have a third eye on his forehead, which was absent from this portrait. Some villagers even turned to me to see if I knew who the figure was. "Could he be Bumo?" I suggested. "[You mean] the ghost master [*gui xiansheng*]?

82   CHAPTER TWO

Maybe," they responded, sounding uncertain. I then asked if he could be Baogendei, the deity of earth/heaven. Villagers replied that Baogendei takes care of water and soil, but the portrait figure could not be him, because for them only the tiny shrine dedicated to the deity of earth/heaven by the entrance of each village constitutes the concrete form of Baogendei. In the end, no one really seemed to know who he was.

RITUALISTIC EVENT PRODUCTION
AND BUYI CULTURAL REVIVAL

While the Liuyueliu annual festival usually focuses on ceremonies for good harvests as well as antiphonal singing (traditionally for matchmaking among young Buyi villagers), the 2013 celebration staged in Wuyang Village that day was intended to evoke something new, something different.[33] Indeed, it was a ritualistic ceremony, an ethnic festival, and a tourism promotion event combined. The legitimacy of the Mo would be ritually evoked and confirmed by the copresence of all the participants at the festival: the deity Baolutuo, village cadres, representatives of the local state, leaders of neighboring communities, and most important of all, the festival-going masses. Among the thousands of fun-seeking visitors were Han urbanites as well as performers and representatives from Miao groups. Reports on the festival later appeared on various news websites as well as online platforms for backpacking and self-guided tours. The portrait of Baolutuo and the ceremony for ritual worship seemed merely to be part of the image making and branding scheme of Wuyang Village, which as a whole aimed to "let the world get to know this ethnic treasure hidden in the mountains," as an online commenter wrote.

This event was a coming together of many interests as well as a complex amalgam of expressions and assertions of sociopolitical meaning that served to signify Baolutuo as the early ancestor of all "fellow Buyi siblings" (*Buyi tongbao*). This kind of event production was, after all, a "ceremony-*cum*-legitimation ritual" (Chau 2006) that combined the expressive power of cultural forms and the ordering force of social institutions. The portrait of Baolutuo continued to look out over the community after that day's event as villagers carried on with their daily routines and occasionally performed for outsiders. The local elites deliberately staged their celebration of Mo on Liuyueliu; hence, common villagers were not the intended audience, nor did they comprehend the meaning behind the staging.

The hierarchical power of ritual literacy further complicates how the masses understand Mo rituals. From my observations across the Buyi region, villagers tend to consider the rituals a natural or self-evident part of their life, without knowing what exactly they mean. And while Mo beliefs and ritual practices have been ingrained in many Buyi regions, there are a variety of perceptions and attitudes toward them. Two basic kinds of religious habitus (Chau 2006, 67)—true believers and practical believers ("half trust and half doubt")—seem to correspond to local realities.[34] Once while I was visiting a Buyi town in southern Zhenning, an illiterate woman expressed deep concern about the disappearance of Mo masters due to the generational gap and social change: "I am so afraid that if I pass away in the future, no one would be able to do the ritual for me." On the other hand, because of the massive influence of state discourse and ideology during the socialist era, some locals maintain a paradoxical attitude toward Mo. Senior males in Wuyang Village explained to me that Mo is "idealist" (as opposed to Marxist materialism). However, it is not contradictory to, but instead parallel to science—one could believe in both, and yet one would only believe in part, depending on practical utility (Harrell 1974). "It is like half-and-half: when you get sick, Mo might cure; but you would have to go to a doctor in the end."

Due to the interpenetration of socialist state power, communal folk rituals have been irrevocably transformed, and traditional practices we see today are "cultural fragments recycled under new circumstances" (Siu 1990a). But we should not assume that what existed before the Mao era was a more coherent and authentic tradition; rather, rituals are a result of inventions and creations adapted by generations of local elites over time, which contributed to both a continuing tradition and a process of change

84 CHAPTER TWO

(see You 2020). Importantly, prestigious males assume converging roles by taking the lead in patriarchal systems, in communal affairs, and as local state agents. Using an age-old idiom called *sanlao sishao*, literally "young and old folks," a prestigious village elder (*zhailao*) in the southernmost town of Zhenning County explained how respected local authorities intersect on a daily basis. "Now, our Buyi village relies on three elders [*sanlao*] — the country elder [*guolao*], village elder [*zhailao*], and the family elder [*fulao*]. *Guolao* are basically village cadres; *zhailao* also include those who lead Mo rituals; and *fulao* take care of the family and lineage."

These authoritative males, in particular, possess and gain social, cultural, and symbolic capital. Right before the 2013 Liuyueliu ceremony in Wuyang Village, for instance, a cultural worker from the provincial level wearing a Buyi-style vest was given the chance to conduct a survey with ritual specialist Master Lu using a form for the Inheritors of Guizhou Minority Nationalities Classic Archives. Possessing scripture records and ritual skills by family inheritance, Master Lu secretly learned the Mo rituals during the Mao era and had been trying to pass down his ritual knowledge to his disciples. In addition, as "memory entrepreneurs," Buyi elite could achieve economic capital not only through tourism display and consumption of cultural traditions but also on the basis of the local ritual economy. As households from nearby villages pay Mo masters to conduct rituals, only sufficiently wealthy families can afford the expenses for grand funeral ceremonies. Around 2006–7, when a prominent Buyi cadre in Zhenning County passed away, his family hosted a grand and costly funeral in his natal village in the mountains that lasted for days. It was attended and acclaimed by local scholars as a rare opportunity to experience "real Mo culture."

As prominent guardians and promoters of their *minzu*'s cultural traditions, local elites seek to excavate the past, however fragmented, to articulate their own uniqueness for new functions and audiences. Interestingly, the reappraisal of Mo rituals seems to connect the Buyi to the more recognized Zhuang and their scholarly discourse rather than differentiating the Buyi narrative from other ethnicities. Some of the most prominent Buyi scholars I have conversed with argue that Mo culture is shared by the Buyi and the Zhuang with common historical origins.[35] They referred to the historical records of Mo culture in Chinese archives that describe connections between the Buyi and the Zhuang, while pointing out how studies have been conducted based on the establishment of the Association for Buyi Studies and the Association for Zhuang Studies, especially after the post-Mao reforms.

Therefore, simply focusing on either the Zhuang or the Buyi might not be adequate for studying Mo culture (Holm 2003), not least because these two *minzu* groups designated by the socialist state were not clearly separated during historical times. Local intellectuals at present are not only speaking to the center but also negotiating their respective positions in various contexts. Many of these cultural revival efforts and reflections are carried out with the intention of positioning the Buyi within the region, as well as within the Chinese state and the Asian borderlands. Reflecting on how other minority elites have interpreted and promoted their culture, Buyi cadres and intellectuals are very aware of local politics and regional history. As ritualistic behaviors flourish at the boundaries between "heaven and earth, center and periphery, my group and their group," perhaps the way of all rituals is "marking such boundaries, playing with them and traversing them" (Oakes and Sutton 2010, 10).

In many parts of China, *minzu* elites are usually those who have experienced the transition from the Mao era to the reform era, who have gained experience and skills in the mass mobilization from socialist collectivization but who also possess memories of changing traditions. That is why some of these key figures behind the initial religious revivals have been former party secretaries who, on the one hand, might wish to expiate past sins (for instance, having participated in toppling temples during the Cultural Revolution) and, on the other, possess the political know-how and connections to jump-start revivals (see also Chau 2006). Various religions and rituals, as well as sacred sites, have flourished with local official

86 CHAPTER TWO

approval and encouragement, in conjunction with commercial tourism as a crucial source of local income and revenue since the 1980s. Especially in the minority regions of southwest China, local elites and officials have been able to use the appeal of religion, even in a superficial form, for local economic and developmental purposes. They present it both as proof of the rich texture of minority culture and as an inseparable part of the national fabric (Borchert 2005; Oakes and Sutton 2010).

As production in the cultural industries is "design-intensive" (Lash and Urry 1994, 112), minority religious activities need to have viewable components so that the state has opportunities to benefit from tourism revenue. In addition to displaying the iconic stone whose shape was said to resemble Baolutuo, Chairman Yang plotted out the possibility of creating a site for worship and a Bumo team in Wuyang Village before I departed the field at the end of 2013. At the time, he was contemplating a plan to turn the Small Bastion up on the hill from Wuyang into a Mo shrine or an ancestral hall by relocating the piece of stone that signifies the legendary Baolutuo. It could, for instance, become a venue to pray for blessings and protection, not only for villagers but also for visitors.

For local elites like Chairman Yang, Mo rituals could even be used to enrich Buyi artistic performances with a *yuanshengtai* feel, conjuring up an aura of originality and authenticity. Incorporating other ritualistic elements of Buyi culture, such as the bronze drum and buffalo sacrifice, Buyi performances could be designed and staged with various props (such as umbrellas and flags), musical instruments, festive costumes, and ritual movements. Mo tradition, to Chairman Yang, is the "core in unearthing [*wajue*] Buyi culture." He told me that only the largest-scale and most comprehensive cultural aspects could be regarded as *authentic*. This economy of authenticity relies on a vision of what the essence of a group is (Borchert 2005, 106). In an age of increasing globalization and modernization, authentic manifestation of a collective identity has to resort to the use of ethnic symbols, which may or may not be derived from everyday life.

Intriguingly, there were also scattered suggestions from local Buyi cadres about setting up totem signs for stone worship by the riverside to echo Wuyang Village's historical relics and stone architecture and manifest the Buyi's spiritual world and sustained relationship with the natural environment. A municipal official working in the cultural industry suggested that establishing materialized forms of totem worship by the riverside would demonstrate a living relic and heritage, drawing a parallel with Window of the World (Shijie Zhi Chuang), a theme park with over one hundred reproductions of famous tourist attractions around the world, located in Shenzhen, the coastal Chinese city adjacent to Hong Kong.[36]

Deeply entrenched in historical memories and social lives, rituals remain central to how sentiments in an ethnic community are mediated based on the shared values and ideologies with which local people connect. Mo rituals remain part of the Buyi's life experience practiced by both elites and commoners. But each speaks a different language, even if both are statist: the socialist state discourse on feudal superstition has been internalized by some local Buyi, while elites and experts in the post-reform era have been working along official lines to institutionalize the rituals. A rich cultural presence based on these expressive practices among ethnic populations has been further reenacted by local elites to create and showcase tangible aspects for outsiders in a context of cultural commodification. Similar to other folk rituals described by Chau (2006, 2), the Mo revival illustrates the intersection of many social actors and forces in local communities and beyond, including the political ambitions and paternalistic interventions of local heritage activists and state agencies and the economic interests of related specialists and stakeholders, as well as the collective religiosity and fun-seeking spirit of the worshippers and tourists.

When I returned in the summer of 2015, the huge signboard of Baolutuo in Wuyang Village had been taken down. By September 2017, the village committee building where the signboard was hanging had been torn down and replaced by a new stone house intended to match the style of the old stone village. However, the Mo icon is still in Wuyang—now incarnated in an almost three-meter-tall bronze statue at the village entrance, where a

FIGURE 4. Bronze statue of Baolutuo at the entrance to Wuyang Village (2015).

performance plaza and a welcome center have been built to define Wuyang Village as a cultural destination (figure 4).

For Chairman Yang, this bronze statue of Baolutuo not only serves as an eye-catcher upon arrival at the village but also provides an opportunity for people to pray for blessings and protection. Creating an ethnic brand requires devising strategies: rituals are supposed to be belief systems and spiritual practices in local everyday life, but they are materialized and visualized as such for the sake of cultural promotion.

CHAPTER THREE

FEMALE PERFORMERS AND
THE SPECTACULAR STATE

THE MUSIC BEGAN. A dozen female villagers stepped out onto the newly built performance stage and started dancing slowly to the sweet and gentle melody they had prerecorded, composed by middle-aged women in the Buyi language. Under an overcast sky, their Buyi costumes appeared all the more vibrant. Ruby- and emerald-colored patches of embroidery decorated their batik clothes indigo-dyed with drip and whirlpool patterns. As the dancers turned, their long ruffled skirts fluttered like the butterflies in the lyrics of the song.

Watching from across the plaza, I noticed a female villager in her sixties standing next to me. She was deeply engrossed in the performance onstage. Intrigued, I turned to her and asked in Buyi, "Is this [performance] good to watch [*?dəi¹ mi² ?dəi¹ jɛ²*]?" She answered in Buyi, with specific words borrowed from Chinese. "Yes, very good. Wearing the Buyi costume to dance looks pretty. The Bunong and the Miao are called minority nationalities [*shaoshu minzu*] too, but only here live the genuinely qualified [*zhenzige de*] minority nationalities."

This was the Lunar New Year celebration of 2013, when the county government initiated a three-day event consisting of cultural and sports activities in Wuyang Village. In hopes of bringing the village to the forefront as a new cultural destination, this festive celebration exemplified a mode of cultural production in which the local state and the villagers joined forces. Following public speeches by county-level government officials, activities for the crowd primarily included basketball games and, more

90 CHAPTER THREE

importantly, art performances. Wuyang villagers enthusiastically signed up to perform songs and dances to compete for small prizes with Han and minority participants from nearby villages and other parts of the county, as well as with staff from a supermarket at the county seat that provided financial sponsorship for the event. That young and old gathered for the event, many of whom had returned from migrant labor for the Lunar New Year, posed a sharp contrast to the tranquility of Wuyang Village during most times of the year.

The female spectator's remark hints at how minority villagers have become adept at comparing culturally genuine ethnic minorities with those who are deemed not authentic.[1] In her comparison of various ethnic groups, the female villager not only juxtaposed the Buyi against the Miao, longtime inhabitants of the same region, but she also seemed to single out the Bunong, who have, in fact, been officially identified as Buyi or Buyizu. Subtle variations in language, environment, and custom (including costuming) underlie this internal differentiation, which still persists among the Buyi in Zhenning County, who are considered to inhabit three subdialect regions, according to ethnolinguists. Through public performances and recreational events like this one in Wuyang, intra-ethnic and interethnic competitions have thus become all the more conspicuous as local peoples seek to distinguish themselves, to outperform other groups, and to attract outside attention.

In our conversation, the female villager highlighted the Buyi costumes with long skirts—rendered even more visible through staged song-and-dance performances—as markers of the uniqueness of Buyi culture. Local women's sense of pride attached to traditional Buyi clothing may derive from the time and energy invested in these items, not to mention the delicate techniques required to create them. To produce a complete ensemble of handmade Buyi costumes requires months if not a year, provided that women can spare enough time from agricultural production to work on them. During the first few months of my fieldwork, I spent hours sitting with the then fifty-year-old Senior Grandma Wu every day to learn batik drawing, as the first step of making Buyi women's clothing, while she played video recordings of village events and performances or Korean or Taiwanese dramas in the background using her television set and videodisc player. It took me months to be able to draw straight lines and tiny dots using a thin metal blade dipped in beeswax that was heated to the perfect temperature; even by the end of my fieldwork, I had not managed to learn to skillfully draw the concentric whirlpool patterns most noticeable on sleeves and skirts. The multicolored weaving on Buyi clothing was an even more complicated task, which Senior Grandma Wu had to practice over and over again with a wooden loom that took up significant space in her bedroom. She sometimes had to consult elder women in the village or learn the weaving techniques by trial and error.

In the local context, drawing batik and embroidering alongside other female villagers is an essential form of sociality, which I experienced with Senior Grandma Wu. I occasionally followed Senior Grandma Wu to her natal village, about an hour's drive from Wuyang, where we sat with her female relatives and acquaintances chitchatting over batik drawing. They did not simply exchange ideas about clothing or the knowledge and techniques of cloth making; they maintained and reinforced social relations through these informal gatherings. At more formal, public settings, posing for pictures and participating in stage performances in traditional costume have also been a delight for many. Local women carefully collected photos (and video recordings) of their costumes and performances, which were either framed and showcased on their walls or stored in safe corners of their houses. Learning to make batik and participating in performances also allowed me to be gradually accepted by female villagers in Wuyang and offered me a particular lens into village life and the domestic sphere.

The elderly woman I spoke to at the 2013 Lunar New Year event believed that only the Buyi, particularly those in the area around Wuyang Village, could be considered genuine minority nationalities. To be genuinely qualified, the female villager implied, is to demonstrate a certain marked difference. "Looking good" (*?dəi¹ jɛ²* in Buyi) through visible difference could contribute to the reputation of local ethnic communities in competitive cultural promotion. At the same time, public performances, featured with

92 CHAPTER THREE

increasing frequency in contemporary leisure activities and ethnic cultural production, might have further reinforced the distinguishing effect of what Buyi women wear. Mostly donned in the past for market days or life-cycle rituals such as marriage and burial ceremonies, women's clothing has now become a visual element evincing a sense of ethnic pride and consciousness through embodied cultural practices that are part of the local Buyi's everyday life. Reinforced by public gatherings and festive events over time, local Buyi have learned "to be ethnic," or become ethnicized, in the language of officialdom (Schein 2000, 257), thus demarcating themselves as Buyi according to state-designated categories.

Staging ethnic performances provided locals, especially female participants, a means to showcase their cultural facets — not least their delicately pleated long skirts. While Buyi male elites were the initial gatekeepers who introduced me to Wuyang Village, it was the women who took me in and taught me the Buyi way of life. Juxtaposed with the male elites and intellectuals depicted in chapter 2 as carrying the authority with the written word that dominates cultural conservatorship (Schein 2000, 205), the female participants at the core of this chapter demonstrate a paradox in ethnic branding: on the one hand, minority women are usually designated as the bearers of cultural tradition, embodying identity markers from language and costume to folk arts and intangible heritage; on the other, they are more often than not rendered marginal in heritage-tourism development processes due to their limited political and discursive power. Women in Wuyang Village have been mobilized to perform their songs and dances in traditional clothing as a public showcase but have rarely been included in either informal or formal village meetings with higher-level officials convened to discuss local development projects.

Ethnic performances therefore serve as one of the few available venues that allow female villagers to straddle the domestic sphere and public displays of Buyiness in a patriarchal society. Singing Buyi songs and staging performances have become a primary way for the women, most of whom are minimally educated, to narrate their changing historical experience and to engage with the state-led development process. Unlike male villagers who had received high school or college educations for the past few decades, most of the middle-aged and senior women in Wuyang Village were illiterate, and even the younger generation seldom graduated from high school, to the extent that a Yang daughter who had graduated from college, earned a white-collar income, and was still single in her early thirties was deemed fairly unusual at the time. But their relatively low levels of literacy or education do not prevent female villagers from combining Buyi cultural forms seamlessly with new ideas and new mediums, or from participating in their own means of ethnic branding. Whether at formally mobilized or informally organized performances that highlight Buyi sartorial and oral traditions, Buyi women present new content and scripts with an attitude that explicitly gratifies the state; at the same time, these performances are underlain by a rooted sense of ethnic self-consciousness and confidence.

Buyi women's performances exemplify how the "spectacular state" (L. Adams 2010) strategically appropriates ceremony, ritual, and expressive culture as the primary means of communicating with its citizenry. Promoting the state's domination over the valence of concepts such as heritage and progress (L. Adams 2010, 5), the party-state's legitimacy and local ethnic identity are simultaneously generated by affective experiences of state-mediated ethnic culture on a symbolic level. Often it is the non-Han women, their outfits, and their songs and dances that contribute most to the spectacular state in China. Ethnic minorities, primarily rural women, presented as "happily singing and dancing people" under the multiethnic rubric in earlier decades (e.g., Gladney 1994; White 1997), continue to be portrayed as traditional, exotic, colorful, and folk-artistic. Catering to the Han gaze, which often belongs to male urban sophisticates, internal orientalism (Schein 1997, 2000) characterizes contemporary commodification and representation of southern minorities, especially in terms of feminized bodies. Having reinforced an unbalanced power hierarchy and "the supremacy of the masculine Han center" since the Mao era (Evans 1999, 74), public culture thus tends to depict the minorities, the folk, and the peasants as feminine keepers of Chinese tradition and the exotic Other against which Han urbanites assert their modernity.[2]

94 CHAPTER THREE

Deemed residual of the past, rural ethnic women have hence carried a double burden, as they are suspended in time as bearers of ancient cultural motifs yet obligated to modernize (Schein 1997). So how do Buyi women make sense of and take part in local processes of ethnic branding? Local women's perspectives and life experiences take us beyond discussions of authenticity in the production and representation of ethnic minority cultures. Sartorial and oral practices not only serve as self-identified ethnic markers but also reveal the social settings in which women effectively prepare, produce, and document performances, sometimes with the help of new media practices such as audio and visual recordings. Female villagers—with generational differences—engage with the influx of bureaucratic attention, the tourism market, and a new kind of (self-)governance through their bodies, performances, and subjectivities. Much like the changing practices of other local social actors, women's song-and-dance performances embody a yearning for an engaged, modern life in the post-reform era.

WOMEN AS EMBODIMENT OF ETHNIC TRADITION? CLOTHING AND TEXTILE ARTS

In changing sociopolitical climates, female members of local communities in China are sometimes regarded as critical to the continuation of cultural traditions as heritage bearers, while they have also been the target of revolutionary forces and civilizing missions (Ka-ming Wu 2015). Questions of embodiment and sartorial decisions are especially at stake (Schein 2000, 209), as the marking of physical appearance, along with costume patterns inherently associated with changing marriage customs and ritual norms, are signs of tradition for ethnic rural female subjects. Contemporary scholars have long considered sartorial traditions as not only an identity marker but also an alternative narrative of community history and collective memory. Clothing and the techniques related to cloth making, especially dyeing and embroidery, have been highlighted in the pictorial pages that begin books on Buyi, from *A Brief History of Buyizu* (Buyizu jianshi) commissioned by the National Ethnic Affairs Commission in 1984 to *The Buyi Ethnicity in*

Zhenning County (Zhenning Buyizu) written by the Wu family in 2014. In addition to their work on the Mo ritual system discussed in the previous chapter, the Wu brothers have invested considerable time in investigating the historical and cultural meanings of patterns and symbols on Buyi costumes, sometimes with the help of their wives and daughters, who accompanied them to interview female villagers. They have planned a series of books on Buyi clothing, the first of which was published in 2022 (Wu Kaifeng and Wu Zhonggang 2022). For many cultural experts, embroidery and batik patterns on clothing could reveal historical narratives that ethnic populations sought to recollect—a kind of "restricted literacy without permanent texts, literature, or documents" that exists in an essentially oral culture (Scott 2009, 227). In today's climate, which favors oral traditions and intangible heritage, women with limited literacy or education who continue to pass down sartorial skills and memories are hence regarded as bearing alternative forms of expertise, creativity, and wisdom in a patriarchal society dominated by educated males.

However, ethnic clothing as an embodiment of tradition may well be subject to attack in times of social change, often signifying the bitter memories of local populations. In late imperial depictions of culturally othered peoples (such as those in the "Miao Albums"), customary dress, music, or dance, along with marital and ritual practices, conjured up a mirror image of civilized conduct of the center. Both men and women of some ethnic populations at China's southwestern peripheries—including certain groups identified as Buyi today—started transforming what they wore (for instance, from skirts to trousers) under Qing rule, either self-consciously or under compulsion depending on the policy of cultural assimilation in specific regions (Xu and Guo 2012; Zhang Shenglan 2014). During the Republican era, sartorial style and hairstyles of ethnic minorities were targeted for eradication and modification. A case of the Guizhou government forcing cultural homogenization happened in 1943, when local authorities forced Miao women to change their hairstyle and dress by using scissors to cut the women's hair and even clothes (Guo Wu 2019, 142–43). Elders in some of the ethnic minority regions I have visited in Guizhou recalled that

96   CHAPTER THREE

officials and soldiers guarding the entrance gates of town seats at the time carried big scissors and awaited horrified minority passersby. Nevertheless, archival records and oral histories depicting forced sartorial changes mostly concern the so-called raw Miao or barbarian areas of Guizhou, which were deemed less subdued human holdouts. The Buyi area near Wuyang Village did not experience such a traumatic past. Up till the early half of the twentieth century, most women in today's Buyi areas near Wuyang Village still wore long, ruffled skirts, sometimes with several layers depending on familial wealth and social occasions (Buyizu Jianshi Bianxiezu 1984, 155–58). Male clothing, by contrast, gradually grew more similar to that of the Han but was usually made from home-crafted indigo-dyed cloth, which men also wrapped around their heads as turbans.

Under the rule of the Chinese socialist state, women's status, along with their social customs, underwent decades of transformation from the Maoist era to market reforms. Doubly oppressed by their status as women in a "backward" non-Han society (Frangville 2012), ethnic rural women became targets for the Communist Party's vision of liberation in ways that symbolized a yearning for the prosperity of socialism. This vision, however, was paradoxical in that emancipating women from domestic bondage and breaking with traditional roles were needed to incorporate them into various political, social, and economic activities for the purpose of collectivization, while old customs, attitudes, and institutions (including gender inequality in family and village life) nonetheless persisted. Cultural representations during the socialist period even demonstrated differentiated visual treatment of Han women and ethnic women, with the latter painted "in gay colors, dancing, waving ribbons, and always smiling"; this portrayal of colorful clothing can be parsed as both celebratory and respectful while also discounting the wearers as serious revolutionary actors (Evans 1999, 73–74).

According to Sara Friedman's (2006) research on Hui'an rural women in China's southeastern province of Fujian, local and regional state actors aspired to act on the bodies of women in order to mold them into liberated socialist citizens by attacking elements identified as feudal, such as distinctive features of women's dress that were thought to hamper labor performance. According to Buyi elders, while those in Wuyang Village were never forced to change their traditional clothing, which remained crucial for life-cycle rituals and staged performances, local Buyi women began to wear plain shirts and trousers on a regular basis and internalized the message that wearing thick layers of Buyi long skirts interfered with agricultural production. Relatively more educated women who moved to nearby townships and the county seat for nonagricultural work adopted a plain jacket or blouse, as old forms of Buyi clothing were becoming impractical among the elite even before the establishment of the People's Republic.

In Hui'an, the pattern of women's extended postmarital residence with their natal families was also regarded as an institutional obstacle under the collective system and was hence targeted for intervention, especially during the Maoist high tide of socialist construction (Friedman 2006). The Buyi historically shared this post-marriage residential pattern—that is, delayed transfer marriage (Siu 1990b)—with many other indigenes in southern China. This marriage custom involved a woman remaining in her natal home after marriage, sometimes until the birth of a child or even permanently. Only when important events, festivals, or busy farming seasons required the presence or assistance of the wife would she stay with the husband's family for a period of time. Buyi families with abundant estates even reserved land for their daughters, which could only be turned over to the husband's family after the daughter/wife went to reside permanently with the in-laws (Buyizu Jianshi Bianxiezu 1984, 162; see also Wu Zhonggang and Wu Kaifeng 2014, 96). In Buyi areas surrounding Wuyang Village, the shift from natal home to in-laws' residence was marked by a change of headwear for the wife, who would shift from wrapping her hair into an updo covered with a kerchief to wearing a hard, heavy headpiece shaped like a carapace (*ts'aŋ³ kan⁵ k'au³* in Buyi) (Wu Zhonggang and Wu Kaifeng 2014, 101–3). According to some, it was a transformation that women were reluctant to adopt. Villagers nostalgically brought up stories of how women used to jump up and down around their houses to evade being forced to put on the carapace-like headpiece. A Wu family member recalled seeing a woman weeping for days before she had to put on the headpiece and move to her husband's home in the 1970s.

This traditional marriage custom in Buyi areas around Wuyang did not become the target of socialist reforms, as in the Hui'an case. In fact, the local land tenure system reserved plots for each household to cope with extended postmarital residence and the possible changes that ensued. Nevertheless, according to locals, significant changes to marriage customs transpired due to the waves of migrant labor after decollectivization. Laborers were first drawn to nearby townships and county seats to work in factories in the early 1980s, and then to cities and coastal areas starting from the 1990s. Since then, traditional institutions and customs around domestic lifestyles have undergone rapid transformation, especially due to the increasing mobility of women. Rural Buyi women no longer followed the convention of extended postmarital residence with their natal family, and many gradually forgot how traditional weddings were prepared and conducted — for example, what types of offerings to prepare for ancestral worship and what kind of wedding gifts symbolized stability and prosperity.

In the post-Mao period, officials have retreated from many reforms directed at local women's bodies, turning instead to a new discourse of socialist spiritual civilization (Friedman 2006). The didactic themes in folk performances since the 1950s — with a dual role of ideologically educating the masses and entertaining high leadership by repackaging official messages in exotic wrappings (Schein 2000, 185) — continue in the present. In Zhenning County, for instance, campaigns such as Building a New Socialist Countryside (Jianshe Shehuizhuyi Xin Nongcun), launched in 2006 and covering a wide range of rural policies from birth planning to village sanitation, have mobilized women by encouraging them to incorporate party discourse into art performances aiming at improving local quality of life, harmony in the family, and spiritual civilization (Lu 2010, 157). Following government regulations in the Buyi-Miao Autonomous County, joint art performances and sports competitions have been held for annual Buyi and Miao festivals such as Liuyueliu and Siyueba, as well as anniversaries of

FEMALE PERFORMERS AND THE STATE 99

FIGURE 5. Buyi women dressed in Buyi clothing sitting in front of propaganda posters about birth planning policy and preparing to perform a song at a Liuyueliu event (2013). One holds the piece of paper with lyrics and chords distributed by the county government.

the county's founding, celebrated every five years since 1963 (Wu Zhongshi 2010, 47), where varied ethnic costumes at public gatherings and celebratory events continue to signify China's "unity in diversity" (figure 5).

Growing mass media and tourist commodification further enhance the recognition of ethnic rural women as "not-quite-Han, not-quite-civilized, and hence, not-quite-citizens" by inscribing that difference on their bodies, whether through adornment styles or marital and sexual practices (Friedman 2006, 247). Considering that Buyi clothing may be inconvenient for farming in the field or traveling to distant market towns, Buyi women today wear traditional garb mostly on two occasions, apart from weddings and burials: attending public performances at the village or county level or posing as photogenic objects for tourists and journalists. For almost all staged performances, female villagers tend to wear the kerchief that is lighter and easier to put on, which formerly signified the status preceding conjugal residence, whereas in actuality most of them are married and have children or even grandchildren.

While women's clothing remains a visible marker of Buyi identity for both locals and outsiders, the cultural meaning behind it is perhaps lost on the younger generations. Mothers and grandmothers almost always needed to help the younger women and girls with putting on the layers of Buyi clothing, which could be quite complicated if not worn regularly. For the younger generations, new sartorial statements might claim modernity in two ways: they displayed affinity with what was considered urban fashion, and they demonstrated economic status, as evidenced by young women's ability to purchase clothing rather than having to rely on what could be made at home (Schein 2000, 248–49). Furthermore, generational differences were evident in the divergent types of performance costumes as well as the songs and dances preferred by Buyi women of different ages. In contrast to elder female villagers, who sang old Buyi tunes in their traditional clothing for performances, women in their twenties to forties—many of whom had been migrant workers—put on rented outfits or fashionable high heels and admitted that while they could understand most of the Buyi lyrics, learning to sing the old tunes could be very difficult. On occasions when local women staged their dances, the old Buyi tunes were often juxtaposed with folk disco music or pop songs (for instance, even the globally popular "Gangnam Style").

Ethnic women's performances are thus by no means essentialized traditional practices reproduced for the cultural economy. During my fieldwork, Wuyang Village experienced a time in which locals were being socialized to package their culture for visitors and to stage explicit identity markers such as traditional clothing and old Buyi tunes, mostly for state-initiated promotional events. The process of ethnic branding for the Buyi suggests that the post-Mao folk cultural revival was important to local identity building, not just for the state agenda, and that self-commodification, far from being tantamount to objectification, was essential to establishing Buyi subjectivity. Buyi women have actively engaged with uncertain sociopolitical environments and defined ever-changing ethnic traditions on their own terms. Therefore, contemporary internal orientalist discourse that aligns the feminine and the ethnic/folk/rural with an authentic realm of tradition risks dismissing the creative initiative of ethnic rural women, who should be considered autonomous cultural agents rather than passive culture bearers (Schein 1997, 80; Ka-ming Wu 2015, 61–62). For minority peasants, customary dress — like rituals — is a matter of everyday practice with its own significations, not simply a vestige of the past that indicates a naturalized sense of continuity with history no longer possessed by the modern urban Chinese. The songs, dances, and media that accompany sartorial traditions are important components of the local performances through which Buyi rural women engage with their changing social worlds as they participate in everyday enactment and negotiation of difference.

ORAL TRADITION IN CHANGING TIMES

About a week before the 2013 Lunar New Year celebration, I joined my host, Senior Grandma Wu, and a dozen women in their fifties and sixties — most of whom had married into the Wu lineage — by a log fire in one of the Wu households after dinnertime to compose a new song for the upcoming state-sponsored celebration. The song was titled "The Small Bastion" (*niaŋ² tɕiɛ² niɛ¹* in Buyi), named after the late imperial stone structure on the hilltop that Wuyang Village once built for self-protection and has proudly preserved as a relic (figure 6). Almost all illiterate, the female villagers nonetheless skillfully rhymed and memorized the Buyi lyrics. They made up a six-minute full-length song over two consecutive evening meetings, each lasting four hours and filled with casual chitchat and jokes, as well as discussions concerning which words were most appropriate.

To show their gratitude for the aid the village had received from local government in the opening line, three women leading the composition of the song had the following discussion:

"Tomorrow, the Han people are also coming, not just the Buyi. Our song has to be clear and understandable."

"So in this line of the lyric, it would be better to talk about how the county government or the Communist Party cares about us?"

FIGURE 6. Small Bastion on top of a hill that has become an attraction in Wuyang Village (2012).

FEMALE PERFORMERS AND THE STATE 103

"Yes. Otherwise, to sing about the leadership of the township would be outdated [*gudai*], not applicable to the contemporary scenario."

Even though Wuyang Village was still under the direct administrative jurisdiction of the township-level authority, the female villagers thought it would have been outdated (or archaic, as they expressed with the word *gudai*) to thank the township. Indeed, most funding for village construction and development actually originated from the county level, and in particular, from the CPPCC (Chinese People's Political Consultative Conference), where Chairman Yang worked until his retirement and through which he continued to bring high-level officials to visit Wuyang Village. Upon further exchanging ideas, the female villagers eventually decided to sing: "Our village has solicitude [*guanhuai*] from the county government [*xian zhengfu*]; our village receives care [*guanxin*] from the provincial CPPCC [*sheng zhengxie*]." All of these terms are borrowed from standard Chinese.

"With such leadership," the song goes on, "our village has built new wide roads. A village gate is constructed to protect the village and make it beautiful. The carpentry and masonry are so skillful, even better than those in Sichuan that have been acclaimed by everyone. We can build skyscrapers in Guizhou like those in Chongqing and Shanghai. This year is 2013, and we have a new parking lot and a performance stage, surrounded with flowers and trees." Considering which words were most suitable and memorable, the female villagers also had a short debate about whether to sing the names of the newly planted tree species in Buyi or Chinese but eventually gave up because not everyone could agree on the specific names of the tree species in Chinese.

The lyrics then continue to depict the construction process in the village: "Upon finishing paving the paths inside the village with stone, dragon and phoenix [*longfeng*] would return to their original position. As the phoenix flies, the layers of stone lead us up to the bastion through winding paths with new handrails. Up in this bastion, which resembles the home of high officials with a big gate in towns, a dragon is guarding our village's treasure." Toward the end, the song becomes moralizing, reminding villagers to preserve the antique relic [*laogudong*] for the sake of the village and never to

104 CHAPTER THREE

TABLE 3. Thematic categories of Buyi songs created and performed in Wuyang and the surrounding area

Category	Examples
Antique narrative	"Legendary Origin-Myth"
Ritualistic/life-cycle	"Marriage"; "Childbirth Blessings"
Ethical/moral	"Against Gambling"
Romantic/love	"Male-Female Duet"
Language-identity	"Learning Buyi-Han Words"
Agrarian life and change	"Irrigation"; "Agricultural Tools"
Socialist agenda	"Socialism Is Good"
Extralocal mobility	"Migrant Labor in the South"
Dynastic comparison	"Before and After the Liberation"
Village promotion	"Thousand-Year-Old Village"

forget it for hundreds of years. It ends with the line: "From generation to generation, we are indeed the 'thousand-year-old Wuyang Village.' Young and old, brothers and sisters."[3]

A song like "The Small Bastion" is noteworthy in that it not only captures the most up-to-date development in the village but also manifests the sediment of time. Reminding villagers not to forget about history and not to discard this village relic, the song builds on the role of singing in locally meaningful ways to educate community members and particularly the younger generations about certain morals. Cosmological and ritual ideas are evidenced in lyrics about the dragon (and phoenix): as in Buyi burial ceremonies, breaking ground or sod (*dongtu* in standard Chinese) for road construction supposedly disturbed the spirit of the dragon in place, which would only return to its original position when the disturbance was completed.[4] Juxtaposed with the bastion that is the age-old treasure of the "thousand-year-old village," new infrastructure development is compared to that of big cities by female villagers who intended to express pride and confidence. In their parlance, these accomplishments might never have happened without the leadership of the party-state, to which locals show their gratitude from the outset of the song—although a couple of women remarked during their discussion of the lyrics on how some of the new trees planted by the government did not survive.

During my stay in and beyond Wuyang Village, I frequently encountered Buyi singing, which remains indispensable to the cultural fabric of local life. In addition to listening to villagers singing at numerous life-cycle events and performances (some of which I participated in), I watched dozens of song-and-dance videodiscs recorded at household feasts and village events. Most of the time, I had the company of Senior Grandma Wu and other villagers, who enthusiastically commented on these video recordings, which we watched over and over again. I have also helped female villagers record and broadcast their songs with the voice recorders I brought to the field. With assistance from the women and several better-educated men in the village, I managed to translate a few Buyi songs into standard Chinese. Table 3 categorizes some of the songs I have encountered but by no means covers the wide variety of songs locals created and sang over different time periods.[5]

In the Buyi language, to "speak Buyi" ($k'a\eta^3 \ ?i^3$) and to "sing Buyi" ($f\partial n^1 \ ?i^3$) indicate a closely coherent set of oral practices. The rhythms of Buyi songs seem to flow naturally through the orality of the lyrics, but very few people could actually explain to me how to "sing Buyi." Passed down by older generations, the tunes of the songs are skillfully formulated based on the phonetic patterns of the Buyi language. Similar to singing practices of other Chinese ethnic minorities (e.g., Ingram 2012), the role of language elements, such as meter, intonation, and syllable structure, is significant in creating and maintaining strict rhyming patterns. While I was asking around for help with translating the Buyi songs, villagers often told me that some of the phrases were hardly translatable into Chinese, and at times even those who had received a school education could only vaguely explain the meaning.

Buyi songs, like the local rituals examined in the previous chapter, have been part of local life-cycle and communal events, serving as a normative realm to define and reflect social customs and ethics. Historically speaking, singing has been strongly oriented toward the realm of life-cycle rituals such as marriage, childbirth, or burial. Songs have also been central to daily settings, communal interactions, and festive events, like guests visiting, feasting, or drinking. Antiphonal singing prevails in Buyi villages; this type of singing mimics dialogue—for example, between hosts and guests or between the bridegroom's and bride's families at weddings. Singing Buyi is not entirely gender specific, as the traditional setting for dating among youngsters (a recreational activity known in local Han language as *langshao*), for example, required both genders to take part in a duet of love songs. Now that dating is carried out in entirely different forms and through modern media communication, such as cell phones, due to outward mobility (especially for migrant labor), none of the younger Buyi men or women I knew ever sang Buyi to find their partners. Rather, some of the songs—including the one now branded as a promotional song of Wuyang Village—were created and sung by male villagers over sixty years old. While most of the Buyi songs we hear these days borrow a considerable number of Han words and expressions, some songs created by educated males have also inserted a few traditional Chinese verses from poems or proverbs.

As a social rather than purely musical activity, singing has thus been carried out at important social venues of local ethnic communities and has major educational significance (Ingram 2011). The original pedagogical function of Buyi singing is intended to convey social norms and moral standards, urging younger generations to follow ancestral guidance. As a form of oral tradition that encapsulates collective memory, some of the songs local Buyi created in Wuyang traced the historical origin of the village or that of Buyi lineages in the surrounding areas.[6] Situated in a multiethnic context of constant interactions with Han populations over time, Buyi women invented a song that explicitly dealt with language and identity, featuring corresponding Buyi and Han vocabulary words, to teach Buyi children Chinese and to teach Han people Buyi.[7] Today, the pedagogical function of singing fits well with state goals, such as preserving historical relics (toward the end of "The Small Bastion"), and continues to be promoted and reinforced through the words of elders.

As an informal means of narrative transmission, such improvised oral performances often reflect their immediate social context and make changes according to it (Davis 2001). During the Maoist era, the Chinese Communist Party (CCP) actively reformed and appropriated folk society through various forms of cultural discourse and popular practices to convey its revolutionary narrative and consolidate its ruling power (Ka-ming Wu 2011, 102). The nascent People's Republic of China implemented its mass propaganda and communication strategy by enthusiastically propagating Chairman Mao's thought among local populations, encouraging people to praise the new regime and incorporate new policy slogans into their oral traditions and art expressions. Early socialist deployment of old cultural and art forms thus served to appeal to the predominantly illiterate rural masses and to communicate state ideological messages (Ka-ming Wu 2015)—for example, through the propaganda folk songs that were prevalent in socialist China.[8]

"Good Flowers Are Red" (Hao hua hong) was selected to represent the Buyizu as a minority nationality group and to be performed in front of Chairman Mao and other central government officials in the late 1950s. "Good Flowers Are Red" harks back to a genre of Buyi folk melodies, and one popular version of its lyrics was originally a love duet that used the metaphor of an indigenous flora species called the Roxburgh rose (*Rosa roxburghii* Tratt). The song was adapted to refer to how Chairman Mao— then eulogized as the "red sun" rising in the East, which became symbolic of the Communist revolution—had helped extricate the masses from impoverishment and exploitation.[9] The main lyric of its chorus goes: "The flowers that grow toward the sun are red." Two Buyi women, Qin Yuezhen and Wang Qinhui, around eighteen years old at the time, sang this song with their agricultural production teams and subsequently participated in the Huishui County First Folk Art Joint Performance in 1956. Endorsed by art experts from the Guizhou Provincial Song and Dance Troupe, the two recorded the song, and it was broadcast by the Guizhou Provincial Radio Station. In early 1957, they represented Guizhou at the Second National Folk Music and Dance Joint Performance in Beijing, earning the song

108 CHAPTER THREE

nationwide fame. For the Labor Day celebration of the tenth anniversary of the People's Republic of China in 1959, official members of the Guizhou Minzu Delegation that visited Beijing reportedly sang "Good Flowers Are Red" to express gratitude to the heads of state (Guizhou Sheng Guangbo Dianshi Tai 2020).

Carrying on its symbolic significance in the post-Mao era, "Good Flowers Are Red" has become a state-recognized artifact of intangible cultural heritage and a desirable brand for local cultural industries. The township in central-southern Guizhou's Huishui County, from which the song originated, even renamed itself after this song, displaying a stone plate engraved with the song's score and lyrics in the public square. During the National People's Congress in 2014, a Buyi female representative who is an intangible cultural heritage inheritor and the self-made entrepreneur of an ethnic textile enterprise sang "Good Flowers Are Red" when General Secretary Xi met with the Guizhou delegation in Beijing (Guizhou Ribao 2014). Even though Zhenning County was not the birthplace of the song, "Good Flowers Are Red" has been consistently staged as the representative song of the Buyi since the Mao era. And yet, as Zhenning County contains all three Buyi subgroups, the performance of the song is usually different from other Buyi regions across Guizhou. At the county's public events, elderly women are often staged together in three sets of typical costumes to indicate the three Buyi subgroups and to showcase the unity and diversity of the Buyi. Each of the three subgroups sings "Good Flowers Are Red" in a different rhythm due to the slightly varied subdialects. Toward the end of the performance, the three groups of performers join together in a grand chorus to sing the song in its most popular form, standard Chinese with a professionally adapted folk melody.[10]

Since the 1950s, writing, speaking, and staging history from the bottom up in China has involved a cultural movement on the grassroots level with attempts to reconstruct historical narrative and let peasants narrate their own life and history (Guo Wu 2014). Rural minorities in the post-Mao era continue to be reified in contemporary representations based on political use of their cultures and the places they live; thus, songs, landmarks, or traditional processions of non-Han societies are inserted into propaganda discourses (Frangville 2012, 65). Many of the contemporary songs created by Buyi villagers—still carrying traces of state ideologies and propaganda—continue to celebrate the successes and achievements of the socialist regime as well as their liberation from the old society. Composed by the villagers in the wake of extralocal attention (especially from the state authority) and partly copromoted by local cultural workers, a particular genre of folk song in local Buyi communities compares transformations over generations, and even over dynasties. Some contemporary lyrics continue to reflect on how policies under Nationalist Party rule oppressed the Buyi people and, by contrast, how the Communist Party and particularly Chairman Mao were so thoughtful to local communities. The songs describe modern development that has extensively changed the Buyi homeland and ascribe these changes to the liberation brought about by the Communist Party. Some of these songs reiterate the achievements of economic reform, agricultural mechanization, and scientific and technological advancement. More recent engagement in the post-reform era includes lyrics concerning the changes brought about by the tourism industry and mass media. For instance, some songs extol how new television sets introduced the village to the rest of China and vice versa—now, the villagers could listen to speeches by the central authority in Beijing from home.

In the context of China's revolutionary change, it was the spirit of dissemination rather than ideological control that was enthusiastically embraced by cultural practitioners (Schein 2000, 178). For many, raising awareness of the changes overhauling Chinese society and integrating ever more members of the populace into the process—whether nationalism, land reform, class struggle, or cultural production—were legitimate within the existing political and cultural system (Schein 2000; see also L. Adams 2010). Therefore, we see the uniformity of historical narratives (from the liberation of the non-Han to the introduction of the reforms) and of cultural forms (such as rites, festivals, and heritage) in the New China.

Some songs, usually performed by female villagers wearing Buyi clothing, were selected as representative of the village to be presented to officials or tourists. The lyrics normally contain words glorifying the village's history and magnificent landscape. This involves a kind of "image engineering" that Emily Yeh (2013, 8–9) suggests encapsulates a view of development as spectacle, which is meant to conjure up the performance of local attachment to the state. According to these lyrics, development is a natural continuation from the Mao era, when cadres and technicians were sent to the countryside to inspect and initiate road and infrastructure construction on the spot (see chapter 5). In response to the official strategy, which seeks to "constitute and cultivate the identities of the subjects involved" in the state-citizen relationship, locals have hence taken part in a reciprocal performance of gratitude to the party-state for bringing the gift of development over decades (Yeh 2013, 16). Many villagers, moreover, have been cognizant of top-down political change all along. During the summer of 2013, when Uncle Yang, who used to be a county-level schoolteacher, was helping me translate the lyrics of a song created in 2010 titled "Thousand-Year-Old Village," we came across a line reading, "Thanks to the brilliant leadership of Chairman Hu [Jintao]. . . ." A neighbor of his immediately chimed in, "Well now, it needs to be changed to Chairman Xi [Jinping]."

Local subjectivity triggered by external transformation, in the meantime, hinges on a reflection on one's own status and experience. As the Buyi area around Wuyang Village has been influenced by the tourism industry of nearby Huangguoshu Waterfall, a top destination in Guizhou for the past three decades, the lyrics in a song named after the waterfall go: "We Buyi are the smartest in that we settled in this treasured land first. . . . We in the countryside who have education are civilized, and we do not need translators even when communicating and doing business with foreigners. Everyone purchases our Buyi dresses as souvenirs and to exhibit them abroad." Expressing ethnic pride and confidence, villagers compare themselves to other regions, even metropolitan areas of China, in lines like "Shanghai has skyscrapers, but we have good masons who build beautiful houses and our village entrance." However, even though villagers use such lyrics to position themselves as equally modern citizens who are fast-forwarding with the rest of the nation, ideologies from the past may still exert a lingering influence on locals' sense of place as the rural-urban divide remains central to their identity (Faure and Siu 2003). They, in effect, recognize and live with this divide: "From the city to the countryside, we await modernization in full force." Buyi singing thus resembles Northern Shaanxi storytelling through musical drama, in which the revival of folk-loric traditions in rural communities remains connected to the socialist past while responding to agrarian change and translocal conditions in post-Mao China (Ka-ming Wu 2011, 103).

Against the backdrop of state propaganda and the emergence of a tourism economy, songs with new lyrics indicating up-to-date transformations have become a significant means of engaging with and reflecting on ethnic rural identity and are repeatedly performed during officials' visits or at public occasions. Indeed, it becomes increasingly challenging to tease out what is traditional in contemporary singing that has permeated informal and formal settings; for many elderly women, songs conventionally embedded in local sociality have lost their meaning now that they are performed for an ignorant or silent audience of visitors (see Ingram 2012; Schein 2000). And yet, with a degree of flexibility, old tunes with adapted lyrics and symbolic value—as seen in the case of "Good Flowers Are Red"—are being appropriated for socialist agendas. Buyi songs, in essence, have consisted of messages that change in accordance with sociopolitical dynamics. Created around meaningful life-worlds through words and rhythms, the wide variety of Buyi songs—many conceived by rural ethnic women—embodies local narratives, imaginaries, aspirations, and desires that are becoming ever more inseparable from broader sociopolitical forces and economic transformations.

DANCE PERFORMANCES AS COMMUNAL PARTICIPATION AND SUZHI CULTIVATION

For staged performances as communal activities or public events, female villagers choreographed dance movements to present some of their songs ($t\,'iau^4\,f\partial n^1$, literally "dancing to the singing"). Though women in Wuyang

CHAPTER THREE

told me that creating movement to go with Buyi lyrics required significant deliberation, my first impression of their choreography was that the dances were simple and straightforward, as they acted out the literal meaning of the lyrics, such as reading books or doing construction work. They deployed dance movements that recalled the Soviet legacy during the Mao era, such as marching with one elbow bent in front of the chest. Indeed, much of the Buyi choreography we see today was developed in relation to agricultural production and everyday life in socialist China, though some scholars believe that Buyi dances were primarily associated with ritualistic activities in historical times. Precisely because of the "feudal and superstitious" nature of such ritualistic dances and the lack of quotidian participation from the masses (*qunzhong*) in the eyes of the Communist regime, Buyi people were encouraged to develop dances related to their agrarian life after liberation (Wei 1981, 118–19). To a large extent, the amateur dance movements in Wuyang Village today resemble those from the 1950s, which generally included basic bodily expressions of rice planting and harvesting, textile weaving, wax drawing, and so on (Wei 1981; Wang Siming 1988).

According to some village elders, the combination of dance and song became popular roughly when folk cultural traditions started to revive in the post-Mao era. While women actively participate in singing and sometimes dancing during feasts and communal events, the state also seeks to stage festive and spectacular performances to mobilize the masses, especially on major holidays and at commemorative events. Female villagers usually team up in performance groups based on relations through kinship and neighborhood networks. This organizational structure, interestingly, overlaps with the socialist-era administrative units at times. Members of the same teams (*xiaozu*) under the village brigade (*dadui*) are grouped together, as was the case when agricultural productivity was emphasized under collectivization. In this sense, local identifications are still shaped by the institutional structures of the Mao era (Schein 2000, 269) and never quite disappeared after the decollectivization reforms. Even at feasts in and between communities, some performance teams named themselves based on their brigade team or place of origin.

FEMALE PERFORMERS AND THE STATE   113

Women, regardless of age, could take part in song-and-dance teams as they wished for entertainment and socializing. Some elders included in-laws or younger family members on their teams, while some women teamed up by age group, from elders to young schoolgirls. In Wuyang Village, those who could spare room in their newly constructed concrete houses would invite other women over to practice their songs and dances, but these activities also took place on the open playground on summer nights, or at public spaces such as the village clinic. When Senior Grandma Wu and the dozen female villagers were rehearsing "The Small Bastion," effective teamwork was at play, even while they engaged in casual chitchat. There were three to four women who mostly concentrated on conceiving and polishing the lyrics, while others plotted out dance movements to match the words. When disagreements occurred, the women in charge of creating the lyrics made suggestions either to focus on nitty-gritty details or to move on. When the scene seemed to lose coherence as the dancers laughed at their own movements, a couple of members tried to get everyone back on track. One woman reminded the others to face the audience during the performance.

As cultural revival in the post-Mao era provides "a focal point for public life in the village and a communal participation long gone after decollectivization" (Ka-ming Wu 2015, 80), singing and dancing on various occasions still very much facilitate sociality among relatives, neighborhoods, and villagers. A village sphere in which affect and subjectivity in group life are produced for and on important social occasions can be understood in terms of "hot-bustling" (*renao* in Chinese; *tsok¹ zaŋ²* in Buyi) sociality—similar to the notion of "red-hot" (*honghuo*) sociality used by Adam Yuet Chau (2006, 148). Differing from boisterous city scenes, hot-bustling sociality is a kind of habitus based on the production of excitement and collective effervescence in village communities. Not only are minority festivals, as multicommunity happenings, popularized as densely peopled, exciting, and carnivalesque (Schein 2000; Chio 2019), but intravillage gatherings have also thrived in this highly local hot-bustling atmosphere. My grandmother, for instance, always felt nostalgia for her old village life and Buyi cultural

114   CHAPTER THREE

practices, despite having spent most of her adult life in the city. She enjoyed returning to her maternal village simply to attend events and observe people singing Buyi songs and liked to watch the performance videos I brought back from Buyi villages. This intimate connection and affective engagement perhaps rest upon "a richly elaborate expressive culture" that has helped foster ties among women in village communities historically and that has also benefited from the articulation of a "countervailing social vision of gender relations" in patriarchal society through narrative traditions, songs, domestic arts, and so on (Watson 1994, 38).

Intrigued by the all-women dance performances, I had a discussion with Uncle Kuan, a folk art enthusiast. Although he mostly focused on animal raising and fruit farming in Wuyang Village, he often reminisced about his days as an itinerant organizer for grassroots performance groups. He explained that local men rarely participated in dancing activities because they—with an entrenched "feudal" mindset—only followed others in drinking or gambling to while away their time.[11] Noticing my intellectual interest in the popularity of dancing among women, Uncle Kuan elaborated on the social function of group dancing for local people: "Dancing used to be just for fun. And then people realized its usefulness for keeping healthy and strong bodies [qiangshen jianti]. It is a social activity that helps keep people full of energy to work and eat and helps maintain good connections between sisters, wives, and neighbors. Also, people could learn new perspectives too. In unity [tuanjie] we can solve problems, so dancing is the starting point of advancement and openness [jinbu kaifang]."

The language of the socialist state deployed by Uncle Kuan implies the gendered subjectivity that is so strongly attached to social progress and advancement—similar to the new lyrics examined in the previous section. Local women were thought to embrace dance activities as a kind of self-improvement that would benefit body and mind. In Uncle Kuan's opinion, by cultivating a healthy lifestyle and interpersonal connections, such sociality might open people's eyes and change old mindsets as well.

Intriguingly, this kind of mind-body cultivation and self-governance through teamwork seems to fit the state discourse about "quality" (*suzhi*) of personhood that appeared in the 1980s, mostly in relation to birth control and education policy campaigns (Kipnis 2006). Through bodily habituation and social involvement, the state has sought to promote the normative value that minoritized subjects, especially those in the rural areas, should possess. During my fieldwork, a township near Wuyang Village started organizing birth control performance teams that incorporated the most up-to-date party-state policies and guiding principles into artistic expressions, serving as a means for the desirable propaganda of "civility" (*wenming*) and "advancement" (*xianjin*) (Yin 2013). From the state's perspective, this could help raise the quality of the rural population and maintain healthy lifestyles by, for example, encouraging participation in or consumption of song-and-dance performances rather than gambling (Nyíri 2009, 157; Oakes and Sutton 2010, 6).[12] In this sense, as the discourse of "socialist spiritual civilization" has become intertwined with the antifeudal orientation of earlier Maoist campaigns (Friedman 2006), Uncle Kuan perceived that local women have been more advanced than men in participating in healthy leisure and recreational activities. Keeping villagers away from tedious and meaningless activities, the dance teams are also deemed beneficial for preserving and branding Buyi cultural traditions and thus continue to receive financial and moral support from local authorities.

The bodily cultivation discussed here is further enacted through performance competitions, which are welcomed by villagers as these occasions also create more hot-bustling sociality. In fact, three days before the state-organized Lunar New Year celebration in 2013, a smaller-scale dance competition was initiated by Senior Grandma Wu's husband, a returned migrant, along with the village doctor and a couple of other male village elders. They each contributed ¥100–¥200 (about $15–$30) out of their own pockets to support the female performers and set up small awards for them. Considered by many village participants to have been more fun than the state-organized celebration, the self-organized event turned out to be rather competitive, and a clear set of standards was used to judge the performances. During the competition, one of the elderly men commented on whether the costumes and dance movements were in good order or uniform (*zhengqi*) enough.

For the state-led celebration, which also included basketball games, the competition included written criteria so as to be fair, whether local women were dancing to hip-hop, disco music, or old Buyi tunes. While teams were formed based on interpersonal and kinship ties, the competitiveness between teams and between communities was evident. The village organizing committee—with only one female representative—regulated the grading system based on such criteria as the *orderliness* of the performers' appearance on the stage, the *healthiness* of the content, the *creativity* of the choreography, and the *uniformity* of clothing and movements.[13] In cultivating national subjects that are "socialist" and "civilized," a vision of the ideal body politic is thus symbolically constructed to promote an understanding of citizenship that makes certain groups responsible for the civilizing of others (Friedman 2006, 245). Local women again assumed a paradoxical role in such practices, gazed and commented upon by men— who were often more educated and inculcated with state ideology—while being positioned as the locus of celebrations of difference.

In the context of socialist epistemology, culture and society are understood as products of ongoing human creative action; hence, the production of minority ethnic identity in China through dance is an aesthetic project because it harnesses the productive capacity of artistic performance (Wilcox 2019). Now that dance has become a recreational activity for socialization and entertainment, local women have become active in mobilizing and participating in these settings. In contrast to posing for photographers or tourists, which is more passive, many female villagers enjoyed not only the hot-bustling atmosphere of dance but also the sense of being part of a group and of a community. Wearing and displaying traditional Buyi clothing made women proud, especially at public events with a relatively greater degree of formality, where Buyi culture was staged side by side with Han and Miao culture. But for performances at family feasts or informal gatherings, local teams (mostly younger ones) rented or borrowed dance costumes that seemed to belong to other ethnic minority groups, or they collectively donned fashionable skirts and high heels. This may have been intended to "[announce] their trendiness with sartorial symbols of urban or imported culture" (Schein 2000, 247) on their own terms. Public performances and celebrations at life-cycle events were thus often staged as a mishmash of old and new. Opened with traditional tunes and antiphonal singing for blessings by elders and closed with contemporary dance music performed by younger women and girls, the performances directly and explicitly manifested generational change.

ENGAGING MODERN MEDIA AS BUYI BELONGING

In addition to attending and participating in song-and-dance performances, Buyi female villagers have incorporated modern media into their everyday lives, allowing their hot-bustling sociality to be captured on-screen. Taped, edited, and produced by locally based semiprofessional or amateur videographers, village videos — visual recordings on video compact disc (VCD) or digital versatile disc (DVD) of village celebrations, local performances, and special events — have offered a site for locals to make their cultural practices visible in a sense beyond the conventional (Chio 2012; Voci 2010). Local Buyi borrowed the Han word *die* to refer to these discs. In Wuyang Village and neighboring Buyi areas, village videos have become a common household object, not least in households, like Senior Grandma Wu's, that are relatively more affluent and better equipped with electronic appliances.

As a much-ignored genre with a vibrant life in ethnic rural China, these event videos document discrete episodes of everyday life such as weddings, funerals, festivals, and bullfights (Schein 2013, 515; see also Chio 2012, 2017, 2018, 2019). Operating outside the hegemonic order and logic of dominant culture in state-controlled or corporate media, these works resist categorization as they draw on different genres of contemporary video practices for locally embedded purposes. Edited by cutting and combining sections of raw original shots, this type of video forms a chronological natural narrative of collective activities. The visual recordings sometimes capture a mishmash

118   CHAPTER THREE

of elements during household feasts and village celebrations—such as traditional life-cycle rituals and antiphonal singing followed by disco-pop songs female villagers dance to. Such video practices, as a domestic form of cultural production and reconstruction, "capture important and memorable moments in family or communal life" (Barnett 2015, 122), particularly those that are seen as distinctly local.

Televisual technologies, in Buyi experience, serve as a symbol of modern life that has been often associated with the urban. A local indicator of lagging behind (*luohou*)—as opposed to being advanced—was that black-and-white televisions, and later color ones, arrived in the countryside only gradually, years after Mao died in 1976, and not many could afford them at the time. This sense of behindness often appears in local articulations of "simultaneously ethnicized and regionalized differences" that conflate the relative quality of a place with the aptitude of its inhabitants (Vasantkumar 2014, 271–72). In the past few decades, state-led expansion has nevertheless led televisual technologies to become more affordable, accessible, and portable, and local societies have adopted and deployed these technologies with relative ease (Chio 2017). Some Buyi villagers recount that they started recording songs and dances first through videotapes and later on through videodiscs. In the days when it was not easy to record an event, villagers spontaneously pooled together money, usually about ¥1,000 ($140) per event. Villagers loved looking at scenes where people were moving (even more than looking at photos), and recordings helped them to memorize and recollect people and events. The Buyi have thus been actively making use of televisual technologies in everyday life for artistic and entertainment purposes. This is also contemporaneous with the rise of a new consumer culture oriented around domestic spheres, not only in Chinese cities but also in many rural areas, which may sometimes be beyond the reach of the state in the post-reform era. The Buyi recordings thus provide a critical space for nonstate actors to make their sense of belonging known and transmissible through grassroots media practices.

Through a word-of-mouth network of family and friends, Buyi videographers were hired to record and edit footage of local life-cycle rituals and household banquets. Copied videodiscs were then distributed informally to, and repeatedly viewed by, relatives, neighbors, and fellow villagers—mostly middle-aged married women. I have spent considerable time watching the videos with them as a recreational activity during spare time when farmwork was not demanding or when they hosted banquets and wanted to entertain guests. Sometimes middle-aged and elderly men in the households, and occasionally children and teens, joined as spectators too. Village audiences usually chose to skip scenes where Mo masters were reciting ritual scripts for blessings. They were likely to skip the antiphonal singing between the host and the guest as well. Many villagers claimed that they could not understand a thing about the ritual chanting or much of the old Buyi lyrics—even though these traditional practices have long been indispensable to Buyi rituals and celebrations and are particularly valorized by state-elite projects of cultural preservation.

Therefore, while the videos captured cultural practices such as the life-cycle rituals that are believed to carry quintessential Buyi traditions, it was usually the more recently choreographed dance performances that attracted the most attention among Buyi video viewers and that female villagers could relate to most. "How could you dance to a song called 'The Reason for Us to Break Up' at someone's wedding?!" Women of the Yang family, with whom I periodically stayed during fieldwork, burst into laughter while watching a video of a relative's event that took place in a neighboring village. Such comments during the viewing of these videos revealed subtle critiques of certain cultural elements as improper for familial or communal occasions. Much engrossed in the videos, viewers also occasionally commented on and laughed at how unsightly ($p\,'ie^1$) some performances were—whether because the choreography involved awkward and offbeat actions or someone suddenly forgot the next move. Villagers often ascribed the unsightliness to lack of preparation. "Good-to-look-at" ($?d\partial i^1\,j\varepsilon^2$) dances, on the other hand, became a resource for local women to learn and imitate new moves, which may have been worth multiple replays.

These videos allowed female villagers to review their own performances from past events. Other than occasionally showing visitors what the village used to look like, these videos were largely for local consumption. The videos captured the natural movements of village women—unlike when they were required to pose for tourists or journalists, which they secretly complained about from time to time. Similar to "screen memories" with the capacity to narrate stories and retell histories from an indigenous point of view (Ginsburg 2002), village videos became vehicles to reenact local cultural life. Senior Grandma Wu, for instance, enjoyed watching herself onstage amid close kin, while other relatives and villagers might join her to relive the celebratory events. That Senior Grandma Wu and her fellow villagers often watched, replayed, and discussed these videos also created a kind of collective effervescence as an extension of the hot-bustling scenes captured in the videos. The elements of entertainment and joy from video consumption (Chio 2017, 47–48) thus reinforced affective engagement in community life.

As a natural continuation of grassroots media once they are produced in local settings, watching and sharing digital recordings are in turn a form of social transaction (Chio 2018). After the elderly women were satisfied with the final version of "The Small Bastion," Senior Grandma Wu asked me to use my digital recorder to record the song for them. I transferred the data stored on the SD card onto a flash drive so as to play the song through a family's audio equipment while the women prepared their choreographed movements. During their onstage performance, with everyone dressed in traditional Buyi clothing for the Lunar New Year celebration later on, I helped them broadcast the song several times using the equipment provided by the village organizing committee. When Senior Grandma Wu and her group members were awarded ¥300 (about $40) by the committee for putting on a team performance, they counted me in as they divided shares, using it to purchase some snacks. A few days later, knowing that I carried around the handy digital recorder, Senior Grandma Wu and a couple of her cohort invited me over to a Wu family's newly built concrete house to record songs for them in a quiet room. Along with "The Small Bastion," they chose to sing and record the five songs they were most proud of, chosen from those they had composed several years before. Senior Grandma

Wu then asked me to help transfer these songs onto a new CD through my computer, copies of which were distributed to interested women. As I continued to observe their creation of songs and preparation for performance on various occasions, the elder women were amazed that I liked to join them all the time—in contrast to other young women my age, who were mostly into pop music. "She is becoming a girl of our village!" Senior Grandma Wu said to the others, warmly including me in their shared hot-bustling sociality.

Having become a technology of reflection, video making and viewing also serve as a means by which locals comment on cultural change and social reality. Both staging oneself in front of the video camera and gazing at oneself through visual recordings suggest a process of inwardly directed self-recognition around what is (not) traditional and (not) ethnic (Chio 2012). While watching Senior Grandma Wu's video collection with us, Uncle Kuan often criticized the inauthentic clothing many women wore in the videos—such as the modernized embroidery, which no longer carried remembered meaning. In some cases, he also disapproved of dance movements—like horse riding—that seemed to be appropriated from other ethnic groups. His criticism echoed my first impression of these village videos, in which female villagers rented colorful costumes that by no means indicated their Buyi identity for group performances and performed songs and dances from a mishmash of genres and styles. As common references to local lived experience, these village videos are not containers of Buyi heritage as a bounded entity, but rather demonstrations of Buyi's ever-changing lifestyles today.

In the context of southwest China, where objectification and commodification of culture may have favored certain ethnic groups over others, the Buyi often find themselves at a disadvantage, as mainstream media or public culture does not pay much attention to the Buyi (Yu Luo 2018a). But the Buyi's deployment of media technologies serves to create new social meanings and aesthetics based on "good-to-look-at" visuals according to their own cultural logics and ideals. When both the content and the creators of media products are China's ethnic rural "others," locals do not

122 CHAPTER THREE

turn themselves into objects of visual media in the ideology of "vanishing natives."[14] Collective self-production and self-representation through media are thus not necessarily about making claims of cultural difference or branding a visible ethnicity, but have shaped what it means to be Buyi in profound ways. Now that women have become consumers of localized media culture driving the demand for video supplies, they have embraced new lifestyles and hobbies as well. Media engagement therefore incorporates the experience, emotions, and subjectivity of those being recorded and those watching later on. The production, circulation, and consumption of Buyi videos, with no established rules, are all part of contemporary culture making, subtly reflecting the performance and representation of difference (Myers 1994). Through quotidian media engagements that are inherently rooted in domestic domains—both household and village—local women navigate their memory, identity, and belonging within larger contexts of interethnic relations and rural transformation.

THE DOUBLE BURDEN OF BUYI WOMEN

Gender and rural differences, as Ka-ming Wu (2015, 63) points out, continue to be two fundamental points of reference by which Chinese modern development has been conceived and legitimated. At China's multiethnic peripheries, these also intersect with Han and non-Han differences writ large in the post-Mao cultural revival since the 1980s. Folk cultural forms have constantly been revived to build local identity, transformed to cater to urban or tourist desires, and reconfigured to generate capital (Schein 2000; Jing Wang 2001). Starting from the early 2000s, the *yuanshengtai* (literally, "original ecology") movement that swept across China further highlighted and valorized grassroots folk art performances, especially in minority regions. Yunnan Reflections, created by the famous dancer Yang Liping in 2003, and Impression Liu Sanjie and Impression Lijiang, directed by the internationally renowned Zhang Yimou in 2004 and 2006, respectively, attracted nationwide attention. These modern art performances combined ethnic, folkloric, and contemporary elements, which were performed mostly by untrained local minority peasants in southwest China (Du 2015). The annual China Central Television (CCTV) National Youth Singing Contest even added *yuanshengtai* as a genre of singing—as a form of unamplified authentic music associated with the natural and the acoustic (Gorfinkel 2012; Rees 2016; Kendall 2019)—to supplement the existing professional categories in 2006. This was intended to be an inclusive gesture for untrained or amateur minority singers from multiethnic regions.

The booming popularity of *yuanshengtai* performances in essence signified the latest version of internal orientalism that feeds on a legible alterity prompted by the pervasive urban desire to preserve and commodify exotic inhabitants and colorful folklore. Interestingly, these *yuanshengtai* performances, promoted as experiments in artistic expression, transpired during the same period as China enthusiastically ratified the UNESCO 2003 Convention for the Safeguarding of the Intangible Cultural Heritage (Rees 2012). The recognition of intangible heritage has designated oral traditions and expression (including language as a vehicle to pass on knowledge, values, and collective memories) and performing arts as two primary categories that capture local people's traditional cultural practices.

These new trends have most noticeably allowed particular ethnic groups and their cultural traditions to gain the spotlight (Yu Luo 2018a). In Guizhou, out of various ethnic groups with their respective ways of singing, the Grand Song of the Dong (Kam) ethnic group (*Dongzu dage*) is perhaps the best known. It was inscribed on the UNESCO Representative List of the Intangible Cultural Heritage of Humanity in 2009, having already received great attention for decades both domestically—including participation in the *yuanshengtai* genre in the CCTV singing contest—and internationally, such as a performance at the 1986 Golden Autumn Art Festival in Paris. Differing from most monophonic traditional Chinese music, the multipart choral style of the Grand Song has been favored in stage performances on a mass scale, which have been widely supported by the Chinese government (Ingram 2012). While much of Dong singing today is the result of artistic processing with greater aesthetic emphasis and melodic interest, it has become a renowned cultural brand for the Dong

124   CHAPTER THREE

people (more precisely, the southern Dong who speak the southern Kam dialect; Ingram 2011). By contrast, the less-recognized Buyi folk singing has only been listed as "intangible cultural heritage" at the municipal and provincial levels (Anshun Shi Wenhua Ju 2009, 327)—with the exception of the recognition of "Good Flowers Are Red" from Huishui County as national-level intangible heritage since 2008.[15] Some local scholars, in fact, felt that the phonic and aural features of Buyi singing were less pleasant to the ear compared to Dong songs, due to Buyi's biphonal resonance, which resembles mechanical sounds. Nor do the Buyi have a famed folk pop star like the Miao's A You Duo, a hometown Miao girl whose reputation skyrocketed after she won first prize in a Guizhou singing contest. She has been enlisted as an image ambassador to elevate the province with her Miao costume styles and unprocessed voice quality, which some praised as *yuanshengtai* (Schein and Luo 2016, 282–83).

A similar dilemma exists for the Buyi in terms of minority dances. A 1981 folklore account of Buyi and Miao social life and customs states without elaboration that the "Buyi's dance lacks both the variety of the Miao and the elegance of the Dai" (Wei 1981, 118). In a Buyi-Miao autonomous county like Zhenning, Buyi are often staged with Miao at the same public events and festivals, clearly signifying the multiethnic composition of the Chinese nation-state. Some Buyi villagers reluctantly admitted to me that the Miao also perform well. A common Miao routine in Zhenning is the *lusheng* (a reed-pipe musical instrument) dance, performed by young Miao schoolchildren.[16] Miao dances seem to require more body movements and skills than those of the Buyi. The county government has also supported teaching Miao dance in schools to promote cultural heritage. By contrast, Buyi performances presented at the county level are mostly singing and are usually practiced by middle-aged and elderly women. Some locals hence lamented the lack of distinctive art forms and how traditions might be at risk as the Buyi pursue modern ways of living. This echoes the historical paradox perceived by the Buyi I foreground in this book—that is, a double bind of being either too late or too early to become advanced as non-Han minorities: too late to catch up with the times or too early to remain exotically distinctive. Thus, while some traditional practices with skillful performances, such as bronze drums and musical dramas in some Buyi areas, have received a certain extent of official recognition as intangible heritage, Buyi cultural and art forms have not garnered widespread influence or publicity.

In turn, as observed in the case of Wuyang Village, local stakeholders have been trying to resurrect traditional elements to be packaged and showcased to draw outside attention. Many of the staged song-and-dance performances discussed here are a primary means of encouraging female villagers to participate in developing cultural tourism and the ensuing economic activity. While such mobilization may indeed empower local women, the cultural economy based on contemporary tourism and leisure consumption still operates on the basis of a rural-urban, Han-minority divide to a large extent, through which women may be subjected to a new kind of inequality as they are only remotely connected to the new world of capital (Ka-ming Wu 2015, 54, 59). For instance, most of the village branding projects were initiated and carried out by male elites and villagers. Unlike places where everyday life has been affected by tourism development, Buyi women at the time did not consider commodifying their culture and embodiment of tradition as a medium for monetary exchange. Many of them enacted distinctiveness whenever necessary and were mostly concerned about the reputation of Wuyang and the Buyi.

As Sara Friedman (2006, 18) suggests, experiences of otherness have not remained static over time and have produced different consequences across generations of village women—from being assigned the emblems of feudal backwardness under socialist propaganda to the marketing of exoticism in cultural commodification. These celebrations of difference align rural women with the devalued element in the Han/non-Han binary and constitute them as objects to be gazed upon and consumed. While most performances in Wuyang were prepared by women, the song created for village promotion, titled "Thousand-Year-Old Village," was composed by a Yang-surnamed male villager who was considered more knowledgeable about village history and poetic lyrics. In this sense, even though certain

126   CHAPTER THREE

art forms have become "intimately affiliated with the domestic sphere," they still serve as a medium of articulation by male intellectuals to discuss cultural origins and traditions in contemporary China (Ka-ming Wu 2015, 34).

We see a disconnect between cultural workers (often male elites), who attempt to establish ethnic pride on the basis of valuable and vulnerable traditions that they are rescuing, and the great mass of villagers (particularly women), who are much more eclectic in their taste. While female villagers have been caught in internal orientalist tropes and may even arguably self-orientalize, they are no longer merely an exotic object of consumption or subjected to a hierarchical gaze, due to the less clear-cut demarcation of *minzu* culture today. Post-reform desires, as sung by the women, suggest that the Buyi, especially the younger generations, do not wish to stick to the "old manners." Local Buyi may choose to perform dances of other ethnic groups or wear fashionable clothes and makeup, but this does not mean they are not Buyi. Enacting a modern subjectivity while presenting themselves as exemplars of tradition, they have come to occupy a kind of hybrid zone in which they act both as producers of raw culture and as participants in its salvage (Schein 2000, 213). Some may find joy in engaging in singing and dancing as a recreational activity with fellow female villagers; others may feel more empowered in the household and village sphere despite an entrenched gender imbalance. Buyi performances leave one to wonder who the intended audience was: the women themselves, their fellow villagers, the Buyi cadres, or the outside visitors?

Simultaneously shaping locally meaningful life-worlds and articulating alignments with party-state discourses, Buyi performances are inherently intertwined with the changing environs. In contemporary China, routinized displays of costumed minorities showcase not simply their colorful objecthood but also their admiring recognition of the center and its rituals (Schein and Luo 2016, 271). Buoyed by the collaborative efforts of Buyi social elites and cultural workers, the "pleasures of complicity" (L. Adams 2010, 191) continue to be forged among performers and artists alike. Economic interests, regional fame, local governmental legitimacy, and communal interests meet during sponsored public events (Chau 2006; Ka-ming Wu 2011), with which folk practices share an increasingly blurred boundary. Self-organized, self-governed performances and competitions have also been staged in Wuyang Village as "our festivals" to maintain a sense of community.

Buyi women may not skillfully reiterate the state discourse or the Han verses used by more educated male villagers, but they have been able to engage in a meaningful space that intersects with external forces to which they constantly adjust. Singing out loud about the positive impact of revolutionary changes during and since the socialist period, they leave behind whatever discontent or hidden transcript (à la Scott 1990) they may have had, including their skepticism about the whole development process. For them, the status of being developed becomes a "moral horizon of a project of self-fashioning" where the work that is done on the self to achieve development involves bodies, desires, habits, and emotions (Yeh 2013, 11–13). In this sense, the circuits of gazing in cultural (re)presentations of minority traditions emphasize reciprocity even as they enshrine inequality.

In trying to control the presentation of their own culture to outsiders, ethnic rural women have carved out ways of life despite the double burden they carry and the internal orientalist representations of them that persist for the sake of ethnic branding and rural development. As the revival of traditions in rural communities today is a process in which villagers must negotiate actively not only with market forces but also with historical resources, the series of Buyi songs and dances locals created illustrates how political institutions and social networks have informed these cultural forms and persisted in local societies. A source of resilience for such artistic or cultural expressions is the possibility of constant renewal and change (Wilcox 2019). In general, women villagers who practiced the newly invented tradition were conscious of seeing tradition as a process of active engagement and reflection, rather than replicating essentialized unchanging practices (Ka-ming Wu 2015). Dominated "neither by their weighty past nor by the subsuming mainstream" (Schein 2000, 271), rural ethnic women remained active and aware in defining themselves while performing in locally meaningful ways.

CHAPTER FOUR

HERITAGE AND IDENTITY POLITICS ON DISPLAY IN THE VILLAGE MUSEUM

"SINCE THE MUSEUM is being set up here in our village, you might want to highlight us more. Many of these objects came from the Bunong areas, not from us Buna. Is it because you are Bunong yourself?" As villagers flocked into the thirty-square-meter unoccupied house in Wuyang Village where Chairman Yang was setting up an exhibit, they leveled this half-joking critique at the relics he had collected. Though Chairman Yang does belong to the officially recognized Buyi ethnic group, he was born and raised in a Bunong area where they speak a slightly different Buyi dialect and dress in a somewhat dissimilar manner from people in Wuyang Village. Slightly embarrassed, Chairman Yang responded, "We are all Buyi anyhow [$zau^2 tuŋ^1 t\,'ai^3 pu^3 ?i^3 na$]."

Over the years leading up to the opening of this exhibit, Chairman Yang gathered objects and relics from various Buyi regions within and beyond Zhenning County. From replica photos of Buyi-related ethnic peoples taken by French missionaries between 1846 and 1925 to modern-day alcohol packages named after the Buyi, his collections were a mishmash of everything one could possibly find associated with the Buyi. I first visited Chairman Yang's collection during my preliminary fieldwork in the summer of 2011, following my introduction to the Wu family by a local scholar. At the time, Chairman Yang was storing and displaying objects in an apartment he owned in the county seat as he gradually built up his collection through a long process of gathering, curating, and organizing. The fact that the Wu family recommended I visit the collection to make my fieldwork complete suggests the effort and pride invested in these Buyi artifacts, as well as their perceived historical value.

As local officials and media workers began to promote Wuyang Village as "an exemplar of the Buyi culture" (Jing 2013, 10), Chairman Yang wanted to establish what he called a Buyi folklore museum (*minsu guan*) in Wuyang, which he hoped would become the "name card" (*mingpian*) for the historical village. Installing a proper Buyi museum was a vital part of village construction and identity making for Wuyang, because it added to the material, visible aspect of cultural heritage that can be showcased to outsiders. The unoccupied house that Chairman Yang selected as a temporary exhibit space originally belonged to a Yang-surnamed family who had relocated to the county seat. It was part of the largest compound of stone houses in the village, where the main cluster of village households meets the old playground in front of the village committee building. Perhaps due to its spaciousness and ideal location, Chairman Yang rented it as a transitional storage and exhibition facility for some of his collections until a new three-story building at the entrance to the village was ready to serve as the official museum.

While such a community-based museum plays a crucial role in branding an ethnic attraction, it also turned out to be a reflexive space for local members around claims to historical knowledge, memory, cultural resources, and authenticity. Right after the 2013 Lunar New Year, Chairman Yang and his assistants spent an afternoon installing some of his collections in the primary house of the compound. Many villagers had returned to the village from migrant labor for the New Year and invited themselves to the exhibit preparation as its first audience members. The exhibit preparation in Wuyang Village that afternoon was not meant to be collaborative or participatory, but the scene grew lively as villagers trickled in. Some approached the objects with respect and appreciation. Some returned with old objects from their own households. Some initiated discussions about where and whom the objects came from. Meanwhile, all were well aware of my presence as a student researcher who was not only interested in studying local Buyi language and culture but also seeking to retrieve my own Buyi identity through immersive learning. The exhibit setup thus also became a site for Chairman Yang and the elderly villagers to offer me a cultural lesson using careful explanations of old artifacts.

The Buyi Museum in Wuyang sheds light on how museums have mushroomed across China in the early twenty-first century. Considered a kind of cultural infrastructure comparable to highways and train tracks, they are pivotal to the country's plan to fast-forward development of the cultural sphere (Gaskin 2014). The recent growth of museums in China reflects a new mélange of heritage preservation and tourism practices emerging from growing receptivity to global trends that converge with domestic issues of cultural commodification and nation building. Because of the increasingly interwoven relationship between heritage and tourism, museums exemplify the convergence of tourism, leisure, and cultural venues, aiming to offer visitors engaging experiences with both educational and entertainment value (Yu Luo 2021).[1]

With a focus on ethnological or folkloric displays, *minzu* museums (*minzu bowuguan*) have proliferated in various locales across the country.[2] They form a recognized category in Chinese museology (Denton 2014, 204–5) and aim to showcase traditional ways of life and colorful aspects of non-Han peoples that are historically rooted and culturally distinctive, often presented as integral parts of a polyethnic nation. Contemporaneously, many ethnic villages are also being "museumized" (Harris 2012, 4–5; Su and Teo 2009, 151) and developed as themed space in their own right, parallel to other cultural and tourist attractions. Both the exhibition of ethnic minorities and the packaging of minority villages as living museums reveal an increasing connection between ethnic branding and place making and contribute to the "impression management" (Handler and Gable 1997) of local cultures in creating and maintaining an authentic image. In so doing, museum practices as such are not only intended to carry historical value in terms of preserving traditional knowledge and collective memories but have also raised a series of issues around identity and representational politics.

Museums display a central dynamic that challenges stereotypical subject-object formation in touristic and museum representations: ethnic minorities, comprised of people of varying status and background, are at once cultural producers and spectators. When minorities represent themselves, what gets reiterated and reworked as their cultural heritage? And more importantly, what effects do such representations produce (Schein and Luo 2016)? Museum practices reveal the subtleties of identity politics and power negotiations involved in the portrayal of ethnic minorities in public culture. On the one hand, the ways humans are coded as exotic, and objects as traditional, continue to underscore the politics of difference at the heart of the effects engendered by museums (Bennett 1995; Riegel 1996). On the other, hegemonic and authoritative claims to cultural resources and knowledge have been increasingly challenged not only by scholars but also by previously marginalized subjects with variegated statuses struggling to make themselves seen and heard (Myers 2006; Sleeper-Smith 2009). Probing into community-based museums in ethnic regions of China thus exposes both the Chinese characteristics and the universal characteristics (J. Adams 2013; Harrell 2013) of contemporary cultural heritage preservation. The cultural politics of and beyond a humble exhibit like Chairman Yang's may help us understand how the conception and critique of museums—a practice that originated in Europe in the nineteenth century (Bennett 1995)—is being reconfigured in the process of ethnic and place branding in twenty-first-century China.

MINZU MUSEUM POLITICS IN CHINA

In 1908 the French Catholic missionary Aloys Schotter stated:

> For the ethnographer and the philologist . . . Kouy-tcheou [Guizhou] is like a *Jardin des Plantes* [Botanical Garden], an ethnological museum. Its abrupt mountains and deep valleys form grandiose boxes where, classed and catalogued, grow multiple samples of tribes. These are the survivors of aboriginal races that constituted China's original population before

132   CHAPTER FOUR

they were pushed back by the Han Chinese invaders. These are the children of the Pre-Chinese; and our Kouy-tcheou is the pre-Chinese province par excellence. (Quoted in Michaud 2010, 198)

These words unveil a longtime fascination on the part of Western explorers with non-Han peoples and cultures in China, who have been seen as embodying both historical continuity and authenticity. Schotter, who visited Guizhou more than a century ago and lived among ethnic populations for decades, regarded locals as "samples of tribes" scattered across a rugged terrain that could be "classed and catalogued." The "ethnological museum" metaphor, in particular, highlighted the curiosity about and romanticization of exotic cultures in nineteenth-century Europe.[3] Museums since then have been critiqued as reifying cultural, racial, and ethnic differences by putting ethnic cultures on display for the consumption of Western metropolitan spectators (Denton 2014). Modern nationalist and culturalist disseminations of museum practices and institutions also imply an inherently hierarchical undertone due to their traditionally aristocratic origins (Bennett 2006, 59; Clifford 1999, 453–54).

This captivation with ethnic cultures of southwest China was not limited to Western visitors alone. Before the establishment of the People's Republic of China, ethnic populations and their cultural artifacts had caught the attention of researchers, officials, explorers, and missionaries, especially those who had firsthand exposure to multiethnic regions. The development of ethnology and museology in China led to the establishment of early ethnological museums, with influence from Euro-American scholarship, including anthropology. The renowned scholar Wu Zelin, among others, emphasized that collection of artifacts was an urgent task because the lifestyles of ethnic minorities had undergone rapid changes. In 1941, Wu Zelin held three exhibitions of minority artifacts in Guiyang, having founded a Miao-Yi Cultural Relic Showroom (Tang 2007, 33). He also helped Xiamen University and Tsinghua University to collect a number of artifacts from non-Han communities. Referencing Franz Boas and research done on the American Museum of Natural History, he argued that museums should generally assume three major roles: preservation of cultural artifacts, propaganda and education, and scientific research (Guo Wu 2019, 164).

Having emerged in the pre-1949 Republican era, public museums in China have since become important venues of nation building and political pedagogy, framing antiquities as national treasures while using them for public education (Denton 2014; Ho 2018).[4] As the modern nation-state based its unity on "occupants of a territory that has been historicized and subjects of a history that has been territorialized" (Bennett 1995, 141; see also Anderson 1991, 179–84), China's governance of non-Han peoples in its territory has also resorted to techniques of bounding and codifying. This inevitably links museum politics to modern Chinese historiography and the construction of national identity. While scholars and officials conducted nationwide surveys to identify *minzu* groups, the Bureau of Cultural Relics at the Ministry of Culture sent out teams to collect tens of thousands of minority artifacts in the 1950s and 1960s (Tang 2007, 34). At this time, the Soviet model of the ethnographic museum made its way to China (Denton 2014, 200), emphasizing cultural difference on the one hand and national unity on the other.

Museums in Mao's China have persisted as symbolic spaces of political legitimacy and propaganda, serving as a venue for experts and intellectuals to work out and disseminate an idealized narrative of the socialist transformation.[5] As historian Denise Ho (2018, 5) has argued, Chinese elites, nationalists, and revolutionaries over different time periods have employed cultural artifacts (*wenwu*) — both objects and sites — to reinforce shared identity or symbols of the nation.[6] Inseparable from the party-state's political propaganda and the rhetoric of revolution, Mao-era exhibitions were grassroots projects. They implied a participatory nature in that, even though they were curated by officials and narrated by docents, artifacts came from the masses and could be extremely humble, while stories came from the people, making the authenticity of their telling intrinsic to their source (Ho 2018, 263). In keeping with this popular linkage, *minzu* museums were steered not only to focus on collections of excavated antiques but also to emphasize common tools and cultural objects. For instance,

134   CHAPTER FOUR

famed sociologist and anthropologist Fei Xiaotong (1988, 103) believed the agricultural tools and porcelain jars he had encountered on his previous investigation tour to Guizhou were worth collecting.

As a category recognized in Chinese museology, *minzu* museums follow a narrative pattern that traces the historical origin of minorities according to dynastic changes in Chinese historiography, displaying visible cultural forms that highlight each *minzu* group as distinct, including architecture, clothing, ornamentations, and festivals. Depending on the scope and scale, some museums follow a model of classifying objects from different *minzu* to delineate their cultural characteristics, while others tend to focus on and promote a single culture. The exhibitions often stressed that certain cultural practices and material objects in minority regions were valuable because they were useful for researching the human past (Guo Wu 2019, 179–80). Persisting through and even after the socialist era, *minzu* museums stressed the Marxist-Leninist teleological narrative of history and how each *minzu* group fit into such a narrative. Representations tended to focus on dance, song, costumes, and aspects of quotidian material culture that were less obviously ideological, merely material manifestations removed from their religious and spiritual contexts (Denton 2014, 203).

Since the mid-1980s, when post-Mao cultural recovery and revival took place, efforts to store artifacts, put collections in order, and mount museum exhibits were part of the collection fever (*shoucang re*) that struck many urbanites and experts, as well as minority people, with an urge to forestall permanent loss in an age of rapid change (Anagnost 1997; Schein 2000). *Minzu* museums have been encouraged and funded by various levels of the government, from the provincial to the prefectural level, some of which were established in or affiliated with *minzu* universities and college institutions. Many museum scholars and staff have continued the convention of collecting common everyday objects from individual households in minority regions as part of their fieldwork. In the meantime, local *minban* (literally, "run by the people," a term that is often opposed to *gongban*, or "official") museums have increasingly enriched the landscape of *minzu*-related museums (Denton 2014, 205). Unlike state- or university-run museums, these local museums have been run by cultural workers, art enthusiasts, and entrepreneurs alike, many of whom see the capacity of museums to pass down historical relics and to realize the economic potential of cultural resources. They intended to serve as local community centers promoting increased awareness of cultural heritage or as sites for displaying ethnic minority culture to tourists.

In multiethnic regions of southwest China, an alternative approach to conventional museums emerged around the late 1990s: the idea and practice of ecomuseums (*shengtai bowuguan*), which stress a balance between local community and the environment (Su 2008).[7] China's first ecomuseum—approved by the Guizhou provincial government with financial support from the Norwegian Agency for Development Cooperation—was established in a Miao village in 1998 after three years of surveying and planning led by museologist Su Donghai. Guizhou has subsequently established ecomuseums in a Buyi village, a Dong village, and a Han historic town. Under this model, which aims to improve livelihood and well-being, a community that has a close association with its original setting becomes the museum per se, an approach seen as integral to cultural heritage protection and sustainable development (Nitzky 2013, 209).

Although new alternatives, such as ecomuseums, strive to empower local villagers as the owners of their cultures by allowing them to represent themselves, questions about the efficacy of museums in emphasizing heritage, memory, and community and its inhabitants—along with local artifacts and architectures—remain unsettled. Contemporary Chinese (eco)museums are situated in a context in which domestic tourism that valorizes ethnic cultural traditions has converged with nostalgia for rural hometowns (*xiangchou*), the new craving for nature, and the prominence of globally championed heritage (see Breidenbach and Nyíri 2007; Blumenfield and Silverman 2013; Chio 2014). Because there has been a growing market of urban romantics who often reimagine remote margins with nostalgia and fascination (Tania Li 1999, 2–4), peripheral regions like Guizhou—deemed a perfect combination of "botanical garden" and "ethnological museum," as Schotter put it—are poised to become new domestic backyards for Chinese

136   CHAPTER FOUR

citizens. In a consumerist economy, ethnic cultures are commodified and displayed to feed and fuel the desires of mostly Han urbanites looking for repositories of both historical tradition and exoticized folklore (Ren 2013). Some have argued that many heritages (*yichan*) have been identified as key resources for building cultural destinations through "the museumification of village and the colonization of lived space" (Su and Teo 2009, 151).[8] Viewing the museum as a metaphor central to the simultaneous processes of cultural commodification and place development, Clare Harris (2012, 4) defined "museumizing" as "the control of territory with the capacity to contain culture within a museum."

These sentiments evoke how ethnographic museums in the West have been heavily criticized in museum studies and anthropology since the 1960s due to the rise of multiculturalism and identity politics (Bennett 1995, 2006; Denton 2014; Myers 2006). By producing knowledge around a group of artifacts as evidence of other cultures and peoples, museum exhibitions and ensuing representations are likely to risk removing expressive practices from their original contexts, extracting them from the rich and dynamic social situations in which they occur. Scholars and practitioners have in turn called for attention to indigenous curatorial traditions and approaches to heritage preservation. Many indigenous communities have their own curatorial traditions or specialized ways of perceiving, valuing, handling, caring for, interpreting, and preserving certain types of objects as cultural heritage on behalf of a community, family, or clan—and thus need to participate in or control curation (Kreps 2008) and to join the dialogic exchange with outside expertise (Sleeper-Smith 2009).

The complexity on the ground in the Chinese context, however, suggests that local governmental bodies are present as both stakeholders (co-owners) and regulators in most heritage-tourism development projects, even those initiated and undertaken by local community members (Nyíri 2009, 163). On a practical level, community-based projects, including museums, often need the help of the local state to sustain financial or institutional support for daily management, even if the museum is privately owned or entirely market-driven. As seen in the development of China's *minzu* museums, intellectuals and scholars have also assumed a predominant role in defining and framing what is to be collected and showcased. In turn, well-educated minority elites, who work for state bureaucracies while maintaining interpersonal connections with their natal communities, often take the lead in documenting local landmarks and collecting historical artifacts. In this way, Chairman Yang came to be one of the key figures in jump-starting Wuyang Village's preservation and development scheme, having planned to implement his vision of a Buyi museum as a concrete vehicle for showcasing the Buyi inheritance. Nonetheless, villagers—while not invited explicitly by Chairman Yang—actively chimed in and joined his preparation of the museum's community setup.

The nuanced relationships between Chairman Yang and the villagers recall the intricate ways in which minority elites have carried out image making and cultural representation of a nostalgic past as well as a distinct ethnicity in the post-Mao era. Focusing on the Miao, Louisa Schein (2000, 238–39) reconsiders the binary between elites and subalterns in China's cultural production and consumption:

> Miao urbanites, cultivated by the central authorities in Maoist times
> and gripped with class mobility longings in the reform era, had come
> to assume the gaze of China's prestigious metropolitan elite. . . . Once
> some Miao had become spectators, gazing reflexively upon others, "The
> Miao" could no longer be a simple category of dominant objectification.
> In turn, the shifting production of the boundary between elites and sub-
> alterns over the 1980s undermined the clarity of both the East-West and
> the Han-Miao binaries. Miao urbanites took up the business of display
> in such a way as to view themselves from an informed distance, and also
> to reproduce the categories of the dominant order.

The way minority elites and urbanites at once reproduce and contest a sense of otherness complicates their part in the production and representation of their own culture (Schein 1997, 91), as they turn the gaze upon themselves, sometimes with self-reflexivity. While possibly facilitating the objectification of one's own culture and reproducing or even reinforcing a rigid sense of cultural difference based on essentialist constructions (Abu-Lughod 1991), such image promotion could be acquiring visibility by soliciting outside attention or catering to urban consumer desires. Recollecting and reinventing traditions in the contemporary context of cultural production and commodification could, in this way, be a tactic to re-create a historical identity aligning with the national discourse of unity while pushing back against an imposed generic inferiority.

For many minority intellectuals and elites, the desire to forestall a permanent loss of culture in the seemingly inexorable process of modernization in contemporary China underlies many current collection, documentation, and reinvention efforts focusing on *minzu* cultures (Schein 2000, 204–5), including both actual museums and "the museum-ifying of villages." Intriguingly, Chinese intellectual traditions, as Stevan Harrell (2013, 287–88) points out, have never made a sharp distinction between "what is old, preserved, and authentic, and what is new, reconstructed, and copied."[9] The perpetual motion of seeking tradition, as seen in the process of branding and promoting cultural heritage, has philosophical roots—such as what Joseph Levenson (1968) saw in Confucianism—in worship of the "eternal yesterday" as an object to be preserved. The Chinese heritage landscape in turn resembles a patchwork quilt where "the land of preservation and the land of reconstruction" meet and mix (Harrell 2013, 289).

In this sense, museums can be deployed by local elites as a desirable means to preserve tradition while being modern, as preservation is not contradictory to development, but rather part of development. As China has enthusiastically embraced the notion of intangible cultural heritage along with identification and safeguarding measures suggested by UNESCO since the early 2000s, museums have become a significant venue to display the material aspects of intangible heritage that carry symbolic value. It is interesting that, although the notion of intangible cultural heritage highlights traditional skills, knowledge, and expressions that are nonmaterial, cultural workers in Guizhou and elsewhere have eagerly sought to collect arts and crafts as concrete objects representing instances of intangible heritage. Heritage preservation and museum management thus become desirable ways for multiple levels of government to fight poverty by obtaining state funding for intangible heritage or tying it to tourism development in once socioeconomically disadvantaged regions.

The phenomenon of culture being operated through the managed development of a locale by political elites (Pinggong Zhang 2007) — and even more so by minority intellectuals and cadres who explore new institutional and cultural spaces as sites in which to reclaim their own culture (Litzinger 2000) — was thus common in the post-reform era, particularly with a focus on the market economy. Asserting his influence on Wuyang Village's physical, cultural, and political landscapes, Chairman Yang has gradually put his idea for a Buyi museum into practice. In the present era of China's cultural development, which seeks to integrate ethnic minorities and rural areas into the modern state and market (Oakes 2006), how is heritage mobilized for ethnic branding and resituated to develop the local cultural economy?

CHAIRMAN YANG'S FAMILY COLLECTIONS AND THE BUYI FOLKLORE MUSEUM

Chairman Yang's enthusiasm for collecting historical artifacts and establishing a Buyi museum emerged well before heritage-tourism development in Wuyang Village. In the summer of 2006, several professors from the School of Arts at Guizhou Normal University visited Zhenning County, hoping to purchase some Buyi costumes for research and collection purposes. They were introduced to Chairman Yang, who was serving as the chairperson of the county's CPPCC (Chinese People's Political Consultative Conference) at the time and who had always been keen to study local Buyi history and culture. Chairman Yang and his wife, who hailed from areas of Zhenning inhabited by different Buyi subgroups, had stored a stack of old Buyi clothing from their parents and earlier generations at home. The variety and antiquity of the clothing amazed the visiting professors: "Your home is like a Buyi museum! Fewer and fewer people are wearing these traditional costumes. These cultural artifacts [*wenwu*] will thus become very precious in the future."

140   CHAPTER FOUR

This incident, which catalyzed Chairman Yang's collection efforts, is recorded in the last few pages of his autobiography, published by the Zhenning County Committee of the CPPCC on his sixtieth birthday (Yang Zhibin 2011b, 335–36), and was reiterated during my interviews with him. A nostalgia for "fading-away tradition" (Yin et al. 2010) undergirds the impulse to salvage and recover fragments of culture before it disappears. This urgent sense of loss is notably felt among contemporary Buyi populations who feel trapped in the double bind I elaborated earlier: similar to the Han but not quite Han. Especially for ethnicities like the Buyi, who have been regarded as topographically and culturally proximate to the Han, the gradual influence of the Han dominant culture, in relation to more recent transformations brought by outward migration and expanding urbanization, results in a daunting identity crisis in a rapidly changing society.

Chairman Yang had been concerned about "the fact that valuable cultural resources have been destroyed, many intangible heritages are constantly disappearing, and few people are willing to carry down the traditions" (Du and Yin 2011). The crisis around disappearing ethnic traditions is entangled with memories from the turbulent Maoist era, which partly explains why local cadres and intellectuals supported Chairman Yang's collection effort from the outset (Yang Zhibin 2011b, 20). As mentioned in earlier chapters, members of his wife's family from Wuyang Village who also became educated elites and local officials have long felt regret and guilt because they were forced to burn many inherited artifacts and ritual scripts during the Cultural Revolution (1966–76), which attacked the "four olds" (old ideas, old culture, old customs, and old habits).

Like those in similar settings where socialist ideologies and policies have lingering effects (L. Adams 2010, 186), Chinese cultural and political elites continue to be subconsciously aligned with the state, which ultimately exerts power over their careers. As promoters of an affirmative version of the nation's history and as its heritage keepers, elites such as Chairman Yang proudly exhibit local cultures, manifesting the great diversity that exists in China's polyethnic nation-state (Denton 2014, 24–26; Vickers 2007, 368). No longer simply preserving his family's old clothing, Chairman Yang began collecting and documenting evidence of Buyi culture, including ritual texts and objects that were avoided for ideological reasons under Mao but later became associated with the rise of intangible cultural heritage. Chairman Yang's collection even includes photos of a Buyi totem pole installed at Beijing's Tian'anmen Square in 2009 to celebrate the sixtieth anniversary of the People's Republic and a two-*jiao* (twenty-cent) banknote with the image of a woman in Buyi headwear issued by the People's Bank of China. These objects demonstrate that the Buyi have both witnessed and contributed to the country's glorious history. They epitomize the Buyi as a part of the "imagined community" that is closely knitted with the rest of the citizenry under the multiethnic rubric, rather than as a point of connection to local cultural history.[10]

While acknowledging the nuanced differences among the Buyi across time and space, Chairman Yang nevertheless embraces a totalizing presentation of state-recognized minority *minzu* culture, intending to demonstrate the Buyi's long-standing tradition. He claims that almost all of his collection dates back at least a few decades and that some objects are over three hundred years old (Du and Yin 2011). Chairman Yang selected black-and-white photos of ethnic peoples from local archives—peoples ethnologically regarded as related to modern-day Buyi—taken by a French missionary before the 1920s, to substantiate the age-old existence of the Buyi. However, no ethnic group had been granted such an ethnonym until 1953, when the *minzu* classification scheme was implemented after establishment of the People's Republic of China (see chapter 1). In this sense, Chairman Yang actually reproduced—literally, through printed copies of these old photos—an essentializing gaze upon local non-Han populations from the past.

By sprucing up preexisting cultural forms and adding new ones where the old ones seem insufficient (Harrell 2013, 290), Chairman Yang seeks to further construct the history of the Buyi in premodern times. He refashioned a bronze drum, which has many musical and ritual uses among the Buyi and many other indigenous populations in southwest China (and southeast Asia), as well as a semimythical figure in stone, used to create a

142   CHAPTER FOUR

common ancestor for all the Buyi people based on traditional Mo rituals.[11] I later learned from others that Chairman Yang spent money to have the bronze drum cast in the neighboring province of Guangxi (given that no craftsperson nearby could do so) and brought the stone shaped like a human head from the southernmost town of Zhenning County during one of his field trips.

Thus, while Chairman Yang gathered many historical relics from his family and his wife's family in Wuyang Village, he also replicated objects found in other areas and purchased objects from Buyi regions outside the county and even from neighboring provinces. Chairman Yang traveled widely in the region, reaching barely accessible places in rural Guizhou, and spent considerable time and money to collect these objects. To save artifacts, from ceremonial objects to everyday clothing, "before they could no longer be found," he even paid several visits to the same place (Yin et al. 2010). At times, he had to convince the sellers that he intended not to resell his purchases but rather to exhibit them for the sake of cultural preservation.

Chairman Yang emptied a one-hundred-square-meter apartment he owned in the Zhenning county seat and added some glass cases and cabinets, as well as audio and visual equipment, to store his collection, which by then consisted of over a thousand artifacts. When I was brought to view his collection in 2011, the objects were stored and displayed by functional categories in relation to lifeways: agriculture/farming, foods, costumes and textiles, bedrooms, handicrafts, religion, bronze drum, and so on. Chairman Yang explained to some journalists at the time that his exhibit began with objects used to meet material needs, such as food and clothing, and then proceeded to things related to spiritual fulfillment, such as ritual scripts (Yin et al. 2010). With little attempt to contextualize the objects in a historically meaningful way, Chairman Yang arranged an array of colorful ethnic costumes—from old and shabby costumes to redesigns for the stage—and various ceremonial and everyday objects all together. Although he tried to categorize the objects by region of origin, the meanings of these objects and the stories they tell remained detached from their contexts.

Manifesting Buyi culture through these collections involves certain practices that can be described as self-objectification. For example, I observed at Chairman Yang's exhibit in 2011 that a bright color photo of Chairman Yang's daughter, dressed in traditional Buyi costume and posed in a commercial photo studio, was juxtaposed with archived images of local ethnic peoples taken by the French missionary. On occasion, Chairman Yang's other family members enjoyed being photographed in their traditional costumes connected to their ancestral home (*laojia*), especially during public spectacles and annual festivals. Some of these family photos were reprinted as the front pages of a 2014 book introducing the various Buyi subgroups in Zhenning County (Wu Zhonggang and Wu Kaifeng 2014).[12] Appearing to be self-exoticizing, these images are nonetheless intended to transmit the memory and knowledge of these local elites, who no longer live in the Buyi countryside yet still feel nostalgia for it.

In September 2009, Chairman Yang received a formal business license from the Zhenning Industrial and Commercial Bureau for his Zhenning Buyi Folklore Museum (Zhenning Buyi Minsu Guan), based in his spare apartment. The naming of the museum as *minsu* (folklore), rather than *minzu* or other terms, intentionally stresses the exhibition's focus on the quotidian and traditional folkways. It also differs from *bowu guan* per se, as *bowu* means "broad [knowledge of] things" (Denton 2014) or "all kinds of things." Chairman Yang has invested over ¥100,000 (roughly $14,000) in the museum. Most visitors to his collection were distinguished officials, scholars, and journalists. While he did not charge a visitor fee at the time, the museum has been a great asset for him. With no intention of selling the objects he has collected (some of which he spent a fortune on), Chairman Yang nevertheless sees potential value in these artifacts, as did the art professors he met in 2006. Chairman Yang believes that cultural artifacts and antiques (*wenwu*) appreciate over time. He once told me that the bronze drum which cost him ¥8,000 (about $1,100) in 2007, for example, would likely be valued at ¥20,000–¥30,000 ($2,700–$4,200) in 2013. Just like elsewhere in the world, antiques are used as a means of investment in China. With the rise of a tourist and leisure economy as part of the post-1980s market reforms, Chairman Yang believes the potential of preserving and tapping these cultural resources is emerging (Du and Yin 2011). Unlike the nouveau riche class whose private museum collections have emerged in the last couple of decades in China (Denton 2014, 26), Chairman Yang has blurred the boundary of public and private ownership. These objects have been reclassified as relics according to the Chinese categories (Harris 2012, 4–5) and have become commodified heritage and, in turn, a new means of amassing wealth through cultural capital.

Similar to the European museum, which is both a product of and a response to a modern memory crisis (Lowenthal 1985, 11; Latour 1993, 69; Urry 1995, 52), the Buyi collection that Chairman Yang is building seeks to restore a link to the past that is deemed lost in transformation. The museum is therefore a powerful instrument of modernity that can be strategically deployed to contain its opposite—the past (Harris 2012, 6). It also embodies severance from history in its tendency to reify the past as an object of both reverence and commercialism (Herzfeld 1991). Chairman Yang's ethnic pride and his longing for the past, enacted by collecting and restoring relics, is inextricably linked to growing market desires for culture and heritage, diffuse concepts contingent upon the contexts in which they are deployed. Subject to multiple ideological forces in contemporary China (Denton 2014, 2–3; Rofel 2007, 71–72), museum displays as such are implicated in a convergence of politicized temporalities: the socialist past with its evolving legacy and the market-oriented present highlighting cultural commodification and fetishism. These entangled temporalities are by no means linear; they reify and reenact a past that is more of a cultural repertoire.

"WHO WE ARE (NOT)": HERITAGE AND IDENTITY POLITICS IN LOCAL COMMUNITY

Wuyang Village's heritage tourism project gelled with Chairman Yang's vision for a Buyi folklore museum in situ; the historical artifacts he had collected could be displayed, along with the age-old stone architecture in the village, as part of the lives of local Buyi. While new tourism infrastructure was still under construction, Chairman Yang gradually moved his collections from his apartment in the Zhenning county seat to the village. He tidied up the residential compound he rented from a Yang family that had moved out of Wuyang Village for migrant labor and used it as an exhibit and storage facility during the transition period. The major house of the compound has a layout typical of old Buyi residences, with two wings on either side of a central living room. Chairman Yang invited Teacher Wei, a Buyi art teacher from the County Cultural Palace who had graduated from the Art Department of Minzu University in Beijing, to design the spatial organization for the display. Teacher Wei suggested putting an ancestral altar, found in almost any Buyi household, in the middle of the central room, surrounded by antiques, including the bronze drum, while the side sections could be used to display costumes and textiles, bedroom furniture and ornaments, and ritual scripts and documents. In this process, cultural experts and state officials collaborated to create a visual space within which real life is simulated but not fully contextualized.

As Chairman Yang, Teacher Wei, and a couple of assistants from the county government were setting up the village exhibition that afternoon, villagers who had returned to Wuyang for Lunar New Year of 2013 started trickling in. The variegated emotions evoked during each individual's encounter with representations of the past (Lam-Knott 2020) offer a particular insight into how locals perceive their history and group belonging. Upon entering the house where objects were being organized for display, villagers generally expressed joy and appreciation. Many said the objects, and the display in general, were arranged in a fine and beautiful way. A woman in her sixties exclaimed that, with the display set up in her village, she was so delighted that she could live for a few more years. A few middle-aged and elderly women even specifically mentioned their gratefulness to the state and the new changes the state had brought to their village (resembling the songs dedicated to the party-state, described in chapter 3).

Villagers reminisced about objects that had been either destroyed or discarded; many of these losses occurred during the Cultural Revolution campaign to abolish the old and establish the new. The eldest man in the village, Grandpa Wu, who was in his midnineties, mentioned that his family used to have a considerable number of Mo ritual scripts, which were subsequently given away or burned. "These," he said, flipping through the ones Chairman Yang had collected, "need to be taken good care of." Elderly women also proudly pointed out to me the entire set of batik-making tools in Chairman Yang's collection, which have become difficult to find, as they knew I was learning to draw Buyi batik at the time. To answer my inquiry about a particular plant species used to make a mat on display, a couple of male villagers tried hard to think of the Han translation for this common and important species' name. They eventually realized that this species, which was once grown by their rice paddies, no longer existed. In the meantime, young returning migrants pulled out their cell phones to take pictures of old objects they rarely saw anymore. Rareness, preciousness, or authenticity is thus communicated through the museum exhibition (Karp 1991, 282). A number of villagers, like Chairman Yang, were also aware of the high cultural and economic value of the objects on display.

Like Chairman Yang's relatives and friends in various Buyi areas, who were actively assisting him in collection and exhibition, villagers spontaneously contributed old objects that held historical meaning and memories for them. Some elders went straight home to find objects left forgotten in quiet corners of their houses. After seeing that Chairman Yang's collection included traps and bows and arrows used to kill wild animals in the age of "barbarians," Grandpa Wu returned to his house and came back to Chairman Yang with an old prong for killing tigers. As villagers spontaneously brought old objects such as an inkstone and a bronze spoon to the exhibit, Chairman Yang delightedly pulled out a piece of paper to record who contributed what, as an acknowledgment of the loan. Nevertheless, I later learned from my host family that although they had donated a few things to the exhibit, they did not, and were not at all willing to, contribute more important objects used for ritual and burial use, because none were sold at the local cyclical markets anymore, and other villagers might still need to borrow theirs. Their concern implies that the boundary separating museum from practical life might be hard to efface.

As Chairman Yang assembled a mishmash of new and old, reinvented and preserved, villagers raised doubts. Gazing at a colorfully innovated piece of women's clothing, an old lady in her eighties grunted, "I don't recognize this [$keu^1 mi^2 zuo^3 kei^1 nei^3$]." To make it more accessible, Chairman Yang explained to her that the costume was a modernized (*xiandai*) version, for the sake of propaganda and on-stage showcase.

More nuanced differences between ethnicities and within the one designated Buyi ethnic group started to emerge. As some villagers and I looked through a few silver ornaments he had collected, Chairman Yang reflected on how the Buyi differ from the Miao, who are well known for their silver artifacts. "Why don't we have as many silver ornaments as the Miao people? Because they are mobile, and they have had to take whatever property with them as they move. We Buyi, instead, are sedentary rice-planters who have been self-sufficient."[13] Positioning the Buyi against the one-time slash-and-burn tribes that the state found difficult to control for purposes of population registration and taxation, Chairman Yang implies mutual reinforcement of cultural pride and state interest, which Harrell (2013, 289) sees as prevailing in heritage conservation in contemporary China.[14] However, Chairman Yang's commentary also raises the question of whether an ethnicity should be civilized or exoticized in the face of cultural commodification today.

Residents of Wuyang Village made similar differentiations among the Buyi, though Chairman Yang tended in the exhibition process to incorporate all of the Buyi subgroups into one through a process of homogenization and abstraction. Noting that the Bunong live in a more remote region of the county where Chairman Yang was born, Wuyang villagers nevertheless realized that some traditional ornaments like wooden chairs might still exist in the Bunong area. "We used to have a lot but threw them all away," my host family in the village explained to me. "They [Bunong] are relatively slow in terms of social transformations." To Chairman Yang, however, Wuyang Village is an area with better-preserved Buyi culture, whereas his home region has been significantly transformed under the influence of Han immigrants.

148   CHAPTER FOUR

Many of the pieces showcased at the exhibit were not immediately familiar to people in the village. Villagers half-jokingly said to Chairman Yang that he specifically brought what belongs to the Bunong to Wuyang because he himself is from that region. Stating the importance of highlighting "us Buna here," some middle-aged women suggested that two versions of the women's clothing should be displayed—one for single women with a kerchief hairdo and another for married women with a carapace-like headpiece—in relation to a unique but outdated custom of delayed transfer marriage specific to the Buyi region around Wuyang Village.[15]

Interestingly, Chairman Yang and his assistants from the county bureaucracy asked for help when they could not figure out how to wrap a Bunong woman's turban. A woman in her thirties volunteered to give it a try. Having married into Wuyang Village from a nearby area, she had observed this kind of triangular turban wrapping at market towns and other events. Standing on a bench to reach the head of the dummy, she started wrapping the cloth into a turban, hoping to make it right. Dozens of villagers, along with staff from the county seat, stood close and watched, pitching in and helping her adjust the headpiece until everyone was satisfied.

Stories such as these about the Buyi exhibit reveal the complexity of producing difference by constructing and remaking a singularized ethnicity. Conditionally consenting to the objects and folklore on display, members of the local community also negotiated the ways Chairman Yang and his exhibition monopolized cultural representations. When cultural "others" are implicated in image making, exhibitions ultimately tell us "who we are and, perhaps most significant, who we are not" (Karp 1991, 15). What further complicated the juxtaposition of Buna and Bunong, of elite and villagers, of us and them, derived from certain (self-)objectifying acts involved in such displays. I noticed that quite a number of young male villagers were staring at the photo of a Bunong woman during the exhibit setup—the daughter of Chairman Yang who works at one of the county government offices. They praised her—"This Buyi girl is pretty"—and started taking photos of her portrait. In this case, even the elite become objects of a gendered gaze.

As a "contact zone" (Clifford 1999) and a "contested terrain" (Lavine and

Karp 1991, 1; Macdonald 1996, 4), a museum is like a storehouse of multiple memories and meanings, serving both a formative and a reflective role in social relations. Making museums authentically ethnic is therefore a "mode of reflection, of self-construction, of *producing* and *feeling*" that ethnicness (Comaroff and Comaroff 2009, 9; original emphasis). The particular kind of authenticity in question is also contested through the presence of both traditional and modernized objects at the exhibit, as well as the convergence of historical relics and human lifeways in Wuyang Village. While the developing ideologies around community-based museums and heritage offer new possibilities for dialogic exchanges, to what extent can the locals being displayed really make themselves visible or challenge dominating idioms in practice?

A MUSEUM OF THE BUYI BUT NOT FOR THE BUYI?

On the last page of his autobiography, Chairman Yang (2011b, 336) writes: "I have always thought that, while the Zhenning Buyi Folklore Museum was founded by me, who invested a certain amount of money, this museum does not belong to me alone. It belongs to the entire Zhenning County, the entire Buyi ethnicity. I am merely taking the lead." While Chairman Yang dominates the production of knowledge and representation through his repository, the sense of "I did this for everyone" implies a kind of "consultative indigenous philanthropy" (Nitzky 2013, 224–25). This can be associated with, on the one hand, charitable practices toward the development of one's hometown and, on the other hand, a yearning for fulfillment and an assertion of influence.

Since retiring from his official position with the county in 2011, Chairman Yang has turned to focus on the heritage tourism scheme of Wuyang Village and worked to incorporate his collections and the folklore museum into the village. Establishment of a village-based museum might contribute to the branding of Wuyang as "an exemplar of Buyi culture" in the mass media, adding to its relatively well-preserved stone architecture, traditional lifestyle, and natural scenery (Jing 2013). During a public speech at a festive event in Wuyang Village in July 2013, Chairman Yang asserted the importance of the folklore museum: "We are hoping to create the 'thousand-year-old Buyi village' so as to seek ways to become better off. We would need to achieve that by protecting and promoting intangible cultural heritage. This would be implemented by the construction of the folklore museum. Outsiders would immediately notice our good things [*hao dongxi*] upon entering our village."

With a rapidly growing number of museums and communities being developed into tourist destinations or preservation sites in contemporary China, many locales have been competing in explicit or implicit ways, highlighting a certain localist impulse that ties pride to profit (Harrell 2013, 293). As museums become an integral part of a burgeoning tourism industry and the increasing commercialization of leisure (Urry 1995, 47; Vickers 2007, 366–67), cultural production falls in the gap between display strategies, state ideology, political economy, and place branding. Unlike the egalitarian sensibility during Mao's Great Leap Forward encouraging "a museum in every county" and "an exhibition hall in every commune" (Denton 2014, 19), each locality now needs to be branded as increasingly identifiable and distinctive to be competitive in the marketplace. Notably, continuing disputes about authenticity and competition for resources in cultural production ensue from differences between and even within ethnic groups (Tenzin 2013). In Guizhou's Buyi areas, for example, a number of villages were named the first Buyi something or the hometown of certain Buyi handicrafts or rituals.

Upon visiting other Buyi museums, Chairman Yang pondered how Wuyang Village's museum could be different. He pointed out to me that some of the other museums did not showcase authentic Buyi traditions. For instance, he noted that a script displayed at a village museum in another county wrongly explained the Buyi's traditional wedding customs, presenting the customs as the same as those of the Han people. This inaccuracy, in his opinion, detracts from the understanding and appreciation of Buyi history and actual customs. He also compared Wuyang Village's museum to the only Buyi ecomuseum in Guizhou, the Zhenshan Buyi Ecomuseum, established in 2000 (Guo Wu 2019, 172–73). "There is too little collection there; no one really visits it. In contrast, ours would be the first/best among the Buyi [*Buyizu diyi*] indeed."

How can one be the first or the best? Differing from village-based Buyi museums in other parts of Guizhou that represent one particular community (Nitzky 2012; Mengqi Wang 2012), Chairman Yang's museum is more ambitious, given the advantage of Zhenning County. While the county does not have the highest percentage of Buyi in the province, Zhenning is allegedly the only county in Guizhou inhabited by all three subdialect groups of the Buyi as classified by ethnologists and linguists. Zhenning, then, has the potential to serve as a convergence zone to showcase both the variety and unity of the Buyi ethnic culture — to become a capital of the Buyi (*Buyi zhi du*) — just as enacted in Chairman Yang's efforts to collect relics and to museumify the village.

Much like how museums display objects with accompanying text, usually on cards or plaques, signboards were installed across Wuyang Village highlighting and directing people to various points of interest, including an ancient bridge and an ancient well. Chairman Yang, along with other officials, has envisioned and constructed Wuyang Village as a cultural destination with a big new wooden gate that defines the beginning of the village for outside visitors, along with a parking area servicing the folklore museum, a performance plaza, an information center, and a guest hotel. While Chairman Yang's collection was temporarily stored in the rented residential compound, new buildings were well under way. The new three-story museum, in particular, was intended to produce an effect of ethnicness by repeating traditional motifs combined with a modern design. This museum would soon be the largest building and the costliest infrastructure project in the village. Chairman Yang stated that the Municipal Antipoverty Office had contributed ¥400,000 ($56,000) in funding for the first floor of the museum, the County Ethnic and Religious Affairs Bureau ¥200,000 ($28,000) for the second, and the County Red Cross ¥200,000 ($28,000) for the third. Many people who work for these government offices or semigovernmental subsidiary agencies have consanguine or affinal relations with Wuyang Village, while some are simply Chairman Yang's former colleagues.

In turn, various state-related agencies have come to make their imprint on the village's physical, visual, and metaphorical space.

As much as the museum becomes a platform from which to join the burgeoning tourism industry and attract investment from various state agencies and subsidiary organizations, it has also been constructed as a material form reflecting the Buyi's cultural attributes. Soon to be part of Wuyang Village's "impression management," the museum is sure to become a site where government officials, intellectuals, artists, and photographers, as well as potential business partners, start their visits to the village. Often combined with major festivals to demonstrate a living museum with living traditions (Karp 1991), moreover, Wuyang's museum exhibits have been integral to all kinds of public activities and events. In July 2013, for instance, when Wuyang Village hosted the annual celebration of Liuyueliu (see chapter 2), urbanites, officials, and minority performers from other areas were all drawn to the residential compound that stored Chairman Yang's collections. A folkloric showcase took place in which Buyi women in colorful costumes from all three Buyi subgroups were arranged to demonstrate their traditional skills of *zongzi* (glutinous rice ball) wrapping, batik making, and textile weaving. In this sense, the museum experience often becomes a model for experiencing life outside its walls (Kirshenblatt-Gimblett 1998, 51). Ethnic incorporation unites all the internal divisions into one; various lifeways, withdrawn from time or history, thus "congeal into object-form" (Comaroff and Comaroff 2009, 12).

In search of cultural roots, Chairman Yang curated his collections on the basis of self-reflection, intending to evoke a collective memory of the past shared by members of the Buyi with varied socioeconomic backgrounds, who have worked toward and negotiated the display of oneself. Inclusive of villagers and elites, who are often related to one another, the settings of folkloric showcases seem to perpetuate the national identification of a unified minority *minzu*, regardless of villagers' contestations over subtle differences like the Buna and the Bunong. The Buyi folklore museum, or Wuyang Village in general, envisioned by Chairman Yang as "the capital of the Buyi culture," serves as a vehicle to gather and value a sense of self.

With rising numbers of visitors, concepts of "the Buyi" and "our village" are notably deployed when villagers refer to themselves in conversations with outsiders, including Han tourists and officials. In one instance, when media reporters came to take pictures of old stone objects to produce a pamphlet for Zhenning County's sixtieth anniversary, villagers directed them to the exhibit not necessarily because it contained what the reporters were looking for but because it was considered a repository of historical artifacts. Not only has cultural tradition become a strong bonding agent for ethnic harmony and national unity (Ai 2011, 130), but the combination of preservation and development may produce the civilizing effect the state hopes to achieve through the potential to produce positive change in tourists as well as "tourees" (Nyíri 2009, 154), by raising rural minorities' cultural self-awareness and self-governance.

Nevertheless, over the course of my eighteen-month stay in Wuyang Village, most villagers had no access to the exhibit inside the residential compound. The doors to this exhibit space were normally locked unless officials or distinguished guests came to visit or public spectacles were put on to showcase the historically rooted and culturally distinctive Buyi. I have accompanied numerous officials, intellectuals, artists, and photographers to the exhibit, which became an ideal spot to facilitate the production of all sorts of photographic and artistic compositions alongside the residents and living scenes that are inherent to the village. By contrast, local villagers were noticeably absent from the exhibit after everyone participated in the initial setup. While some heritage tourism projects may empower villagers and allow for ownership of their own culture to become a reality (Nitzky 2013; Su 2008), questions arise of who really owns properties and resources, or whether such ownership is public or private. "Do we have to pay a fee when we enter for a visit later on?" A casual question raised by some villagers while watching the preparation of objects for display in the rented house reveals the paternalistic attitude they suspected local officials would adopt.[16] Having emerged earlier in the era of planned economy, property rights related to cultural heritage have been a vaguely defined government monopoly (Silverman and Blumenfield 2013, 18). Moreover, the intervention and dominance of state actors in the local heritage context reveals a common situation observed on the ground in China: leaders have little actual faith in the people's ability to know what they need and what is desired (Harrell 2013, 292). Cultural strategies for development in contemporary China, as Tim Oakes (2006) explains, further introduce a capital logic that presents new challenges to village governance and initiates new struggles between different actors.

The timely Buyi folklore museum with its atemporal exhibit presents a timeless people. In museum exhibitions as well as museumized villages, objects—and even local inhabitants—are enshrined either as relics of a vanishing culture or as witnesses of cultural richness (Varutti 2008). As people look to peripheral places where the past might be found, or marginal peoples who might possess something distinctive, the Others become closer to the general public through exhibited cultures yet are still kept at a distance. Museums turn cultures into objects as materializing and visualizing embodiment (Macdonald 1996, 7), while communities and landscapes are also increasingly becoming territorialized heritage incorporated into regional development and governance. This parallels Tony Bennett's (1995) understanding of the modern museum as a venue of discipline, surveillance, and spectacle, as museum representations and practices focusing on ethnic minorities engage the production of modernity through an intertwined temporal and spatial configuration in the Chinese context.

This complexity recalls the case of the Smithsonian's National Museum of the American Indian, which opened on the Mall in Washington, DC, in 2004. While its "community curators" were all Native Americans, it was still considered by some as a museum "of the Indian, not for the Indian" (Lujan 2005). The museum has been critiqued as an exercise in cultural propaganda that emphasizes the positive and glosses over the negative, while risking stripping culture of its historical context, reproducing stereotypes, and lacking full inclusion and appreciation. As James Lujan (2005, 516) suggests, the museum will probably always be more important "as a symbol of what it represents than as an actual museum."

In the context of post-Mao reforms, heritage and museums—as memory making and nostalgic practices—often underscore the relationship between nation building and mass consumption. The staging of the Buyi folklore museum, and the museumifying of Wuyang Village itself, aim to highlight a meaningful locality for commercial culture but also for state legibility. Just as the museum exhibit implies a certain timelessness, the production of the site assumes the village as a bounded entity and a totalizing concept, aligned with a powerful state and a burgeoning market-oriented logic. In contemporary China, development secures a position as a critical criterion in evaluating and judging the social status of a place (Mengqi Wang 2012, 429)—as does heritage preservation.

Close attention to identity politics and power negotiations embedded in museum representations and practices can contribute to a rigorous examination of the intersection of heritage and tourism, however local such museums may seem. As demonstrated through the case of Wuyang Village, cultural production and identity politics are implicated in ethnic and class status, state ideology and intervention, and commercial development potential. As the Buyi folklore museum creates a nexus between cultural production and consumption, and between expert and lay knowledge, Chairman Yang plays a pivotal role in assisting the state by placing the ethnic, rural "other" within a "civilizational hierarchy" (Bennett 2006, 59).[17] Negotiated by local Buyi with their variegated social positioning and embodied experience, who sometimes view themselves at a conscious distance, the cultural representation of this village-based museum at once reproduces and disrupts the subject-object binary. But where shall we draw the line indeed (Harrell 2013, 290)? Villagers and bureaucratic elites originating from minority communities, integral to producing cultural displays of themselves, may be insiders and outsiders simultaneously. As a (post-)modern vehicle for cultural production and representation, community-based ethnic museums in China thus complicate the East/West duality as well as the binary within—that of Han and minorities, elites and subalterns.

When I left Wuyang Village in December 2013, the three-story folklore museum was still under construction. But Chairman Yang was already envisaging an outstanding interior for the museum and the nicely designed exhibition rooms, along with modern hi-fi and projection equipment. Initially, there was hearsay that Chairman Yang was planning to arrange for a villager to manage the exhibition house as a daily part-time job. He wanted to have someone reliable, not necessarily someone capable of speaking standard Chinese; nonetheless, he explained that it would be nice to have someone more genuinely local to explain the Buyi culture and objects. This person would be in charge of preventing objects from being stolen and keeping the museum tidy and would be paid ¥300 (approximately $50) per month. Chairman Yang claimed that he was not as concerned about the objects being stolen as fearful that one would not be able to find them anymore if they were gone.

The next step for Chairman Yang might be redesigning and commodifying some of the local handicrafts into touristic products and souvenirs. When I revisited Wuyang Village in the summer of 2015, the village museum, with its exhibition of Buyi folkloric cultures, had been integrated into a visitor center catering to tourists. The interior design and spatial organization, still under construction at the time, resembled an official art gallery or a professional cultural exhibit. The visitor center had been registered as a business corporation (*faren qiye*) and had begun showcasing and selling tourism products such as ethnic minority dolls. The township government that administers Wuyang Village was considering organizing a bid for investors interested in developing the village. If Chairman Yang were to collaborate with external investors, the preservation and development project in Wuyang Village might initiate new struggles over ownership among villagers, state actors, and entrepreneurs. In many other ethnic communities in China's southwest, locals are beginning to lose control of their economies, cultures, and lifestyles. Some say these communities are meant to feel like living museums, but no one genuinely lives there. Whether and how the Buyi museum in Wuyang might stay viable and closely engaged with the villagers therefore remains an unanswered question. But for now, the village has a new landmark—a storehouse with tangible artifacts to showcase who the Buyi are.

CHAPTER FIVE

MODERNIZING RURAL INFRA-STRUCTURE AND BRANDING A HISTORICAL VILLAGE

"THIS IS SO DIRTY. The visitors who come would just take a picture with poop in it. . . ."

We were on our way one afternoon to harvest some vegetables planted by my hostess, Senior Grandma Wu, in her family field when Yun, her youngest daughter-in-law, noticed a pile of buffalo droppings in the middle of a brand-new concrete road that had been rebuilt and paved using county government funding in 2011. One of the few accessible paths for motor vehicles to move in and out of the once secluded Wuyang Village, the road ran along the foot of limestone hills, eventually leading to one end of the village. The road was first built in the mid-1970s by a socialist-era work team dispatched by the Guizhou Provincial Communist Party Committee with help from faculty and students from provincial college institutions, and it remained a pebbly, and sometimes muddy, path that had been used and renewed over the past few decades. Until recently, animal excrement did not seem to be much of a problem. However, in accordance with the Building a New Socialist Countryside campaign, a policy initiative set out in 2006 seeking to increase rural income and living standards, the new concrete road had become the fresh and bright face of Wuyang Village.[1] Anything incongruent with this image, such as livestock droppings, was deemed undesirable. Yun, whose perspective on the abundance of city life was shaped by her earlier experience of migrant labor in coastal Guangdong,

158   CHAPTER FIVE

welcomed the new development in Wuyang and believed that its face should be welcoming too.

Yun and I then looked to one side of the road, where irregularly shaped rice fields belonging to various households were gradually being turned into equally variegated concrete houses. Having mushroomed in number over the past five years, these new structures were built using migrant remittances and looked fairly different from the old stone houses to which Wuyang owed its uniqueness. Built on wooden stilted structures and fortified by stone walls and overarching gabled roofs, the original houses in Wuyang formed rows along the gently sloping hills, all facing almost the same direction, toward the strip of land in the basin that had been cultivated as rice fields. With many younger generations of villagers switching from farming to migrant labor, new multistory houses were popping up on families' fields next to the road. Using concrete bricks, cement, and sand as their primary construction materials, villagers improvised structures that varied in shape and height without any architectural plan, sometimes leaving very little space between buildings. While these new residential structures may have meant better living prospects for the villagers, their incongruous sizes, orientations, and styles caused quite a headache for local government officials, who had hoped to highlight the traditional stone architecture in branding Wuyang Village.

Roads and houses in Wuyang exemplify the most direct changes to physical environments and local lives in China's countryside, as well as the tensions surrounding infrastructure development. While infrastructure has always been a focal project for the Chinese state, village planning and landscaping with the goal of modernization have become key to Building a New Socialist Countryside. This was one of the central government's foremost priorities for the Eleventh Five-Year Plan (2006–11), targeting the problem of the "three rurals" (i.e., agriculture, farmers, and villages) by seeking to increase rural incomes through a mixture of infrastructural investment, agricultural specialization, expansion of social welfare, and accelerating urbanization (Perry 2011; Looney 2015).[2] This civilizing project frames the landscaping and redevelopment of rural environments as critical, regarding them as "dirty, chaotic, and poor/backward" (Bray 2013; Rosenberg 2013); it was a logic that Yun and many other villagers I encountered picked up on. The village environment—defined as the quality of village infrastructure, sanitation, and housing—is a noticeable aspect of rural development (Looney 2020). To build a civilized countryside, then, rural environments need to be tidied up, as infrastructure improvement and hygienic installations are important in creating neatly designed and manicured villages. These ideas rose to further prominence when the New Socialist Countryside campaign was extended in 2012 into the nationally promoted Beautiful Countryside campaign (Meili Xiangcun), aimed at sanitizing and beautifying rural landscapes.

Intriguingly, this process of village redevelopment witnessed the marriage of two governmental discourses, one on urban planning and another on rural development (Bray 2013). A technical, design-oriented approach to spatial planning was understood to mark the difference between the built environments of urban and rural areas; hence, rural China started to apply the logic of civilization through functional zoning and landscaping. The significant redevelopment of the rural built environment was not just about concrete infrastructural needs but took place alongside the development of education and hygiene as well as the improvement of population quality (*suzhi*) and quality of life (Steinmüller 2013). Frequently appearing in the Building a New Socialist Countryside campaign, the *suzhi* discourse plays a central role in the contemporary construction of Chinese citizenship. It involves discussion of how to produce the ideal citizen as well as what to do about the less-than-ideal citizen (Anagnost 2004; Jacka 2009). A concern of critical importance both to the socialist market and to socialist planning is the regulation of human bodies and human conduct to bring forth a quality that is up to standard for a modern society (Yan 2003, 20). In the context of China's tourism growth, the state exhorts middle-class leisure travelers to demonstrate healthy forms of consumption and serve as ideal models for their rural hosts to emulate, in the belief that urban tourists can help raise the quality of the rural population by, for example, insisting on clean toilets and attentive service (Nyíri 2009; Oakes and Sutton 2010).

160 CHAPTER FIVE

In line with this model of citizenship defined by orderliness and governability, urban planning—regarded as a mechanism to regulate land use and modernize the built environment—has thus been extended into the rural hinterlands, contributing to the promotion of urban-rural integration. Paradoxically, the effect of this urban-rural integration policy may have been less integration and more distinction in terms of spatial imagination, as local governments and rural leaders have striven to refashion a rural aesthetic that kindles the urban desire for a visually consumable countryside (Luo, Oakes, and Schein 2019). Recognizably pastoral or rustic villages are sometimes rendered providers of environmental amenities for urban centers (Wilczak 2017), creating a new leisure environment for consumer citizens. In minority regions, the redevelopment of towns and villages has also meant a visual beautification and re-ethnicization of the landscape, with an emphasis on refurbishing houses in uniformly traditional and symbolically ethnic styles.

Managing village appearance is thus the most tangible aspect of ethnic and place branding within the broader context of rural development in contemporary China. To make a locality stand out through its look and feel, the makeover plans of many minority regions involve landscape engineering and imagineering that cater to both the tourist gaze and the party-state vision. Local officials, to safeguard their political careers and satisfy their superiors, have devotedly guarded the desirable image or appearance of the villages—what locals might call "face projects" (Steinmüller 2013)—as potential proof of their success in developing and improving rural landscapes. Whereas villagers are interested in achieving desired standards of living and quality of life, officials may pursue specific modes of infrastructure development and rural spatial planning, starting from the facade of the houses, with proper building materials, architectural styles, and locations. These "image projects"—symbolic projects in strategic locations to improve physical appearance and built environment—are prioritized over local lives, since the former demonstrate local government's achievements in more visual and direct ways (Feng 2017, 53). The right kind of village appearance could offer an impressive experience to outsiders—not only tourists who bring in cash but also visiting officials who come to inspect the progress of local development.

In a village like Wuyang with a historical feel that is considered distinct and valuable, there are particular challenges in installing new infrastructure and redeveloping rural environments. The village is caught in the paradox of *kaifa*, a Chinese term that implies the discovery of a locality and the utilization of its resources for the purpose of development. Most prominently featured in China's Open Up the West (Xibu Dakaifa) campaign in 2000 to accelerate inland economies, *kaifa* has been a key term in the parlance of local government and business partners targeting Guizhou's ethnic rural regions. However, for sites deemed to have significant heritage value, *kaifa* entails not only a degree of disturbing what needs to be preserved as historical but also a confrontation between normative visions of socialist progress and a reality that is never clear cut.

To *kaifa* Wuyang Village means that it needs to preserve its traditional appeal while promising modern hospitality. Mindful that tradition/modernity and preservation/development are highly loaded and contested pairs that are by no means binary oppositions, my examination focuses on local usage of these terms in negotiating the forms and future of the physical environment and village landscape. In a parallel case, where the sprawl of Ho Chi Minh City in southern Vietnam blurs the lines between city and countryside through rapid spatial transformation, local residents persistently conceive of their personal situations and social space in terms of opposed temporal categories — the traditional rural past and the modern urban future — which they move between (Harms 2011). As these "competing models of temporal hierarchy also coexist *within a condition of simultaneity*" (Harms 2011, 118; original emphasis), social actors exalt the past and the future concurrently, as the peri-urban setting is both condemned as a site of underdevelopment in need of progress and celebrated as a site of tradition threatened by development.

Ethnic rural regions of China face such a spatiotemporal oscillation between ideal categories, given the paradoxical goal of local government to create an "integrated urban and rural system in which city and countryside

162   CHAPTER FIVE

play distinct roles" (Wilczak 2017, 50). When it comes to urbanization and modernization, the countryside needs to fall in line. However, these processes do not mean eradicating the countryside; the goal is to make the countryside more like the countryside.[3] Village-based preservation and development schemes in Wuyang thus entail changing and contested configurations of time and space in everyday life, most directly manifested in infrastructure construction. During my fieldwork, local Buyi were experiencing a process of simultaneous oscillation in which they are still caught, impelled to valorize tradition and then to take part in modernity, as the tensions between these opposed spatiotemporal categories take on material form in the local branding process.

STATE-MANAGED PLANNING OF VILLAGE LANDSCAPES

Ever since it attracted the attention of local authorities in 2009, Wuyang Village has been regarded as a desirable site for cultural preservation and tourism development. Aside from the aspects of Buyi culture I examine in previous chapters, the physical forms of Wuyang's age-old stone architecture and its ambient landscapes became a critical component of place branding, deemed to offer aesthetics that could increase the village's appeal to outsiders. However, the historical feel of this Buyi village posed a dilemma for township and county cadres who wanted to initiate development projects that could aid the poor (*kaifa shi fupin*). Improvement of local living standards would almost assuredly require a thorough upgrade of public infrastructure, a process that would transform, perhaps radically, the pristine villagescape that had been well preserved for years. Many of the local officials I conversed with during my fieldwork had reached an unspoken consensus that, for the time being, infrastructure should be improved piecemeal. No one dared to change much, concerned that it would be irreversible once historical elements such as the old stone architecture were gone.

Infrastructure not only provides convenience in everyday local life but also leads to evolutionary ways of thinking in relation to societal progress, as possession of roads, electricity, and running water has come to define civilization itself (Larkin 2013). But for a "thousand-year-old Buyi village," infrastructural development conflicts with the ideal of preservation. This paradox was manifested in a public speech by a highly respected county official born and raised in Wuyang, given during the Lunar New Year Festival in February 2013, when neighboring villages were invited to Wuyang Village for a joint celebration. Director Wu from the County Gazetteer Office reminded the entire community of its "economic and cultural value" to mobilize villagers to support the village branding project: "It is time [for us] to resort to rural ethnic policies to transform the local economy. . . . Longtime isolation, lack of development, and the absence of urban industries have created this historical village, this treasured place of fengshui [*fengshui baodi*]. But without people to discover and develop [*kaifa*] it, it would remain nothing. Because state investment and support are limited to merely jump-starting infrastructure construction, we need [to rely on] our own grassroots funding, techniques, and management."

The village's historical relics and traditional lifestyles, in Director Wu's opinion, have benefited from longtime isolation; however, without becoming known and consumable for visitors, their value would not materialize. Wuyang Village is then caught in a state of oscillation, juggling the preservation of the old and the development of the new, while the *kaifa* process relies heavily on the sustainability of state support and funding. In Guizhou, when sites being developed for tourism are distributed in modest villages and are small in scale, government-supported development has depended on relatively minor infrastructure investments and market-promotion activities (Donaldson 2011).[4] The paradox lies in the idea that villagers need help from the state to pursue progress yet cannot afford to wait for and depend on top-down sponsorship to meet their needs. Ideally, government support would be accompanied by the mobilization of grassroots participation. The means through which villagers are mobilized for development recalled methods deployed in the socialist era, when the masses were convened and instructed during public events such as the one described above. As Elizabeth Perry (2011) has suggested, the Building a

164   CHAPTER FIVE

New Socialist Countryside campaign was a continuation of earlier developmental policies that had long been in place, which adopted and adapted revolutionary campaign methods to elicit widespread engagement. In contemporary state-managed campaigns, it seems that grassroots officials, rather than ordinary peasants, have been the main actors. For instance, ad hoc leadership groups consisting of work teams (*gongzuodui*) of cadres from the village, township, and county levels have been established to organize and guide rural programs related to socioeconomic development and to facilitate grassroots implementation (Steinmüller 2013).

During the initial stage of *kaifa* in Wuyang Village, local bureaucracies and grassroots officials deployed functional zoning and spatial planning to map out their vision for transforming local landscapes. In 2011, when the County Cultural Bureau submitted an application at the provincial level to grant Wuyang Village status as a heritage preservation unit (*wenwu baohu danwei*), the county and township governments also reached out to the provincial research institute for urban-rural planning and design.[5] The institute assisted in measuring and mapping out the physical environment surrounding the village and envisioning and designating various functional zones for residential and leisure purposes. But county government officials were dissatisfied with the design, which, regardless of professional expertise, was in need of refinement and readjustment before it could be used to attract potential investors. This was because the design should have aimed for protective development (*baohuxing kaifa*)—a mode of *kaifa* that was supposed to cause minimum damage to the historical relics in the village.

In 2012, a joint office was established for the preservation and development of Wuyang Village. It consisted of working units that collaborated to survey and plan village landscapes, in conjunction with cultural support, environmental protection, poverty reduction, transportation, and infrastructure construction. This joint endeavor aimed to create a Buyi cultural experience zone (*wenhua tiyan qu*), where visitors could have a taste of authentic Buyi ways of living. Many county and township cadres, enthusiastic supporters of Wuyang Village's development, originally hailed from the village. Funding was raised by county-level state agencies as well as the township government, which was directly in charge of project implementation. This coordinated planning was evident in the establishment of the folklore museum, examined in the previous chapter, which became part of the village's cultural development project.

Local authorities regarded such collaborative efforts as necessary because one of the biggest challenges in village-level development, or planning as a whole (*tongchou guihua*), was the limited funding available, which could be insufficient for large-scale construction and a recurring obstacle to efficient distribution of monetary resources.[6] At the same time, dealing with land as property has also raised puzzling issues, as initial construction has mostly focused on public spaces such as village roads and playgrounds. Subsequent development might require the use of spaces occupied by households and owned by the village collective under the current land tenure system, which might produce tension.

The mixture of governmental organizations involved in Wuyang Village's development demonstrates the paternalistic role the Chinese state has continued to play in the post-reform era while acting as a custodian for its people's welfare. Most of the infrastructural development I observed during my fieldwork in 2012 was funded under the Case-by-Case financial subsidy scheme, after Wuyang was designated a model village by the Zhenning County government in 2011.[7] The development projects included a road linking the village to the intercounty road and the paths that connected households, water supply and drainage, and sanitary facilities, including public toilets, garbage dumps, and garbage cans. In addition, the scheme included measures to improve village appearance, such as installation of solar-powered streetlamps, signboards, a village gate, a performance plaza, and a parking lot, as well as plans for greening and afforestation (figure 7).

Overall funding for the subsidy project was ¥2.1 million (about $300,000), and almost eight thousand laborers were mobilized according to the county government. Subsequently, more ad hoc subsidies came along, including one from the County Red Cross intended to implement a disaster management humanitarian project and capacity-building efforts based on a village-level public evaluation in July 2013. In a more recent plan of action drafted by the county government in July 2015, ten county-level state departments were listed as participants in the coordinated planning for Wuyang Village; most of these were bureaus in charge of a particular dimension of development, such as housing and urban-rural construction, environmental protection, transportation, ethnic and religious affairs, forestry, and agriculture, as well as poverty reduction and reform.[8]

In many villages, public infrastructure and utilities targeted by the Building a New Socialist Countryside campaign to achieve *xiaokang*—which can be translated as "moderate prosperity"—include housing, electricity, telecommunications, sanitation, roads, and water (Bray 2013; Steinmüller 2013). Among the infrastructure features deemed conducive to achieving a relatively comfortable status in Wuyang were roads, housing, and village appearance.[9] As subsequent sections further explore, these forms of infrastructure shed light on the underlying paradoxes in developing a historical ethnic village and the subtle power negotiations involved. While villagers

FIGURE 7. The wooden village gate with an ethnic design under construction (2012).

MODERNIZING RURAL INFRASTRUCTURE 167

participated in and were affected daily by infrastructural development, the construction processes were heavily critiqued by the villagers themselves, as well as by some local officials who had originally had high hopes for development.

Undoubtedly, the Buyi villagers understood that development takes time. In a way, investment in and construction of infrastructure is a rite of passage for the experience of local development—or, in the words of a male villager, a formality (*guochang*). As bureaucratic auditing of government subsidies takes considerable time, multiple government agencies at various administrative levels were still devising plans to *kaifa* Wuyang Village when I returned in the summer of 2015. Given the rapid turnover in local bureaucracies, it has never been clear to most villagers which governmental bodies were in charge of which aspects of development, and transparency in funding (thought to total ¥4 million, or $550,000) and the use of other resources became particularly contentious issues. A development dream embraced by the Chinese state and its citizens—a dream hinging on the hope for a better future and a celebration of the past (Harms 2011, 91, 157)—entails both opportunity and precarity for locals. Whether their sacrifices are worth it for this development dream, locals have been subjected to ongoing uncertainty over which they have little control and yet are still trying to navigate.

In this case, while infrastructure presents the visual environment of a place to outsiders, what's more important is that it embodies the senses, desires, and imagination of various groups of people who live around and create associations with it. Just like the roads, architecture, and even accessory installations, such as the public signboards in Wuyang Village, infrastructure is seen, heard, discussed, smelled, touched, and in a nutshell, experienced. Such sensory politics embodied in infrastructure through meaningful everyday encounters with space (Dourish and Bell 2007; Fennell 2011) are particularly important for Wuyang Village, as discourses and actions oriented around public infrastructure have been a point of contention ever since the initial stages of its *kaifa,* which both provided hopes and left doubts.

168   CHAPTER FIVE

THE ROAD TO DEVELOPMENT: DRIVING TOWARD MODERNITY?

Roads, which have both practical and symbolic value, compress travel time and promote unimpeded circulation, while exemplifying a common visual and conceptual paradigm of what it means to be modern (Harms 2011; Larkin 2013). New roads in mountainous hinterlands of China are significant not only because they improve the transportation of goods and services in and out but also because they channel cheap rural labor toward nearby cities for low-skilled work, as well as to the coastal-based factories and construction sites that have fueled China's economic development (Harwood 2013). Villagers, articulating their feelings and desires, often brought up the topic of roads and the lack thereof when assessing whether places were suitable for living. As I hiked with villagers for half a day to the closest weekly market, many lamented the steep hills and narrow mountain paths. They noted that the historical advantage of an easy-to-defend terrain had become a conspicuous disadvantage, an intolerable hardship. Roads were inevitably associated with good living (*ʔdəi¹ kwa⁵*) while their own lives were difficult (*ʔja¹kwa⁵*) as they inhabited and farmed steep slopes, carried buckets of water or manure on muddy trails, and lived far from town centers. Even children in Wuyang Village believed improved roads would make their lives more manageable and bring benefits to the village in the form of more tourists.

Roads thus not only shape the embodied experiences and ambient conditions of everyday life but also transmit the desires and dreams of individuals and societies.[10] Guizhou's road building has received dramatic state investment over the past decades as part of China's national growth strategy, with expressway connectivity joined by the rapid emergence of high-speed rail lines crisscrossing the province. The passageway culture (*tongdao wenhua*) that has marked Guizhou's identity as the crossroads and thoroughfare connecting the interior heartland to farther reaches of southwest China since the late imperial era has thus seen new incarnations in roadways (Luo, Oakes, and Schein 2019).[11] Critically, building infrastructure in karst areas can be hard work; the rocky hills in these areas constitute recalcitrant topography from the state's perspective but nonetheless possess arcadian beauty in the eyes of urban romantics. Building in this context requires technically advanced engineering with a stress on "man's will to conquer nature," a key indicator of societal progress during the Mao era (Scott 1998; Shapiro 2001). Slogans like "digging roads through mountains, building bridges across waters, and subduing the rugged terrain," for instance, were still highlighted as goals at a high-speed railway construction site near Wuyang Village in 2013.[12]

A key development priority in Guizhou has been construction of the rural roadways that are vital for the village-level economy. Spending on such road construction was deemed effective because it met many of the conditions that link roads to poverty reduction, such as stimulating the production of cash crops and encouraging economic diversification (Donaldson 2011). The history of how roads came into being in Wuyang Village exemplifies the party-state's decades-long involvement in driving developmental progress in rural areas. Around the mid- to late 1970s, a work team dispatched by the provincial party committee constructed the initial road from scratch. At the time, teachers and students from Guizhou University and Guizhou Agricultural College formed a major part of the labor force and were paid according to their work points under the socialist regime.[13] Later, in the 1980s, a Wu-surnamed villager became head of the Zhenning County Agricultural Bureau and allocated funding to improve the road surface. Similar situations have transpired in recent years, as funds for new road improvements have been raised by Buyi elites at the county and municipal levels in the hope of lending a hand to their hometown. As the material characteristics of infrastructure—the hardness of the road, the intensity of its blackness, and its smooth finish—produce sensorial and political experiences (Larkin 2013), the main road that links Wuyang to the outside world has witnessed several phases, from mud and sand to concrete and asphalt. Along with establishment of an irrigation facility and distribution of crop varieties and fertilizers, road construction has become associated with socialist modernity, as praised by female villagers (for example, in a song titled "Reform and Opening Up Is Really Good," which celebrated the post-Mao transition to a socialist market economy).

To improve and widen the outbound road connecting Wuyang to the Zhenning county seat was a key infrastructural priority in the village's *kaifa* process, mostly for the purpose of bringing in more tourists. The bulk of the construction was carried out by a manual labor team from the county seat that consisted of rural Han and Bunong. As in earlier years, local residents sometimes assisted in government-organized infrastructure projects, including terracing land, improving irrigation, and building rural roads. Villagers normally took on these projects during the agricultural off-season, taking advantage of the opportunity to supplement their income without the work interfering with agricultural production (see also Donaldson 2011). Even those who did not directly participate or earn income welcomed such interventions. During my fieldwork, construction took months and resulted in messy road conditions and scattered construction debris. At times, we had to trek along narrow paths across rice fields or unpaved, muddy roads to return from the county seat. But villagers seemed to bear with these inconveniences, based on a belief in sacrificing the present to welcome a better future.

Though the outbound road was under improvement, some puzzling problems remained. Not situated along a major road in the first place, Wuyang Village would need a much wider road to accommodate two-way traffic if it were to increase its tourism capacity. However, not only was the outbound road adjacent to many of Wuyang Village's rice fields, which lay on relatively flat land amid the rough limestone hills, but the original passage connecting the village to the county seat also passes by two Han villages. I was told that these two Han villages did not wish to cooperate to widen the road without receiving greater compensation for expropriation of their land, even though it would have helped them transport their agricultural produce to market. Eventually, the road had to take a circuitous route to circumvent the Han villages, and it was still narrower than a regular two-lane road.

Apart from their technical functions, roads can be an image project that affects certain impressions of a community as well. For this reason, the roads in Wuyang Village were transformed in beautifying (*meirong*) ways. To match the stone architecture in and around Wuyang, and also to cover up culverts that prevented the muddy paths from further dampening, local authorities came up with the idea of paving the village paths with flagstones. The Yang family who temporarily hosted me took charge of these paths, while a contractor from the county seat was called to construct similar stone-paved paths that led to and ran along the riverside.

The Zhenning foreman who oversaw paving the stone paths revealed his perception of this infrastructural development project in a historical village when I went to observe their construction process. One of the construction workers was bewildered by the fact that Wuyang wanted to pave the roads with stones: "Why not just pave cement roads, which would have cost half as much?" The foreman chimed in, "A scenic area needs special features. Without using stone, how could it correspond with the name 'thousand-year-old Buyi village'?" When a male villager suggested smoothing some irregularly shaped stones, the foreman responded by emphasizing the importance of maintaining the original stones (*yuansheng shi*) of the historical village.

Despite the Zhenning foreman's awareness of the historical feel of the village, his construction work was later strongly criticized by villagers, who regarded this infrastructure as a public project for the entire community. Cousin Yang commented:

> The Han people are not so conscientious about their construction here, especially the construction of the riverside paths managed by the Zhenning boss. They did not use enough cement underneath to stabilize the flagstones, which could be really fragile if stepped on frequently. So now the local authority has made them start over. To rework would actually cost more for the boss, as they have to repair and rebuild, and then the workers ask for extra wages. Working so perfunctorily, they would just leave upon finishing the construction. But the road is left there for villagers and visitors.

172 CHAPTER FIVE

Cousin Yang took over the task of paving village paths himself (see figure 8). In contrast to the Zhenning workers, the Yang family members he summoned were seriously concerned about the quality of construction. After placing underground pipes to collect wastewater in an effort to sanitize the village environs, the Yang brothers-in-law and other relatives brought back flagstones from nearby hills to cover the surface of the village paths, aligning and laying the stones with clay underneath. The newly paved roads looked nicer but were not necessarily smoother, due to the varied stone shapes and the uneven foundation of the original paths.

For Cousin Yang, such a project in the village not only necessitated considerable manual labor but also required him to be prepared for the uncertainty of internal funding. He had to pay for the construction materials up front to build the village paths, which ended up being more than ¥10,000 ($1,400). He was reimbursed only after the construction passed inspection and endorsement. This arrangement, as explained by some villagers, prevented them from taking control of large-scale construction projects, such as the village entrance and parking lot. Instead, contractors who benefited from personal networks with the county government were the only ones able to invest a few hundred thousand yuan in such projects.

Better roads could potentially allow residents of Wuyang Village to increase their access to markets and information while also introducing this cultural destination to the outside. But the development dream encoded in roads cannot be realized without a price. While symbolizing modernity for once-isolated rural communities, roads and the resulting experience of modernity can also be treacherous and dislocating (Harwood 2013). It was very common for Buyi villagers unused to traveling by motor vehicle to have physical reactions to doing so. Once while returning in a minivan to Wuyang Village from the weekly market at the county seat, I overheard several elderly Buyi women discussing their fear of throwing up in the car, claiming that "the Han have no carsickness" ($pu^3\ ha^5\ mi^2\ ka^2\ zu^6$). Longing for a modern lifestyle requires the Buyi to catch up with the mainstream both physically and mentally but often leaves them frustrated. Healthy and energetic young males recalled how painful it was to get carsick and

FIGURE 8. A male villager paving stone paths to match the stone walls of local residences, echoing the historical feel of the village (2013).

CHAPTER FIVE

fatigued on overnight buses or trains with standing room only, which were the cheapest options for travel to the coastal regions. While new roads offer the possibility for a younger generation of villagers to learn to drive and purchase new motor vehicles to transport villagers and goods, safety issues have nevertheless emerged for those who spent a few thousand yuan for a motorcycle, which is more common and affordable. Dreadful stories of people injured in vehicle crashes have been frequent enough to show that danger, not just pride, is associated with increasing mobility.

The paradox of roads, providing both opportunity and precarity, is also associated with the timing of the village's development. When the then fifty-three-year-old Senior Grandpa Wu, the male head of my host family, returned from migrant labor for the 2013 Lunar New Year, he walked around the village with me to see what had changed over the year he was away. I asked him how many years of history Wuyang Village had — whether it was six hundred years as recorded in genealogy or, as in the official branding, a "thousand-year-old village." Overlooking the village from the hills, he responded, "Six hundred years perhaps? Who cares how many years [it has been here], as long as we get good roads to use." Like everyone else, he believed that transportation and mobility would be possible only with roads in good condition.

However, as we continued our walk, Senior Grandpa Wu implied that only after the main road had been improved did new, modern houses explode in number: "If we had built better roads much earlier, we would have never remained the historical village." When broader and better roads become available for vehicles, they usually have a decisive impact on settlement patterns (Steinmüller 2013, 68). Villagers tend to start building houses made of concrete blocks, as these materials can then be transported by truck to the villages, and new houses spring up as close as possible to the roads for better accessibility. Road construction in Wuyang Village therefore needed to come at the right time, neither too early nor too late. If the road had reached Wuyang sooner, modern development might have drastically transformed, if not destroyed, the historical village — especially through new housing that would change the village's appearance. If the road had not reached it soon enough, villagers would have lagged behind in terms of socioeconomic progress. This, in fact, offered a justification for local cadres who jump-started the *kaifa* process at a particular juncture for Wuyang Village, hoping to strike a balance in the spatiotemporal oscillation between preserving tradition and becoming modern. Preservation, in this sense, ideally serves as an integral part of development rather than an oppositional force (Harrell 2013).

Roads are almost always the first thing built during the *kaifa* process in rural villages. Roads stand as "an iconic marker of similar abstractions" in glowing, idealized slogans using terms such as "the party-state," "investment," "development," and "modernization" (Harms 2011, 157–59), while their material effects and functions are transforming contemporary rural China in tremendously influential ways. While synergizing state-driven modernity with market potential, roads also connote uncertainties and challenges. Whether experiences around roads concern the well-being of individual villagers or the quality of life of the entire village, in practice they confront idealized visions of progress with the messy realities of development.

A PATCHWORK OF OLD AND NEW HOUSES

While some public projects require mass mobilization and support from the local state, individual households in Wuyang appear to undertake one type of infrastructure development relatively spontaneously: building new houses (*ku⁶ zen² muə¹*). For rural residents, each house represents its respective family to the outside world, serving as the "most immediate materialization of the expectations and aspirations linked to the family" (Steinmüller 2013, 93). During my eighteen-month stay, I witnessed a proliferation of new reinforced concrete houses in Wuyang Village, replacing the agricultural fields and woods that surrounded the village. I was also invited to many family banquets celebrating the inauguration of these new residences. Firecrackers set off at the outset of family banquets often publicly announced the completion of new houses in the village, showcasing the pride attached to housing projects. They were unequivocal proof of the time, energy, and money invested.

Hans Steinmüller (2013) noticed during his fieldwork in rural Hubei that two types of houses represented, respectively, tradition and the countryside versus modernity and the city. This distinction was especially pronounced when spelled out to an outside visitor such as a government guest, a tourist, or an anthropologist. Wooden houses carry associations of backwardness and inaccessibility despite being regarded as the idyllic, carefully preserved dwellings of a mountain people, whereas concrete houses serve as visible signs of progress and development in the built environment. Likewise, the different styles and patterns of house construction in Wuyang correspond to the socioeconomic transformations locals have experienced. Wuyang Village was originally an array of residences neatly laid out in rows facing almost the same direction, each consisting of houses, yards, and sheds, with collective spaces close by, including rice fields, vegetable gardens, and orchards. The architectural style, featuring stone foundations and wooden interiors that can be dated to at least a hundred years ago, was a modification of the original stilted houses, whose wooden pillars allowed the structure to stand at a distance above the ground and protected against damage from the humidity of the soil.[14] Stonework was added to the exterior of the houses, including the overarching gabled roof—a result of local need to fortify these houses against brigands during the Republican era.

The old houses in Wuyang relied on an art of carpentry that many villagers told me was almost forgotten, and the siting of houses was strictly determined according to *fengshui* knowledge often only possessed by the Mo ritual masters.[15] Therefore, these old residences would be nearly impossible to reconstruct once fragmented or destroyed. As road conditions have improved in recent years, villagers have started building new multistory structures, funded through money in addition to agricultural income. These new houses are mostly made of concrete blocks and plastered walls strengthened with steel bars, with concrete floors on the ground level and concrete ceilings (figure 9). Some villagers invited ritual practitioners to conduct a simplified ceremony before breaking ground, but the situating of new houses was primarily constrained by the size and orientation of the land each family possessed close to the main road.

These residences from various time periods in Wuyang Village became a core challenge in tackling the balance between preservation and inheritance, on the one hand, and *kaifa*, on the other. While a key goal of Building a New Socialist Countryside was modernizing and urbanizing the rural built environment in China (Bray 2013; Rosenberg 2013), houses are perhaps the most important aspect of village appearance when it comes to branding a locality with *minzu* characteristics. As recounted by a female representative from Wuyang who visited the well-known Xijiang Thousand-Household Miao Village in southeastern Guizhou, "good-looking houses" (*zɐn² ʔdəi¹ jɛ²*) that offer a direct and immediate visual experience have become a primary magnet for tourists, sometimes supplanting the quest to see other ethnic cultural practices. The old stone houses in Wuyang Village were foregrounded as a significant inheritance that should be preserved, as such vernacular architecture deeply impressed the artists and photographers looking for inspiration for their art. Some artists and travelers I interviewed placed a particularly high value on the old stone houses that condensed the traditional wisdom of local people inhabiting this particular environment, even compared to eco-friendly practices in other parts of the world.

Over the past decade, the trend of constructing new concrete houses has moved too swiftly for local state agencies hoping to preserve the original appearance of Wuyang Village. In 2009, the county government forbade any changes to the old stone houses. As a result, most of the village could no longer be modified, with the exception of a couple of households that had already been partly turned into cement structures. Meanwhile, any new houses built with concrete bricks beyond the old village had to have an exterior made of stone rather than plastered with lime powder or ceramic tiles. In addition, a roof made with layered stone shingles had to be added, so as to maintain a uniform look for the entire village.[16]

Establishing new residences near roads and on relatively flat land may in fact provide convenience for elderly villagers who find it difficult to climb slopes to reach their old houses. More importantly, villagers need

FIGURE 9. Traditional stilted house (*top*, modified from the original stilted structure), allowing residents to keep cattle, horses, pigs, chickens, and other livestock on the ground level, compared to a newly built bungalow (*bottom*) (2013).

new spaces because the number of family members per household has been growing, and some of the old stone houses have gradually become unstable due to age and infrequent repair. As villagers have increasingly moved away for office work or migrant labor, unoccupied old houses become dilapidated and even dangerous for their inhabitants. In 2010, the township government began to allow villagers with old residences specified as "dilapidated houses" (*weifang*) to apply for funding to construct new houses outside the scope of the original village. This subsidy, which varies from ¥6,000 to ¥10,000 ($800–$1,400) per household, is only granted when a qualified new house is completed.

Some middle-aged male villagers further explained to me the implicit reason for the rapid appearance of new residences: not only have people become migrant laborers and gained more disposable income in recent years, but the new construction is a precautionary measure to prevent local authorities from taking back the land. Villagers were unsure about future policy and knew they only had the right to use the land temporarily. Some may have heard of or witnessed other regions of China where land requisition for modern development involved monetary compensation. Therefore, aside from accommodating a growing population and improving living standards, the new houses also reflected insecurity about future prospects under the vague vision of *kaifa*. Villagers may plan to use the built residences in the future to claim pieces of land they technically do not have individual ownership over. As some put it, "The rice is cooked [*shengmi zhucheng shoufan*]. What is done is done."

Construction of new concrete houses, for many male villagers, did not require professional skills but could be learned through observation. The basic cost of constructing a new house was around ¥50,000–¥60,000 ($7,000–$8,000). Concrete bricks, wood, and stone could all be purchased in the Zhenning county seat, although stone from nearby quarries could be cheaper. A number of villagers asked carpenters or masons in other villages or the county seat for help when structuring the building and finishing the roof. Some builders continued to follow traditional house-related rituals to confirm the *fengshui* of the location and the orientation of doors and

180   CHAPTER FIVE

windows, as well as selecting an auspicious day to break ground. However, the structures and building methods of these new houses diverged from the old houses, which required symmetry as well as carefully laid out wood and stone materials. Villagers were primarily concerned that building rectangular houses would waste land. To use every inch of their land, many houses were constructed right next to each other, without even leaving space for a person to pass or for a window to open. The space between some houses and the main road was also quite narrow. In addition, some builders simply did not follow the correct angle of a construction plot or added two to three stories to the homes to make more use of vertical space. The tomb of the Wu family's ancestors, dating back to the late Qing and situated between the old village and rice fields, thus found itself amid newly built trapezoidal or curved concrete houses. The irregular shapes of crop fields and other family land resulted in a patchwork of new houses, which irritated local government.

Officials and experts invited to Wuyang Village for consultation purposes were frustrated that these newly constructed houses looked so unplanned. During a November 2013 meeting in the village committee building's unused classroom, chaired by the district chief of the township government in charge of the area, a message was conveyed to Communist Party members from Wuyang and three adjacent natural villages. The district chief started off with an admonition about the uncoordinated planning of tourism development (with a focus on Wuyang Village) that worried him considerably:

> Comparing now to ten years ago, we indeed have much better public infrastructure. But the main problem is construction without any order [*luan da luan jian*]! A "thousand-year-old village" relies predominantly on its antique feel [*gu se gu xiang*], its scenic beauty, which is why everyone comes to visit. But you see, all the new houses are being built now, one right next to another, right next to the road, which is rather narrow to begin with. Cars would not even be able to make turns and pass one another. You think those in Beijing or Shanghai don't know how to build better and more stylish ones than yours?! Villages around here all have

old stone houses, but once new cement bungalows emerge, the original appearance [*yuanmao*] would be disrupted. Go ask some youngsters these days—how fast internet travels! Once anyone puts up photos of our villages with rough road conditions and chaotic houses, the entirety of China would know. We would receive a definite no-no online, and no one would be willing to visit anymore!

This fretting over visually incongruous structures reveals the contradictions of timelessness versus modernization. Warning against creating a homogenized countryside with a generically contemporary appearance that is no longer ethnic or historical, the discourse above indicates that Wuyang Village welcomes infrastructural development and high-velocity connectivity but not mimicry of modern big cities.

The urgent need to regulate new construction, which had been growing rapidly, was a shared concern among officials at all levels from the county to the provincial state agencies. One dilemma, however, was that before these changes transpired, local government did not have enough funding or time to carefully repair the historical architecture. Nor were local authorities able to relocate villagers out of the old village into a new residential zone with high-density townhouses, as seen in other instances of Building a New Socialist Countryside (Hillman and Unger 2013, 3), which would have required considerable money and spare land. Some local officials felt that it was necessary not only to plan and control the building of new residences, but also to remove human activities entirely from the core residential area of the old village, which distinguishes Wuyang Village from many other villages and modern cities. After decades or even centuries of inhabiting these old houses, villagers and their basic livelihoods had become obstacles to preservation and had to give way to the "de-peopling of rural landscapes" (Wilczak 2017). Traditional architecture was treated almost like wilderness, according to past conservation strategies of protecting dehumanized landscapes, but houses, in fact, need human habitation (*renqi*) to prevent dilapidation.

The local state thus regarded the chaotic clusters of new houses as a sign

182   CHAPTER FIVE

that the quality (*suzhi*) of local residents needed improvement. Villagers were deemed shortsighted and self-interested, which was less than ideal. Cultivating their mindset was a goal that joined that of enhancing agricultural facilities and constructing infrastructure. Local officials hoped people would start to realize that preserving the original landscape of Wuyang Village was to their benefit. The new concrete houses in Wuyang Village thus symbolize unpleasant chaos, just like the uncontrollable urban villages in coastal China, which are "uncivilized, messy, and disorderly" (Bach 2010, 425), the removal of which is thought akin to removing "the city's cancers" (Siu 2007, 335). For example, while villagers regard ceramic tiles as a technique to beautify their new modern houses, photographers and cultural experts suggest their removal.

In early 2014, locals were ordered to stop all housing construction, regardless of the stage of construction. Apart from the unsatisfactory appearance, local authorities might have also been concerned about the huge cost required if the state decided to take over the land and needed to compensate these partially completed new houses. As a result, some elderly couples were residing in new houses without doors or windows, and villagers used the foundations of unfinished buildings to plant vegetables. The entire village was waiting for further notice and funding to continue development projects. The people were suspended in uncertainty. Some villagers considered secretly completing the half-finished houses, but local authorities had coded and photographed each house to ensure they remained unchanged. By the time I returned in the summer of 2017, several villagers were assisting in a new government project to develop an area one kilometer from the original village for uniformly designed townhouses. The plan was to move part of the community to these new residences, which would also offer board and lodging for future tourists. This served to keep modern houses away from the village's core area, which needed to star in the branding of Wuyang as an eye-catching destination. To render local populations and the landscapes they inhabit more manageable (Tania Li 2007), village development therefore involves spatial zoning of rural China that resorts to technical solutions.

HAS MODERNITY ARRIVED AT THE BUYI VILLAGE?

During the Lunar New Year celebration in early 2013 when Director Wu stressed the importance of *kaifa* for Wuyang Village, Chairman Yang, who had initiated Wuyang's public infrastructure development upon retiring from his official position in the county government, described three dimensions he regarded as needing attention to attract more tourists and potential investors. First, preservation efforts should focus on the stone and wood architecture and the river, both of which he hoped would gain more protection from provincial and even national-level authorities. Second, the sanitary environment in the village needed attention: "The Buyi is an ethnicity [*minzu*] that pays much attention to hygiene [*jiang weisheng*] of not only the village, but also of each individual household. We dislike not old things, but dirty things. So we need to make the guests feel the cleanliness [*ganshou jiejing*]. Anything affecting village hygiene, such as chickens, ducks, or dogs, shall not be reared."

The third dimension he stressed, in relation to the second, was to be "civil and polite" (*jiang wenming limao*). Here again, the discourse of *suzhi* by regulating human bodies and conduct (Yan 2003) permeates the infrastructural development process, seeking to present a neat and tidy village. The attention to hygiene and civility not only emphasizes becoming model citizens to comply with a modernizing China, but also recalls the high socialist era, during which nationwide campaigns against infectious disease called attention to hygiene and sought to transform rural residents, who typically stood for backwardness.[17]

While infrastructure investment serves as a precondition for socialist modernism and for material, and thus ideological, progress (Pedersen 2011), Chairman Yang's speech illustrates that merely expanding public infrastructure or the hardware of development is far from enough. The focus on civilization is not, however, solely in the mindset of elites and officials. At times, residents of Wuyang Village described other populated Buyi villages in nearby areas as places where "no civilization has really arrived," even if those villages had been reached by roads much sooner than

184   CHAPTER FIVE

their own. A male villager in his midtwenties who was helping his parents with farm work in Wuyang recalled his visit several years previously to the natal village of his young wife, where he was shocked by its appearance: "Their village had no water [at the time], but moreover, their village paths were not only muddy but also filled with dog feces, diapers or even sanitary pads that had been strewn everywhere. . . . Our Wuyang Village, on the other hand, is referred to as a civilized village (*wenming cunzhai*); no one dares to throw filthy things around."

Though both Buyi elites and villagers from Wuyang consider themselves clean and tidy, what seems paradoxical is the continuing need to cultivate the minds and bodies of the Buyi. One may ascribe the idea that the Buyi care more about cleanliness than various other ethnic groups, especially the "out-of-the-way hill tribes," to the prevalent discourse of the Buyi being more sinicized (*hanhua*). But even if the Buyi have been more conscious of catching up with the Chinese state and mainstream society, their lifestyle is still considered not fully ideal, perhaps partly due to their rural status. Once at a family banquet in Wuyang Village, a female villager in her sixties explicitly told others that the reason she would not join the table I was sitting at was because she considered me a Han girl. She said, "The Han are cleaner; they would be disgusted by our appearance." Ethnic difference alongside living conditions thus embodied the discourse around cleanliness—with a connotation of civilization—caught in a Han/minority, urban/rural hierarchy.

One major proposal for transformation that was raised by Chairman Yang and shared by other cultural experts was the separation of human beings and domestic animals. On separate occasions, a Fujian businessman who came to assess investment potential and some Sichuan professors who visited for artistic inspiration had advised villagers to move the animal pens outside their households, where more space was available and collective management of livestock was possible. In their opinion, not only did raising domestic animals produce unpleasant smells, but the bodies and droppings of domestic animals could carry germs, the effects of which could be worsened by the presence of flies and other insects. Thus, villagers should no longer raise pigs, cattle, or poultry from a sanitary standpoint, especially if the village households later intended to offer accommodation and catering to tourists in a *nongjiale* (peasant guesthouse).[18] Some of the villagers agreed with this suggestion, while others considered secretly raising a few animals.

It surprised many when Chairman Yang, himself a Buyi, suggested that villagers should no longer keep livestock. Not only have domestic animals been indispensable for agrarian communities, but they are also important in ritualistic and festive activities. What's more, in the traditional stone and wood residences and stilted houses typically seen in ethnic areas, which local authorities fought so hard to preserve in Wuyang Village, the ground level is normally used for cattle, horses, pigs, and chickens, while the level above is for human residence. The ground level is covered with grass and grain husks, allowing animal excretions to be mixed into manure for crop farming. Sometimes, even humans discharge from the living quarters into the pen below through removable wooden planks. In this way, domestic animals have indeed been part of the household unit, crucial for local livelihoods, socio-ecological integration, and domestic economy.

In Richard Handler and Eric Gable's (1997) discussion of Colonial Williamsburg, horse droppings, euphemized as "road apples," are an evocative symbol of natural disorder in a tidy and elegant historical community. "Road apples" coexist with white picket fences in the carefully managed outdoor museum of Colonial Williamsburg, representing mutually contradictory paradigms of a collective past while adding to its authenticity. In contrast, animal excrement is deemed undesirable in Wuyang for material, symbolic, and perhaps aesthetic reasons. Although certain domestic animals could potentially be regulated through managed space and techniques, dogs still run freely around the village, and cattle need to be led to and from the fields, if not farther to the markets. The concerns of some officials and villagers were that the brand-new roads and paths both in the village and beyond—an expression of cleanliness (Larkin 2013, 336–37) and the "face" of Wuyang Village—might be continually threatened by not only dust but also what is, in fact, organic dirt.

186   CHAPTER FIVE

Women in Wuyang Village, who play the role of housekeepers in charge of domestic labor, are thus constantly summoned to tidy the paths and the communal playground, especially before the start of public events or the arrival of officials.[19] Like animal husbandry, another hygiene issue that affects the aesthetics of public space involves the increasing garbage scattered across the village. The consumerist culture sweeping across rural areas has resulted in a tremendous amount of plastic packaging and other disposables. When I arrived in Wuyang in the summer of 2012, I noticed that, on a hill slope not far from the village where people used to maintain dense forests, tons of garbage had accumulated over time, some of which was burned by villagers from time to time.

While recycling systems have yet to be improved, garbage cans and garbage dumps had been installed in the village by early 2013. Funded by the Case-by-Case financial subsidy, three garbage dumps shaped like huts with blue roofs were built at the village's major intersections, and dozens of orange tin trash cans were set up at approximately every three hundred meters across Wuyang Village. Rather than hiding these facilities containing dirty materials, local authorities made them visible to exemplify the modernizing process that was transpiring in the village. In 2014, a red-lettered signboard warning of a ¥200–¥500 (roughly $30–$70) fine for littering was mounted at the top of the slope once covered with trash.

The look of the trash cans was, however, criticized by officials and visitors for being too new and discordant with the supposedly historical village. To match the historical and pristine feel of the village, the criticism went, trash cans should be made of local natural materials (like wood). The bright orange color stood out harshly amid the stone architecture but was one of the few options available to Chairman Yang with limited funding. The function of the trash cans was further called into question by village residents: more like a decoration (*baishe*) than anything else, the trash cans hardly made the environs cleaner but were themselves malodorous. When discussing why villagers were still burning trash instead of using the garbage facilities, a village cadre explained that the trash cans were for collective (*gonggong de*) use, while individual trash needed to be managed

MODERNIZING RURAL INFRASTRUCTURE   187

on one's own—otherwise, law enforcement would blame the villagers for unhygienic conditions. In turn, some villagers wondered what the real use of these trash cans was and whether they had been installed purely to demonstrate that civilized human conduct could contribute to maintaining sanitary conditions.[20]

These ardent efforts to sanitize the village have been accompanied by other modernizing and beautifying measures so as to manifest the village's advanced awareness of environmental protection and *suzhi* cultivation. In Building a New Socialist Countryside, urban planning is often seen as an appropriate tool for solving a range of intractable rural problems (Bray 2013), and educating peasants through the "scientific concept of development" (Perry 2011) is regarded as key. As in other Buyi villages promoted as energy-sustainable sites, two dozen solar-powered streetlamps were erected along major paths across Wuyang Village in late 2012.[21] Villagers noticed that these streetlamps automatically lit up as the sky darkened and turned off as the dawn came without using grid electricity. They mostly appreciated the convenience that these lamps brought, as they no longer needed to carry a flashlight or feared walking outside after dark. Nevertheless, these lamps, also purchased by the county authority through the same Case-by-Case subsidy as the trash cans, were censured by officials and tourists as too modern for the historical feel of the village. The blue poles of the solar-powered lamps, together with the messy electricity cords that already sprawled above and across village households, were visually unpleasant.

These constant tensions around old and new, rural and urban appeared inherent in the subsidiary construction to support public infrastructure. If the whole point of attracting tourists was indeed to showcase the traditional appearance of Wuyang Village and to let people get away from the modern pressures of living in cities, then some of the new changes seemed contradictory. Wuyang Village replaced a patch of high-density forest, which earlier visitors praised as showcasing the area's natural beauty, with a brand-new parking lot to accommodate and welcome visitors at its entrance. This lot was partly a result of Chairman Yang's personal vision and investment but was seldom used during the period of my fieldwork.[22] The parking lot, as

188   CHAPTER FIVE

well as the new roads, was bordered with new tree saplings neatly planted in rows, contributing to the greening of the village environment.

While the countryside is seen as a desirable space to nurture health through outdoor activities in nature, local government also set up an area with fitness equipment for peasants to exercise (*nongmin tiyu jianshen qicai*) in a corner of the parking lot. Along with a performance stage and a basketball court that are part of the parking lot, the fitness equipment was intended to enhance the material and spiritual life of villagers who are already doing farm work all day long. Basketball games, often accompanying festive celebrations, can be a collective activity conducive to mass mobilization. New wooden signboards with conspicuous slogans about birth control and societal progress, erected by the township government and the County Red Cross along the main road that leads into Wuyang Village, further symbolize the state's endeavor to improve local *suzhi*, or quality of life.

In addition to hygienic installations and recreational infrastructure, the makeover of Wuyang Village involved various efforts to promote cultural branding. Directional signs were installed to indicate the locations of ancient sites associated with local history and culture. Multiple attractions, including a stone bridge, a well, and two bastions, were labeled with the added value *gu-* ("ancient" or "aged"). Points of interest across the village were showcased like museum displays with explanatory texts, usually on signboards or plaques (as part of the museumification process delineated in chapter 4). Villagers also pointed out to me that officials and developers used select Han characters with a historical feel but decontextualized meanings to phonetically denote Buyi names. For instance, the crystal meandering river that runs by Wuyang—upstream of China's largest waterfall, Huangguoshu—was originally named $\m#ellipse{}o^1 lo^5$ in Buyi, which a few village elders remembered as referring to the abundance of fish in the river swimming in circles. Because Buyi does not have a written system, local officials decided to use a Chinese word that best resembled the pronunciation of $\mathellipse{}o^1 lo^5$ as a replacement. The Chinese word chosen was *suoluo*, which actually denotes cyathea, an ancient fern species that has supposedly existed since the age of the dinosaurs. In the end, "Suoluo River" appeared on the signboards, intending to echo the historical feel of the stone bridge and the village in general. The original Buyi meaning was lost in translation.

The "thousand-year-old Buyi village" has thus encountered a number of tensions in its creation as a historical site and a cultural destination. When my fieldwork approached its end in 2013, local elites were discussing plans to deploy efforts to turn back time, such as recovering riverside mills in future development, and some suggested that existing construction (such as stone paths and facilities) should also be redone to look less modern. But perhaps not everything from the past is desirable; thus, careful curation is required for contemporary valorization. When some county officials came to inspect Wuyang Village in 2012, they questioned whether the immediately obvious slogans like "Long Live Chairman Mao," written in vermillion paint on many of the old stone houses during the socialist years, should be covered up. Chairman Yang answered, "Well, it is history, after all. It shows the age of the village."

THE UNEASY PROCESS OF *KAIFA*

The infrastructural development in Wuyang Village has come at an uneasy time. According to local authorities, neither preservation nor development can wait. For some officials and intellectuals in Guizhou—considered underdeveloped as a whole—*kaifa* is a necessary action, and maintaining a delicate and sustainable balance between conservation and development may be the best way to help boost economic growth and reduce rural poverty (Yu Luo 2018b). The reality is that the conflicts between historical preservation and commercialized development encapsulate a fundamental tension between timelessness and progress (Duara 1995; Oakes 2012), inherent in the impulses of China's nation building. Trapped between the need to maintain an idyllic past and the desire to progress and civilize, Wuyang Village exemplifies the dilemma of many ethnic, rural communities that can be neither traditional nor modern enough—but are perhaps uncomfortably both. Unlike those in peri-urban areas that are neither city nor countryside (Harms 2011), the spatiotemporal oscillation rural villagers in China have experienced derives from the contradiction between remaining distinctly rural and following an urbanized framework to improve use of space and quality of life, among other aspects.

Wuyang Village is inevitably caught in a dual process described by Jenny Chio (2011, 60–61), whereby the rural is brought closer to modern China through infrastructural development but is simultaneously characterized as distant to serve as an attractive destination for domestic tourism. To be both livable for villagers and presentable to visitors, *kaifa* needs to strike a balance between the village's original condition and a manicured landscape. Uncle Kuan, a male villager in his fifties, critiqued how inconsistent construction had spoiled the signature look of the historical village, as he counterposed the adequately antique (*yuangu*) with the overly modernized (*xiandaihua*). Intriguingly, Wuyang's new infrastructure connectivity had intended to redress the local experience of remoteness, but it also forced Wuyang, and many other ethnic villages, to compete with those already known as cultural destinations by fixing and commodifying just that remoteness. It is precisely when socio-spatial compression and mobility unsettle the urban-rural and Han-minority binaries that localities are pressed to recapture remoteness as legible, marketable, and ultimately profitable (Luo, Oakes, and Schein 2019).

In branding and developing Wuyang for heritage tourism, the appearance of the village hence became a primary focus. Accordingly, the local government decided on village makeover plans while new infrastructure projects, especially roads and sewage systems, were being built. New concrete houses and village paths, viewed as visual markers of modern development, were surfaced with stone. This entailed a preference for aesthetic uniformity in housing and infrastructure design, with an ethnic or historical touch. This kind of ethnic theming, as Tim Oakes (2020) argues, is not merely a branding ploy or a "face" project but a deliberate project of social engineering in Guizhou's small cities and towns. As villages and towns are being rendered visible leisure spaces, this process might be a key technique or strategy in relation to governing populations, often an unfinished and contingent project.

"Without trash cans, would the village not be sanitary? Without street-lights, would people stop walking?" A middle-aged male villager's critiques of the perfunctory and performative transformations brought about by these new infrastructure projects certainly resonate with the viewpoints of many. While the ongoing infrastructure projects may well create new social meanings (Larkin 2008), villagers sometimes recall traditional ways of life they maintained for a long time. When water and electricity were unstable during my fieldwork, villagers resorted to old wells and kerosene lamps, both of which would soon become outdated. The paradox of the new concrete houses proliferating in Wuyang is that while these new residences may be more spacious, they are sometimes less comfortable than the old stone and wood structures, which allowed for better ventilation and temperature control. Old Buyi clothing, for instance, become damp and spoiled easily when placed in the closets of new concrete houses. At times, locals feel nostalgic for the rice fields and forests they consider to have been more pleasant and scenic in the old days before infrastructural development began.[23]

Local government promises new public infrastructure, which many rural residents may not have equal access to nor fully enjoy the benefits of. The extent to which villagers can participate in construction projects or receive subsidies partly depends on their personal relationships with leading cadres in the township and county government. For an underfunded local state, the urgency to develop infrastructure risks less careful design, and thus incomplete and wasteful investment. And even after infrastructure has been constructed, maintenance also requires work. When I returned in the summer of 2015, weeds had grown up between the paved stone steps to the Big Bastion, trees had toppled over, roads remained unrepaired after damage by mudslides, and roadside saplings obstructed the way into the village. In addition, the custodian role the government continues to play necessitates coordination of various bureaucratic sectors, yet such a process can be complicated and ineffective.[24] For both local authorities and residents in Wuyang Village, development entails a long process, which the Buyi must endure as they wait for the murkiness of their situation to clear up. To wait and see is a common strategy in the face of changeable

192   CHAPTER FIVE

state policies and the trickling down of governmental support. However, waiting may feel like being in a state of oscillation or even suspension.[25] As villagers informed me in the summer of 2015, "the funding has not arrived yet and the plan to *kaifa* is suspended for the time being."

Faced with the challenges of scaling up development in modest villages when subsidies and start-up funding remain limited, Buyi elites encourage improvement of the integral quality (*zonghe suzhi*) of the villagers. Infrastructural development in Wuyang Village promised a better quality of life inherently tied to this cultivation of human quality, or *suzhi*, mobilized by the socialist mode of state-led planning and the burgeoning market. The paradox of grassroots participation lies in the idea that villagers need the state's help to pursue socioeconomic progress, yet simply waiting for and depending on top-down aid is not sufficient. From the viewpoint of local officials, villagers cannot be expected to take the initiative to tap into emerging market opportunities when they do not sense any immediate prospects; therefore, cultivating *suzhi*, especially a modern mindset and human conduct, goes hand in hand with reconstructing the village's physical environment and improving local infrastructure. A common situation observed on the ground in contemporary China is that leaders have little faith in the people's ability to know what they need (Harrell 2013, 292). In turn, the structure and transmission of funding continues to lack transparency, and what were once claimed to be grassroots initiatives end up in the hands of local cadres. Villagers hence feel dispensable and grow skeptical about the promises of local authorities, despite the perceived success of public infrastructure.

In contemporary China, a kind of infrastructure fetishism characterizes the maelstrom of fast-moving socioeconomic development and modernization. Locals are caught up in the longing for and dreams of a better future made possible by new infrastructure. These infrastructure projects, like a facade, are encoded with meaning and imagination attached to modernity, which is deeply political. Deemed the key to attracting more attention and market potential, these transformations could ideally transmit a positive message about the community to outsiders. Yet the unintended consequences of the *kaifa* process appear to be beyond the state's control, similar to how the patchwork of old and new houses became a chaotic assortment. A focus on rural infrastructure and landscape in ethnic minority regions thus reveals the fuzzy realities that confront the ideal vision of a market-driven state. With limited prospects in agriculture and increasing outward migration, villagers might hope to take part in commercial development and become more entrepreneurial, as some of them have turned their land into small parking lots or barbecue grounds. This kind of pragmatism in a rapidly changing countryside is also demonstrated by the fact that rice paddies, crop fields, and forests, which had long been maintained for local subsistence, are now being turned into new houses, possibly marking the transition of devalued agriculture into desirable urbanization. Urbanizing and modernizing the rural, therefore, is not simply enforced from the top down; rather, the process entails spontaneous responses from local society.

When I last visited Wuyang in September 2017, tremendous changes were transpiring in the village. A four-meter-tall stone archway by the main county road indicated the turn into the village for visitors; there was a new road to Wuyang Village, running from the county seat along a different route from previous ones, wide enough for two cars to pass. As it approached the environs of the village, the road crossed a section of the river once only reachable by foot, where I used to swim with the Yang sisters near a small waterfall flowing over an old stone dam. Along this section of new road, a small public square with facilities akin to a visitor information center and some barbecue stands were taking shape. There I encountered some familiar faces building houses at a new village complex that was under construction. Since the local government had decided to dismantle dozens of houses deemed to negatively affect the village appearance, some villagers would be relocated to this new residential area once they moved out of the original village.

The primary area of Wuyang Village had undergone a reconstruction to standardize its appearance. Concrete houses that villagers had constructed in recent years were required to have exterior decoration featuring wooden carved windows and stone-piled roofs in uniform patterns. Quite a few households had hung a plaque indicating *nongjiale* (peasant-style bed and breakfast), and one household was to become a Buyi batik workshop where visitors could learn the skill. I also noticed two new vendor stalls in addition to the one store in the village, with signboards indicating "specialty [*tese*] food and crafts." Some original structures, such as the village committee building and the clinic, had been replaced with bungalows imitating the style of old stone houses. A number of dilapidated and half-complete houses in the village had also been torn down. In addition, the uniform landscaping and planning had resulted in newly paved paths throughout the village connecting sites of interest, with flowerbeds serving as decoration along the way.

The paternalistic nature of local governance affected not only the living space of the village but also villagers' everyday routines. As I greeted and chatted with villagers, they informed me that local government had bought out both the old residence of the Wu family—which might be turned into a bookstore or a hostel—and the entrance area to the village where Chairman Yang had helped build the museum as well as a performance plaza and a visitor center. The local authority had also regulated tourism-related behaviors such that parking was only permitted outside the village, and no recreational activities, such as swimming or barbecuing, could take place near the old stone bridge. At the time of my visit, none of the villagers were farming their fields, except for small scattered plots where some villagers were still able to plant vegetables, because the local authority had requisitioned all the land in the village to prepare for unified tourism planning. Villagers received compensation for their land and for refurbishing or relocating their residences. My longtime hostess, Grandma Wu, for example, had received money to refurbish the interior of her family's stone house with wooden floors and walls, install a toilet and a shower, and provide three comfortable bedrooms for guests. As villagers have been eagerly adapting to modern lifeways, they are also asked to maintain the visual appeal of their village, thus participating in both tangible and intangible aspects of ethnic branding. In transforming the material world, locals may well be transforming themselves.

CONCLUSION

IN AN AGE WHEN LOCAL lives are becoming increasingly similar to the rest of the society, ethnic branding is not easy. Endeavors to mark one's difference tend to rely on a few limited cultural domains. Indeed, several key dimensions of ethnic branding on which this book has focused epitomize what can be observed in many ethnic communities across China and perhaps in other countries as well. These include ritual and religious revivals, cultural performances and spectacles, museum exhibitions of historical artifacts, and revamped villages. The promotion of material and visual aspects works in tandem with symbolic and discursive elements—such as historical narrative and distinct lifestyle—to build a cultural persona of ethnic peoples and their communities.

What the Buyi case adds to a typical scenario of ethnic branding is that both the condition and the solution of ethnic branding are paradoxical for them. A most telling instance is that, since my last visit to Wuyang in 2017, the village has been contracted to and managed by a tourism company under the government's supervision, one of the many lessons it took away from the Xijiang Thousand-Household Miao Village. The development model of Xijiang was considered so successful that Wuyang representatives went to learn from those who had engineered and operated it. Intriguingly, the end goal of marketization is to make Wuyang a famed Buyi village similar to Xijiang as a renowned Miao village. As competitive branding has become unavoidable, cultural difference must be carefully crafted. But for the Buyi, several intersecting paradoxes from their historical and

196   CONCLUSION

contemporary experience have led them into a situation in which branding themselves is simultaneously urgent and challenging.

The first is a temporal paradox that underlies the national history of China and projects onto its ethnic hierarchy. The fundamental drive toward civilizational advancement at its frontiers has experienced a more recent reincarnation in the pursuit of nation building, such as in measures of socioeconomic progress during and after the socialist years. But at the same time, rapid changes in China have driven a desire to find roots in cultural purity, to salvage traditions, and to search for Chineseness. This paradox has influenced local identities and livelihoods as minority groups juggle their material realities and symbolic positions in the changing environment of multiethnic regions of southwest China. Mostly residing by rivers and living off rice paddies, the Buyi have become both culturally cosmopolitan and physically sedentary over time. Thus, they are considered more advanced among non-Han groups. However, in a cultural economy that favors both the traditional and the exotic, the Buyi strive to make their profile more visible and yet face the contemporary predicament of branding a unique identity in competition with other ethnicities. The case of the Buyi thus encapsulates a double bind in which minority populations may be either too late to catch up with the times or too early to remain culturally distinctive.

In relation to this temporal paradox, a spatial paradox lies in the emblematic features of the frontier and the rural in China. At once peripheral and central to the identity construction of Chineseness, the frontiers—and similarly, the countryside—have become spaces deemed in need of improvement and, paradoxically, threatened by development. This paradox is manifest in the way remoteness is simultaneously derogated and celebrated in an age of increased mobility and socio-spatial compression. Wuyang Village's new infrastructure connectivity was intended to bring villagers and tourists closer, but it also urged Wuyang to differentiate itself from other villages by highlighting and marketing its remoteness, which has contributed to its distinctly historical feeling.

The spatial-temporal paradox is the reason we see frequent negotiation of what is to be preserved and what is to be improved. The story of Wuyang Village, and that of the Buyi in general, demonstrates the alternation between the traditional and the modern — a most evident paradox for minorities striving to showcase selective difference in contemporary China's cultural economy. This is not to suggest that tradition and modernity are irreconcilable binary forces; indeed, they are inseparable, complementary, and even converging.[1]

But in China's ethnic politics, standards, values, and hierarchies are often set by those in the dominant category, whether Han, state, or urban. Minority experiences are thus at once focal in themselves and also never free of China-wide frames of reference that structure contemporary mainland life.[2] Therefore, ethnic groups who are neither mainstream nor the most unique may find themselves busy figuring out how to avail themselves of the traditional culture they have been eager to restore while also needing to march with the rest of the country as modern citizens.

Against this sociohistorical backdrop, the Buyi not only find themselves in a conundrum that ensues from social classifications of identity, temporality, and space, but are also caught in a paradoxical attempt at ethnic branding. More often than not, ethnic branding hinges on cultural essentialism, which is at odds with the fluid and changeable nature of identities and cultures. While seeking to brand a quintessential ethnic identity, the Buyi's historical experience, based on their constant, strategic interactions with other ethnicities and with central authorities, continues to inform present-day experience. The Buyi continue to reference modes of cultural promotion and socioeconomic development emanating from others, just as they have historically thrived on cultural borrowing. Ethnic branding therefore turns out to be a case of everyone joining the race to champion cultural distinctiveness and yet trying to be different in similarly generic ways.

After Wuyang was commissioned to the tourism company, I continued to follow my informants' WeChat accounts, where they sometimes posted updates about the village or shared videos by tourists. In a video shot by a travel blogger in late 2018, a small tour group took electric sightseeing cars into the village, where they were greeted by tour guides playing drums at

198 CONCLUSION

the entrance, followed by a team of senior female villagers dressed in Buyi costumes who arranged a welcoming ceremony and offered homemade liquor to the visitors while singing—a scene akin to those in many other ethnic villages. Tourists then circled around to follow the dance movements of the tour guides, tried Buyi snacks prepared by female villagers, tasted water from the old well, and wandered around the revamped village now decorated with explanatory signboards and potted plants.

As Wuyang welcomed hundreds of tourists on a daily basis and thousands on national holidays, its commodification intensified. In 2019, an advertisement for Wuyang's bonfire parties on WeChat caught my attention. Packaged into a ceremony intended to pray for blessing and harvest, the bonfire party included dance, singing, and ritualistic elements. The ¥158 (about $22) per person included the entrance fee to Wuyang as the scenic site, the electric sightseeing car fee, a nutritious all-pork meal, the bonfire party, and a free docent for tour groups. In the summer of 2020, a Yang sister posted a video about the inauguration ceremony for a business called Wuyang Barbecue. Dozens of villagers dressed in traditional costumes, as well as invited folk singers, were performing by the riverside, which had been refitted with steel railings as a guarantee of safety for tourists and residents. In a 2021 official video where a female representative of Wuyang proudly introduced the achievements of her hometown's rural development, tourists followed new boardwalks that led them into the middle of the rice paddies to appreciate the scenery and to take pictures. When night fell, there was not only a bonfire party but also a dazzling light show in the massive new wetland park by the river, where visitors could pay to stay in a glamping zone consisting of a dozen white tents with modern amenities.

Similar to many minority villages I had visited in Guizhou, Wuyang initially attracted a small selection of backpackers who wanted to explore the beauty of hidden gems that were out of the way for most people. However, like other sites, Wuyang did not follow an artisanal or boutique approach intended to be exclusive (and perhaps more expensive) for consumers. This is because a non-mass, hand-crafted approach could never achieve the large-scale effects prioritized by the government.[3] In creating an assembly-line mode of touristic experience including the bonfire party, Wuyang has fallen into what Naomi Klein ([2000] 2010, 36) suggests is the cruelest irony of branding: most campaigns start off by seeking out authentic scenes and important causes so as to infuse their brands with meaning, but the expansive nature of the branding process ends up making such cultural events lose what they need most—a sense of authenticity with which to associate their brands.

On the other hand, impressive and arresting visual cultural elements—even if they are not authentic—have become a must in ethnic and place branding, mostly for the sake of gaining profits from one-time tourists and cultivating a potential pool of regulars. The more visually attractive elements and entertaining cultural activities there are, the better. Drawing on a complex of representational strategies, certain visual motifs are in turn considered expedient to the reputation and potential success of a locale by shaping popular understandings. For instance, in 2020, two poverty-stricken counties in Guizhou attracted nationwide attention with vanity projects that became highly controversial.[4] These ostentatious building projects included an almost one-hundred-meter-high tower complex with a mix of Shui, Buyi, and Miao architectural elements in southern Guizhou, as well as a giant statue of a Miao goddess that stood eighty-eight meters tall in the province's southeast. Though public opinion expressed the suspicion that such big spending had either usurped poverty alleviation funding or become a debt trap, the local governments invested heavily in constructing these scenic spots as cultural landmarks for publicity, which allegedly cost millions, if not billions, of yuan.

With the intention of attracting visitors by creating a striking impression when they first lay eyes on these built structures, branding seeks to establish things that are more appealing to the public gaze, or bigger in size or scale. It may in turn entail a process that is subject to arbitrary judgment and preference. Even for Wuyang, its signature feature, frequently referenced by outsiders, is not necessarily the Buyi villagers and their way of life but the distinctive style of Buyi stone buildings. Had Wuyang not retained its old stone houses and vernacular architecture as its selling point, it might

200 CONCLUSION

never have embarked on a journey toward heritage tourism development, which earned it titles as a provincial-level cultural relic protection unit and subsequently a 4A national tourist attraction.[5] Nor would it have received acclamation as one of the best-preserved Buyi villages in China and become the only Buyi village included among the Top Ten Ethnic Minority Villages in Guizhou (though at least half of them are Miao villages).

Branding, rooted in molding and staging an appealing presence, is therefore about seeking recognition and crafting status. However, as this book has suggested, ethnic branding in the Buyi case is not simply intended to make an impression on outsiders, nor is it merely a story of developing local tourism. Whatever ethnic branding has created in the process locals would have to live with, and perhaps feel strongly attached to. During the Spring Festival of 2023, several of my informants, including a Yang sister I had stayed with in the village and one of the elite Wu family members, shared a WeChat video from Zhenning News Station of a busy bonfire party in Wuyang. The video aimed at signifying the return of "hometown's New Year vibes" (*jiaxiang de nianwei*) after the COVID-19 pandemic. At least a hundred or so people, some dressed in Buyi clothing and others holding cell phones with flashlights, were huddling together, dancing and jumping in a big circle around a bonfire, almost as if they were at a club. As they shared the video on WeChat Moments, my informants added titles such as "My Village" or "My Ancestral Home" (*laojia*), demonstrating pride as Wuyang gained publicity and popularity.

In a way, ethnic branding contributes to strengthening emotional ties with one's home place and ethnic identity, adding greater purpose to local experience. Various local participants and social actors have contributed to producing and highlighting a meaningful Buyiness in their own terms. Chairman Yang and the Wu brothers have been key figures in jump-starting development projects in Wuyang Village, which initially relied on support from governmental agencies that had since turned into entrepreneurial efforts. As local Communist Party cadres who retain an ethnic minority status and yet have benefited from state-run education, these Buyi elites are cultural brokers who have become inseparable from both the bureaucratic

CONCLUSION   201

system and the local community, while becoming astute about the contemporary market potential of ethnic cultures. Over different time periods, they have been drawn into sociopolitical tides over which they have little control, such as when they had to sacrifice Buyi historical relics for personal and family safety during the Cultural Revolution. These experiences did not pull them away from the state but instead taught them to work carefully within permissible parameters. With mixed guilt and nostalgia, as well as hearts keen to assist in the development of their rural home, local Buyi elites in the post-reform era have looked back to the past—for instance, by way of retrieving the Mo rituals and establishing a museum to store Buyi artifacts. They hope to reclaim historical memories and cultural pride, while being motivated by potential socioeconomic gains in the future, however uncertain that future is.

Although they lack institutional resources and discursive power, villagers are eager to make the best of their circumstances. They have relied on the slow trickle of information and any interpersonal connections they have been able to obtain, despite limited transparency about what the local government was planning. Local residents, and especially returned migrants, initiated negotiations with bureaucratic agencies so as to put into practice their visions of services catering to tourism and rural-based industries, such as mushroom planting or fruit gardening, to engage the market economy. Illiterate Buyi women have enthusiastically participated in singing and dancing, wishing to manifest their ethnic distinctiveness with pride and to have a share in the promise of future development potential. Although staging rituals and establishing the museum were not their ideas, villagers spontaneously took part in crafting these refashioned traditions. From contributing old objects from their own households to devoting resources and time to paving stone paths, Buyi villagers have undertaken the branding of ethnicity and locality in their own ways. In a similar manner, they voiced their subtle critiques of ongoing transformations in the village, with regard to whether they themselves were adequately represented as Buyi or whether certain changes have taken place at their expense.

As local Buyi have been vying for the ethnic resources available to them and prioritizing certain cultural practices to foster ethnic branding, I have taken part in unraveling how they envision their sense of belonging and craft their lives on an everyday basis. My presence in the village reminded both local officials and community members that I could be part of ethnic branding—for instance, by helping to spread the word about Wuyang. More importantly, they acknowledged me as someone trying to find a connection to her culture and history by reimmersing herself in the Buyi way of life. Thus, when presenting Buyi as my subjects of research, I also set out to engage with myself in critical ways. The learning process I was involved in reveals the navigation of different vectors of difference in relation to identity and becoming.

My background, which is relatively sinicized, is a metonym for Buyi identity writ large as it oscillates between material, educational progress and ethnic, cultural distinctiveness. This layered, situational nativeness could contribute to a more refined analysis of the multiple forces of boundary making or destabilizing in ethnic identification. It has allowed me to situate the configuration of ethnicity in shifting fields of power and meaning, as well as a long history of change and continuation. Tenzin Jinba (2022) points out that the recent call for decolonization in anthropology will become possible only when the idea of native(s) and the existence of non-Western native anthropologists are taken seriously. He foregrounds the shifting identifications and hierarchical relationships of anthropologists to specific communities in order to reflect on various hegemonies. In this sense, my self-presentation as a native anthropologist—most noticeably in the gradual transition of local Buyi changing my appellation from "that Han girl" to "one of us"—sheds light on what I learned from the field and how I have changed, and more significantly, how selfhood is constructed and how subjectivity is involved in local experiences.

So, what are the implications of a study of ethnicity like this? Ethnicity is a mode of existence that is clearly dependent on conscious fashioning and constant negotiation; it involves both how outsiders describe it and how those who inhabit such categorizations make sense of it. The persistence of the fundamental human desire to objectify one's identity in terms recog-

CONCLUSION 203

nizable to others is why ethnicity still matters "as an analytical construct, a political resource, and an affective anchor for identity" (Shneiderman 2015, 5). At the same time, we cannot lose sight of how ethnic subjectivity, collective memory, social space, and interpersonal relationships are being reconfigured through ethnic branding in everyday local life. With a critical part of it being meaningful self-making, ethnic branding offers a timely way to go beyond previous discussions of cultural production and identity construction.

In what I have observed in present-day China, ethnic identities, along with folk traditions, are not just appropriated by but commingled with and reproduced through the state-market mechanism. In an official WeChat account for Wuyang called "Thousand-Year Buyi" that has been activated since 2018, many posts mentioned "rural revitalization and poverty allevi- ation through the support of industries" (*xiangcun zhenxing, chanye fupin*) and how "resources" could be turned into "assets" when everyone in the village is mobilized to support tourism.[6] The official account documented a combination of events, from ethnic festivals to official visits to tourists' craft-learning experiences, demonstrating a common mode of cultural industry development in the region that incorporated research, education, and entertainment. This exemplifies a moment when ethnic rural lives are still greatly affected by the state in early twenty-first-century China, but the state is less determinant than in earlier decades as it relies on, and yet tries to rein in, economic stimuli. Furthermore, ethnic branding is one significant dimension of a critical juncture at which new discourses and practices in cultural development have not only ensued from China's domestic demands but also come into dialogue with global ideals and visions. As ethnic rural peoples are increasingly intertwined with regional and global economies, local identities and livelihoods become implicated in mass nostalgia consumption.

The story of the Buyi and of Wuyang Village is a bittersweet one, as China has experienced considerable transformation brought about by state outreach, by capital and development. In a context where rural tourism and cultural industries seem more expedient than agricultural production in

204 CONCLUSION

bringing in potential socioeconomic benefits, ethnic branding might be one of the few available paths out of historically inflicted poverty or marginalization for minority peoples. As much as it is a self-construction, ethnicity is also shaped by larger socioeconomic and political forces. Many of the means to advance socioeconomic welfare and political profiles — from improving rural income and living standards to identifying widely acclaimed cultural heritage — have bestowed new meanings on the presupposed ethnic categories designated by the Chinese state and adopted by respective *minzu* groups. For many minority populations, clinging to the historical label of ethnicity and highlighting permissible difference provide the only hope of negotiating themselves out of perceived obstacles to achieving a better life.

"Let the murky water settle and the clear water rise," the Buyi elders in Wuyang told me. As they are flung into powerful sociopolitical currents and face uncertainty, local Buyi find security and comfort in the limited capacity in which they can maneuver. They actively deploy ethnicity as a means of claiming identity and resources, accepting their label and status. But in a process of "treading water," they have to be acutely aware in order to let the murky situation settle, to see how to respond to sociopolitical changes, and to draw on others' lessons. Success or failure in a competitive field of ethnic branding that locals may have little control over is thus hard to determine in this case. Nevertheless, emotional feelings are evoked and lived experiences are transformed by the desire to access one's culture and brand one's difference. This inherently complicated story of contemporary China involves a moment with plentiful opportunities but also unpredictable circumstances. It is the locals' commitments and investments, along with the struggles and setbacks they experience in life, that make the Buyi who they are.

GLOSSARY OF CHINESE CHARACTERS

Bafan 八番
Bai Miao tu 百苗图
baishe 摆设
Baiyue 百越
ban xin ban yi 半信半疑
baohuxing kaifa 保护性开发
baozhuang 包装
benwei zhuyi 本位主义
Biandanshan 扁担山
bowu guan 博物馆
Bu Zhuang lianmeng 布壮联盟
Buyi/Buyizu 布依/布依族
Buyi wenhua de yangben 布依文化的样本
Buyi Xuehui 布依学会
Buyi zhi du 布依之都
Buyizu diyi 布依族第一

cehua 策划
cehuazhe 策划者
chongbai 崇拜
Chu Sihai 除四害
chuangzao 创造

Da Song Guo Guang Nan Xi Lu 大宋国
  广南西路
dadui 大队
datong xiaoyi 大同小异

dazao 打造
deng xia hei 灯下黑
di san tuyuqu 第三土语区
di yi tuyuqu 第一土语区
Dian Qian yixiandao 滇黔一线道
dianji 典籍
die 碟
di'er tuyuqu 第二土语区
Dong/Dongzu 侗/侗族
dongtu 动土
Dongzu dage 侗族大歌

faren qiye 法人企业
feiwuzhi wenhua yichan 非物质文化遗产
fengshui 风水
fengshui baodi 风水宝地
fu 府
fulao 父老
fupin 扶贫

gaitu guiliu 改土归流
ganbu 干部
ganbushang shidai 赶不上时代
ganlanshi 干栏式
ganshou jiejing 感受洁净
gaoceng zhishifenzi 高层知识分子
Gelao 仡佬(族)

206 GLOSSARY OF CHINESE CHARACTERS

geng xianjin de Buyi 更先进的布依
gexing 个性
gongban 公办
gonggong de 公共的
gongzuodui 工作队
gu 蛊
gu se gu xiang 古色古香
Gu xie jing 古榭经
guanhuai 关怀
guanxin 关心
gudai 古代
guge 古歌
gui xiansheng 鬼先生
guihuazhe 规划者
Guizhou Zuiju Meili Minzu Cunzhai 贵
    州最具魅力民族村寨
guochang 过场
guojia 4A ji lüyou jingqu 国家4A级旅
    游景区
guolao 国老

hanhua 汉化
hanren yihua 汉人夷化
Hanzu zhu chengtou, Buyi zhu shuitou,
    Miaozu zhu shantou 汉族住城头，布
    依住水头，苗族住山头
hao dongxi 好东西
"Hao hua hong" 好花红
hexie shehui 和谐社会
hexie sixiang, datong yishi 和谐思想，
    大同意识
honghuo 红火
hongya tianshu 红崖天书
Huangdi 黄帝
Huangguoshu 黄果树
Hui 回(族)

jia Buyi 假布依
jiaguwen 甲骨文

jiang weisheng 讲卫生
jiang wenming limao 讲文明礼貌
jiangshan 江山
Jianshe Shehuizhuyi Xin Nongcun 建设
    社会主义新农村
jiaxiang de nianwei 家乡的年味
jinbu kaifang 进步开放
jingdian 经典
jingwei 敬畏

kaifa 开发
kaifa shi fupin 开发式扶贫

langshao 浪哨
laoban 老板
laobiao 老表
laodage 老大哥
laogudong 老古董
laojia 老家
laomo 老摩
Li 黎(族)
Liuyueliu 六月六
longfeng 龙凤
longqi 龙气
luan da luan jian 乱搭乱建
luohou 落后
lusheng 芦笙
Lutu 渌图

man 蛮
Meili Xiangcun 美丽乡村
meirong 美容
Miao/Miaozu 苗/苗族
Miaojiang zoulang 苗疆走廊
minban 民办
mingpian 名片
minjian 民间
minsu 民俗
minsu guan 民俗馆

minzu bowuguan 民族博物馆
Minzu Quyu Zizhi Fa 民族区域自治法
minzu ronghe 民族融合
"Minzu tuanjie hua shengkai" 民族团结花盛开
minzu xuehui 民族学会
minzu yishi 民族意识
minzuxue 民族学
Mo wenhua yanjiu 摩文化研究
Mogong 摩公
Mogong shijia 摩公世家
Mojiao 摩教
Mojing 摩经
Moshi 摩师

niutou 牛头
nongjiale 农家乐
nongmin tiyu jianshen qicai 农民体育健身器材

Po Sijiu, Li Sixin 破四旧、立四新

qiangshen jianti 强身健体
qiannian Buyi guzhai 千年布依古寨
qunzhong 群众

renao 热闹
renqi 人气
renwen shizu 人文始祖
rouhe 柔和
rulin cun 儒林村

sanlao sishao 三老四少
shang shanqu 上山区
shangmian 上面
shaoshu minzu 少数民族
shehui fazhan 社会发展
shehuizhuyi jingshen wenming 社会主义精神文明

shejizhe 设计者
sheng zhengxie 省政协
Sheng Zhengxie Shuhuayuan 省政协书画院
shengmi zhucheng shoufan 生米煮成熟饭
shengtai bowuguan 生态博物馆
shengtai wenming 生态文明
shenling 神灵
Shijie Zhi Chuang 世界之窗
shiju minzu 世居民族
shoucang re 收藏热
Shui 水（族）
shui de wenhua 水的文化
Siyueba 四月八
suoluo 梭罗/桫椤
suzhi 素质

ta zu 他族
techan 特产
tese 特色
tongbao 同胞
tongchou guihua 统筹规划
tongdao wenhua 通道文化
tonggu 铜鼓
tuanjie 团结
tudigong 土地公
tuntian 屯田
tusi 土司

wajue 挖掘
weifang 危房
wenhua jianshe 文化建设
wenhua re 文化热
wenhua tiyan qu 文化体验区
wenhua zijue 文化自觉
wenming 文明
wenming cunzhai 文明村寨

208 GLOSSARY OF CHINESE CHARACTERS

wenwu 文物
wenwu baohu danwei
　文物保护单位

xia shanqu 下山区
xiamian 下面
xian 县
xian zhengfu 县政府
xiandai 现代
xiandaihua 现代化
xiangchou 乡愁
xiangcun zhenxing, chanye fupin 乡村振
　兴、产业扶贫
xianghua 向化
xianjin 先进
xiansheng 先生
xiaokang 小康
xiaozu 小组
Xibu Dakaifa 西部大开发
xinan guanhua 西南官话
xingxiang 形象
xinyang 信仰

Yi/Yizu 彝/彝族
yi zu 夷族
yichan 遗产
yiren hanhua 夷人汉化
yishiyiyi 一事一议
you wenhua 有文化
Yu 禹
yuangu 远古
yuanmao 原貌
yuansheng shi 原生石

yuanshengtai 原生态
yuanshi 原始

zhailao 寨老
zhanyong 占用
zhengjiao heyi 政教合一
zhengqi 整齐
Zhenning 镇宁
zhenzige de 真资格的
zhishifenzi 知识分子
zhongbu shanqu 中部山区
Zhongguo Chuantong Cunluo 中国传
　统村落
Zhongguo Minjian Wenyijia Xiehui 中国
　民间文艺家协会
Zhongguo Wenxue Yishujie Lianhehui 中
　国文学艺术界联合会
Zhongguohua 中国化
Zhonghua minzu 中华民族
Zhongjia 仲家
Zhongyang Minzu Fangwen Tuan Xinan
　Fangwentuan Disan Fentuan 中央民
　族访问团西南访问团第三分团
Zhongyang Minzu Xueyuan 中央民族
　学院
zhongyuan 中原
Zhuang/Zhuangzu 壮/壮族
Zhuanxu 颛顼
zhun zongjiao 准宗教
zonghe suzhi 综合素质
zongjiao 宗教
zongzi 粽子
zuo ziji de zhuren 做自己的主人

NOTES

INTRODUCTION

1. According to the Sixth National Population Census in 2010, Buyi population has decreased from the 2000 census (from 2,971,460 to 2,870,034) and placed tenth among the non-Han groups; before then, it had been the ninth largest minority group in China.
2. In anthropological research on brand making, natural and cultural (or even spiritual) attributes are used to indicate authenticity and guarantee quality (e.g., Manning 2010; Wengrow 2008). Selling or trading on Guizhou has similarly rested on highlighting certain qualities of its life-nourishing environment (Oakes 1999).
3. Schein (1997, 77) has described a pre-tourism moment in which locals were socialized to commodify their culture during her fieldwork in Guizhou's Miao communities in the 1980s and 1990s.
4. Existing studies have focused much on the entrepreneurial, corporate nature of ethnic branding through ways in which cultural difference carves out specific niches of value production (e.g., Comaroff and Comaroff 2009).
5. Scholars such as Abu-Lughod (1991) and Narayan (1993) have discussed in detail the complexity "halfie" and "native" anthropologists encounter in fieldwork and ethnographic practices and how it affects the process of knowledge production. Critiquing against ideas like "halfie" in postcolonial and subaltern studies that entail political complicity or intellectual naïveté, Tenzin (2022) suggests that the idea of native(s) should be taken seriously as a multifaceted, multilayered engagement to facilitate critical dialogue.
6. The proverb in Chinese is *Hanzu zhu chengtou, Buyi zhu shuitou, Miaozu zhu shantou*. Similar proverbs have also existed among other multiethnic regions in southwest China, where the Zhuang, Dai, and Dong are stereotyped as living by water, and the Yao live on mountaintops.

NOTES TO PAGES 9–12

7. Historians, anthropologists, and geographers have identified Zomia (van Schendel 2002) as a distinctive region, which is notably absent from Eurocentric and Asiacentric historiographies, area studies, and classic nation-state frameworks (Formoso 2010; Jonsson 2010). Michaud (2000, 2006, 2010) refers to an overlapping but slightly different area as the Southeast Asian Massif.

8. Hostetler (2001, 2006) has examined how Guizhou's petty officials in the eighteenth and nineteenth centuries created a typical hierarchy among culturally alteric peoples through ethnographic caricatures and pictographs in the "Miao Albums" (*Bai Miao tu*, or "Illustrations of the Hundred Barbarians").

9. Scholars have argued that swidden cultivation is not an evolutionary predecessor of wet-rice cultivation; as part and parcel of an integral agro-ecological system, both have been cultivated at the same time by the same peoples, in the uplands as well as lowlands, with ancient roots (Keyes 2010; Dove, Jonsson, and Aung-Thwin 2011).

10. Scott (2009, 102) points out a similar stigma that Vietnamese attached to those without an ancestral place: such people were vagrants and uncivilized, "people of the four corners of the world."

11. *Hanhua* can be translated as Hanification, whereas the Chinese translation for sinicization is sometimes *Zhongguohua* (see Jing Wang 2021). I use "sinicization" and *hanhua* interchangeably to indicate the long historical processes of incorporating local indigenes into Chinese society and the social and cultural changes experienced in Buyi areas under Han influence. Scholars have noted that sinicization is a simplistic narrative that by no means takes into account the various phases of military occupation, imperial expansion, civilizing mission, and moral transformation that have transpired on China's southwestern frontier (Herman 2007). The naturalized connection between the highly malleable Han identity and Chinese culture/civilization is equally problematic (Mullaney 2012, 4–6). Mindful that sinicization is premised on a unidirectional and ahistorical understanding of ethnogenesis that may undermine its analytical usefulness (Crossley 1990; Leibold 2007), I treat sinicization as a discourse that has taken on a particular life in everyday usage.

12. Borrowed from the Japanese term *minzoku* in the early twentieth century, *minzu* was an attempt on the part of Chinese intellectuals to build an ideological basis for a modern nation-state. The *minzu* classification scheme not only drew on the precedent of Republican-era surveys but also made direct reference to the Soviet Stalinist model of nationalities, which were defined based on four common criteria—territory, language, economy, and psychological nature. Chapter 1 discusses in detail the politics of *minzu* classification and the implications of creating these state-endorsed *minzu* categories.

NOTES TO PAGES 12–16   211

13. Ka-ming Wu (2015) discusses the Chinese notion of *minjian*—folk knowledge and practices of rural peasant society—as foundational to Communist Party propaganda and nationalist politics even before the establishment of the People's Republic of China.

14. A term raised by antecedent anthropologists like Fei Xiaotong to urge the reflexive understanding of Chineseness, "cultural self-consciousness" (*wenhua zijue*) was headlined and elaborated upon in the 2013 special issue of *Guizhou Daily* that spotlighted the six hundred years of history of Guizhou since 1413. See Wang Xiaomei (2013).

15. The post-Mao reform years also marked a phase in which fifty-six ethnic groups—a number symbolically reinforced in national celebrations, school curricula, and public representations—were officially confirmed based on a national census after decades of relentless efforts at specifying and consolidating *minzu* categories.

16. This tendency is arguably influenced by the tenacity of the Cold War lens (Farquhar and Hevia 1993) and assumptions borrowed from Western racial and ethnic politics (Schein and Luo 2016).

17. Guizhou's officials have often regarded culture as both a rich vein of untapped economic ore and a salve for the social instability wrought by decades of uneven growth (Oakes 2006, 2009). According to Donaldson (2011), tourism as a development tool appeared in the Seventh Five-Year Plan (1985–90), and Guizhou became the first province to explicitly tie tourism to poverty reduction in 1992. Subsequently, Guizhou's cultural development coincided with the Open Up the West (Xibu Dakaifa) campaign implemented by the state after the turn of the twenty-first century, seeking to assist the development of interior regions (Goodman 2004).

18. Scholars have pointed out a regional shift from development to eco-development as East Asian governments acknowledge that environmental sustainability is a critical component of economic growth at the turn of the twenty-first century (e.g., Haddad and Harrell 2020). The Chinese state is increasingly seeking to legitimize its role in preserving both biological diversity and cultural transmission (McLaren et al. 2013). Evidence of its enthusiasm to embrace heritage preservation, China was the sixth among the hundred-some nations to ratify the 2003 UNESCO Convention for the Safeguarding of the Intangible Cultural Heritage (Rees 2012, 26–27).

19. Nyíri (2006) has argued that the uniformity of Chinese tourist sites is a direct result of the state's ultimate authority to determine the meaning of landscape and to control culture even in a highly commercialized sphere of everyday life.

20. An informant of Chio (2014, 70) notes that the situations of two villages carrying

out tourism activities were "similar, with minor differences" (*datong xiaoyi*): what these villages were experiencing was simultaneously similar to other rural ethnic tourism destinations and specific to their own circumstances.

21. The concept of double bind, tracing back to Bateson (1972), denotes a situation in which every move—even though it seems commonsensical—could be made ineffective by the moves that others make in response.

22. In an earlier work, Clifford (1988, 288–89) notices the "predicament of culture" in the case of the Mashpee Indians, who were asked to prove their identity and yet had relatively permeable group boundaries due to intermarriage, migration, sociolinguistic changes, and amalgamated values. More recently, scholars have criticized how neoliberal multiculturalism (e.g., Hale 2006) creates ambivalence for indigenous communities. For instance, in Povinelli's (2002) research based in Australia and Cattelino's (2010) research in the United States, indigenous peoples must fit into the preconceived expectations of settler states to achieve recognition, but the settler states struggle to reconcile ideals of equal citizenship with claims to political distinctiveness and different forms of citizenship by indigenous peoples.

23. Cornet (2010) has discussed the experience and positionality of a foreign female researcher in ethnic rural Guizhou. See also Turner (2013) about the ambiguity of gender role that nonlocal female ethnographers take on in highland Asia.

24. The Provincial CPPCC Painting and Calligraphy Academy (*Sheng Zhengxie Shuhuayuan*) is a subsidiary agency and social group under the Chinese People's Political Consultative Conference, a political advisory body consisting of representatives from various sectors of society. "Top 30 Charismatic Villages of Guizhou" (Guizhou Zuiju Meili Minzu Cunzhai) was a selection of ethnic villages conducted across various social media during the Ninth National Traditional Games of Ethnic Minorities held in Guizhou in 2011. In August 2013, Wuyang Village was selected as a "Traditional Chinese Village" (Zhongguo Chuantong Cunluo) by the Ministry of Housing and Urban-Rural Development, the Ministry of Culture, and the Ministry of Finance.

CHAPTER ONE. **BECOMING BUYI IN A MULTIETHNIC HINTERLAND**

1. The song "Minzu tuanjie hua shengkai" was orally translated from the Buyi into Chinese by Uncle Kuan. The English version was translated from Chinese by the author and edited with the help of Cheow-Thia Chan.

2. The 1982 Constitution of the People's Republic of China reaffirmed and developed earlier regulations and systems concerning the practice of regional autonomy for ethnic minorities in areas of high concentration through administrative powers

NOTES TO PAGES 27–32   213

and autonomous agencies, which laid the foundations for the Regional Minzu Autonomy Law (*Minzu Quyu Zizhi Fa*).

3. See a detailed review of Guizhou's governmental operations on *minzu* culture and arts in post-Mao China, compiled for the Fifth Minorities Art Festival of China, held in Beijing in the summer of 2006: https://www.neac.gov.cn/seac /c100639/201205/1096341.shtml (last accessed on January 14, 2025).

4. During the Hundred Flowers campaign in the mid-1950s, intellectuals were encouraged to discuss nationwide problems and minority activists could even criticize Han chauvinism (Spence 1990, 569–73).

5. *Benwei zhuyi* can be literally translated as "sectionalism" or "provincialism" in other settings.

6. Fieldnotes, September 19, 2012.

7. Skinner (1977, 214–15) grouped Guizhou with its neighboring province of Yunnan into Yun-Gui, a macro-regional borderland joining the Upper Yangzi and Middle Yangzi socioeconomic macro-regions.

8. Since the early 2000s, local Chinese scholarship, such as that of Yang Zhiqiang (2018) at Guizhou University, has started to conceptualize this passage zone—known historically as the "one pass threading through Yunnan-Guizhou" (*Dian Qian yixiandao*)—as the "corridor of a historical Miao frontier" (*Miaojiang zoulang*) developed on the basis of an old horse trade route with post stations, which extends from today's Hunan all the way to Yunnan.

9. In the areas of Guizhou that my study concerns, the Buyi have had long-term interactions with the Yi (Lolo) people, who held native chieftainship from the fourteenth to the seventeenth century (Herman 2007), and with the Gelao, who are deemed some of the earliest local settlers. In some rituals to celebrate wet-rice cultivation and irrigation, the Buyi initiate by worshipping the ancestral Gelao (*pu³ zuŋ²*) (Wu Zhonggang and Wu Kaifeng 2014). In this sense, defining "indigenous peoples" would be challenging in China, given centuries of fusion and reshaping among ethnicities (Elliott 2015). A term commonly used to define local ethnic populations in Guizhou is *shiju minzu* (ethnicities who have resided for generations).

10. During the Republican era, *yi zu* in standard Chinese was used to cover a range of Guizhou's Tai-speaking groups (Chen [1940] 2004, 3–4), including present-day Buyi, Dong, and Shui.

11. Detailed depictions of the Zhongjia, widely considered the Buyi's forebears, were included in the *Republican-era Guizhou Gazetteer* (Zhongguo Difangzhi Jicheng Bianji Gongzuo Weiyuanhui [1948] 2006, 13502). See also Luo Zhengfu (2010, 149–50).

12. Primarily a series of rituals inherent to ancestral worship, life cycle, and cosmology, Mo beliefs and practices are somewhat syncretized with Buddhism, Daoism,

NOTES TO PAGES 32–34

and Confucian thought. Many such ritual scripts and practices also exist in the Zhuang region in present-day Guangxi (Holm 2003; Kao 2014). Though preserved ritual scripts date back to the late Qing or early Republican era, local experts inferred that these scripts were created no later than the period between the Tang dynasty (618–907 CE) and the Song dynasty (960–1279 CE). See chapter 2 on how local elites interpret history and construct knowledge and cultural heritage based on the Mo scripts.

13. Interviews with the Wu brothers, June 2013.

14. As to the question of from whom the Buyi ancestors learned such house-making skills, local cultural elites vaguely offered "another ethnicity" (*ta zu*) (Yang Zhibin 2011a). When I inquired later, they conjectured that "they must have been the Han with more advanced skills." But there is also a suspicion that the so-called other ethnicity was related to a certain Tai-speaking group who built stilted houses off the waters. As the Wu brothers suggested, the text also described a few other groups (with the prefix pu^3) that could not correspond to any modern-day counterpart.

15. Between 1700 and 1850, at least three million settlers moved to the southwest provinces; by the nineteenth century, the Han proportion of the twenty million inhabitants of this zone increased to 60 percent, which approximates current ethnic proportions (Lee 1982, 284–86, 295–96). For the five hundred years under the Ming and Qing, campaigns for assimilation or "suppression and extermination" were nearly constant (Scott 2009, 138, 140). See also "Yang Mingshi zouchen suiding Miao jiang zhi ce zhe," an imperial edict dated 1736 and included in the *Edited Volume of the Archives on Miao Rebellions in the Early Qing Dynasty* (Zhongguo Diyi Lishi Dang'an Guan, Zhongguo Renmin Daxue Qingshi Yanjiusuo, Guizhou Sheng Dang'an Guan 1987, 163).

16. See Scott (2009) on statecraft that often required sedentarized agriculture.

17. The centralized bureaucratization with its transition from indirect to direct rule was marked by the *gaitu guiliu* policy, which replaced native chieftains with state officials (Herman 2007).

18. Weinstein (2014, 129) makes the case that being "no different from the Han" did not confer the same status as being Han, and this also suggests that the Buyi were indeed still different from the Han in the eyes of Qing officialdom.

19. See Luo Zhengfu (2009, 2010) for the use of Chinese characters in personhood naming, as well as ancestral altar and genealogy writing. Most Buyi genealogies traced ancestries back to the central plains (*zhongyuan*) with tenuous links to key Chinese historical figures; meanwhile, one genealogy of my relatives even included an alleged conversion from the original Han to the "barbaric" Buyi after migrating to Guizhou.

20. Some Wuyang villagers recalled that their great-grandfathers were graduates of

NOTES TO PAGES 34–39 215

the Republic of China Military Academy (also known as the Huangpu Military Academy) from the 1920s to 1940s.

21. "Yi" (夷), in this context, was the historical term generally used to address "foreign" peoples, sometimes connoting non-Han groups at the peripheries as "barbarians." It differs from the Chinese character used for the socialist-era designation of the ethnic group Yi (彝), as in Yizu.

22. Tian might have been an underground Communist Party member who was not only conducting research in Zhenning but also networking with minority elites in the 1940s when he met the mother of the Wu brothers, a teacher with profound knowledge about the Buyi. As the nascent People's Republic regime was eager to cultivate minority cadres, Tian thought of recommending the Wu brothers' mother, whom he had unfortunately lost touch with. They accidentally reunited when the delegation came to Zhenning; after that, Tian frequently paid visits to Zhenning and discussed research with Wu's mother. Interviews with the Wu brothers, July 2015.

23. Today's Zhenning County (xian) inherits only one-fifth of the territory its antecedent Zhenning Prefecture (fu) administered during the Qing era (Ma Guojun 2010, 107–8). According to the 2010 National Census, the Miao is the largest non-Han population in Guizhou, and the Buyi the second largest. But in Zhenning County, the Buyi comprise 38.41 percent of the overall population and the Miao only 10.41 percent, whereas the Han take up 46.78 percent in total (calculated based on the 2010 Guizhou Provincial Population Census).

24. In spite of historical adjustments from time to time, there are five de facto levels of local government in contemporary China: province, prefecture, county, township, and village. Under China's Law of Regional Minzu Autonomy, regions, prefectures, and counties can be autonomous and associated with particular minzu (Yeh 2013, 203).

25. Bouyeix, Bouxnaz, Bouxnongz, and Bouxloeh are romanized transcriptions according to one standard transcription system for the Buyi and Zhuang languages. The final "x" in Boux indicates the fourth tone in both Buyi and Zhuang, which is not pronounced as a consonant; the final "z" in Bouxnaz and Bouxnongz indicates the second tone in Buyi and Zhuang, and the final "h" in Bouxloeh indicates the sixth tone. See Holm (2003).

26. "Bunong," as it is used in this book, is not to be confused with the Bunong people, a highland ethnic group in Cambodia where it borders Vietnam, nor with the Bunun people in Taiwan.

27. Diamond's (1988) research shows that stories about the Miao poison (gu) have been repeated, expanded, and rarely questioned in official documents and in an outpouring of travel accounts, books of strange and wondrous tales, miscellanies of "fact," and works of exotic information about the peoples of China's

216 NOTES TO PAGES 39–50

border regions through Song, Ming, and Qing and into the Republican period. Diamond considered the narratives of the Miao poison as a means through which the Han authority sought to harden ethnic and cultural boundary against the perceived threats to a moral civilization, through a kind of Han fantasy, or rather, anxiety.

28. The northwest area under Zhenning's jurisdiction was dominated by a Lolo chieftain (*tusi*) family during Qing and inhabited mostly by the Buyi and the Miao; here, the relatively high-altitude terrains have been conducive for cropping and husbandry combined. See Ma Guojun (2010, 107–8).

29. The invented Buyi script has, however, been used seldomly by a very limited number of Buyi intellectuals.

30. Interview notes, September 15, 2012 (italics mine).

31. Holm (2003) suggests a different regional cartography altogether based on dialect distribution and river systems, given that the Northern Zhuang share more traits with the Buyi than with the Southern Zhuang.

32. As anthropologists have suggested, *minzu* identification—based on a performative act of naming—gave the state-endorsed categories a life of their own; it was driven more by political efficacy than by a concern for local people's sense of ethnic identity (Gros 2004; Yang Zhiqiang 2009; Cheung 2012).

33. Elman (1991) argues that the Ming-Qing period civil service examinations were a means of political, social, and cultural reproduction for the prevailing social system more than a mechanism providing social mobility.

34. For ethnography on how everyday life in contemporary rural China is characterized by an increased sense of moral challenge and uncertainty with arbitrary cultural forms and moral frameworks, see Liu (2001) and Steinmüller (2013).

35. The local Han dialect in Guizhou belongs to the Guizhou-Sichuan-Yunnan varieties of southwestern Mandarin (*xinan guanhua*). Mutually intelligible with standard Chinese to a great extent, *guanhua* is the most widespread and most used topolect of the Han language.

36. There are a few *minzu* autonomous areas, where bilingual education in standard Chinese and ethnic language at school is encouraged and enforced.

37. "Miao" (or "Miaozi") is a derogatory word in parts of southern China even today.

38. Similar dynamics among other ethnic groups have been widespread in various regions of southwest China (see, for instance, Harrell 2001b; Cheung 2012). Sum et al. (2022) point out that overlooking such interethnic phenomena results from the obsession with an oversimplified dichotomy of minorities versus the Han state.

39. In Chinese official discourse, the Han often act as fatherly figures or older brothers who will lead minorities in the construction of a socialist modernity (Tenzin 2013, 48).

CHAPTER TWO. MO RITUALS, BUYI EXPERTS, AND POST-MAO CULTURAL REVIVALS

1. Liuyueliu is a festival celebrated by several ethnicities, including some Han people in southwest China, with various legendary narratives that explain its origins.

2. Ren (2013, 65) suggests that while minority cultural experts were intellectuals (*zhishi-fenzi*) and cadres (*ganbu*) as part of the socialist cultural workers, now they play more the part of designers (*shejizhe*), planners (*guihuazhe*), or strategists (*cehuazhe*). In understanding the efforts of Qiang scholars and entrepreneurs in Sichuan Province to articulate ethnic difference, Yanshuo Zhang (2021) coined the term "entrepreneurs of the national past," as they are largely incentivized by an ethnopolitical desire to claim cultural integrity and indigeneity for minority groups in national narratives.

3. Besides lineage formations, temple networks, and sectarian movements, official elite models such as community compacts, model neo-Confucian lineages, or local academies or poetry associations are often absorbed and adapted to local needs by emerging social groups (Dean 2009, 185). On the other hand, Shahar and Weller's (1996) volume documents the existence of other domains that allowed Chinese gods to challenge the prevailing power structures and traditional mores of Chinese society.

4. Focusing on a rural minority community in north-central Yunnan, Mueggler (2001) has discussed the drastic transformations of local political institutions and the ritual realm, accompanied by memories of conflict and suffering inflicted during Maoism and the decades thereafter.

5. Siu's notion of "state involution" differs from Duara's (1987) usage of the same term, which focused on the early twentieth century, when the state's fiscal and functional growth gave rise to an inefficient and uncontrollable "entrepreneurial brokerage" structure consisting of tax collectors, middlemen, and bullies.

6. Note that Holm (2004, 14–15) points out the four basic kinds of literate male religious practitioner in Northern Zhuang villages—Daoist priests, Buddhist priests, ritual masters ("military" priests of the Meishan School of vernacular Daoism), and indigenous Mo specialists. A similar situation exists in the Buyi villages, where members sometimes use both Daoist priests and Mo masters for life-cycle rituals. While many locals were well aware of the differences between a Mo master (sometimes referred to as *Buyi xiansheng*) and a Daoist practitioner (*fengshui xiansheng*), they were not capable of articulating such differences.

7. Holm (2003, 21–23) summarizes the Bumo as ritualists who conduct divinations, expel troublesome spirits, and make sacrifices: "The Bumo perform a wide range of rituals on behalf of the living, including exorcisms, sacrifices and healing

218   NOTES TO PAGES 61–68

rituals on behalf of people, domestic animals, and crops. Many of these rituals involve calling back lost souls. They also select auspicious days for weddings, funerals, and house-building, and conduct divinations by means of eggs, chicken thigh-bones, and divination blocks. Unlike spirit-medium masters, Bumo do not go into any form of trance." However, according to at least one of the Wu brothers, they had seen a ritualist in a state of trance mediating lost spirits when they were young.

8. Holm (2013, 770) notes that the widespread availability of primary education in the Zhuang- and Buyi-speaking areas since the eighteenth century has provided a relatively broad basis for the practice of writing local languages using Chinese characters.

9. The six ways of forming Chinese characters are self-explanatory characters, pictographs, pictophonetic characters, associative compounds, mutually explanatory characters, and phonetic loan characters. For the Tai-speaking groups in southern China, Chinese language served as a primary vehicle for Buddhist and Taoist teachings and fulfilled the bureaucratic and cosmological needs of native chieftaincies (Holm 2004, 1). As Holm (2003, 47–49) explains, Mo masters sometimes used standard characters for phonetic and semantic readings; sometimes they created entirely new characters to represent words in their native tongue.

10. Interview with an official at the Anshun Municipal Cultural Industry Office, May 27, 2013. See also chapter 1.

11. According to the Wu family, their grandfather had passed away at a young age and thus did not have the chance to become as knowledgeable.

12. According to Holm (2003, 23) and Zhou Guomao (2006, 2), *mo* in Zhuang/Bouyei means "to recite (scriptures)."

13. Following Harrell's (1974) observation, Chau (2006, 67) proposes four basic kinds of religious habitus (à la Pierre Bourdieu): intellectual believers, true believers, nonbelievers, and practical believers ("half trust and half doubt").

14. Interview with Buyi scholar Luo Zhengfu, November 2013. See also Zhou Guomao (2012, 2–7).

15. According to Chairman Yang, although local Buyi were still conducting buffalo sacrifices while the People's Liberation Army was liberating them in the 1950s, some of the ritual procedures had already incorporated Han Chinese elements, and some ritual language had gradually become a mix of Buyi and Chinese.

16. Interview with Master Mo in Libo County, Guizhou, July 2011.

17. To annotate the oral Mo rituals, a newly created romanized Buyi script system based on the Latin alphabet was promoted (Zhou Guomao 2012, 3). This was never a successful project among locals. See also chapter 1.

18. According to some Buyi elites in Libo, local authorities in other Buyi areas did not

think to apply before they did. But in these other regions, the Buyi have generally been using the acknowledgment from the State Council as a means to bring public attention to the self-created scripts.

19. The Chinese Folk Literature and Art Society (Zhongguo Minjian Wenyijia Xiehui) is a collective membership under the China Federation of Literary and Art Circles (Zhongguo Wenxue Yishujie Lianhehui).

20. Fenggang Yang (2011, 157) has offered an explanation of some "alternative spiritualities without a religious label": a semi-religion is oriented toward the supernatural but has underdeveloped beliefs and organization, which describes folk or popular religion in China; a quasi-religion has a diffuse social organization, for example, ancestor worship.

21. Harrell and Li (2003) have examined stories of the ancientness of Yi writing as a kind of script game to assert historical precedence among Yi scholars and elites.

22. Da Song Guo Guang Nan Xi Lu, a place-name that existed in the southern part of China during the Song dynasty, for instance, was recorded in a Mo scripture.

23. When translating this ritual script, in fact, Chairman Yang and his colleagues were striving to define the most accurate narrative. The end of the script discusses the issue of who would take charge of Guizhou and could lead to two different interpretations: one suggests that, on behalf of the emperor, the Buyi master in charge of Mo rituals would govern Guizhou, the other that the Buyi, who were becoming prosperous and well educated (with a sense of upward mobility), would take charge of Guizhou. As I later confirmed with Chairman Yang, it was ultimately understood to mean that the Buyi took charge of Guizhou for the emperor.

24. Many of the native officials and chieftains in the regions under examination here were ethnically Zhongjia, while some had ethnic backgrounds that roughly corresponded to today's Han, Yi, or more rarely Miao (Herman 2007; Weinstein 2014; see also Gong 1992). Faure and Ho's (2013) edited volume unravels how legends and rituals shed light on the intersection of imperial administration and chieftain-dominated local culture in China's southwest.

25. China has been quick in setting up its own institutional framework regarding the inventory system for intangible cultural heritage (ICH), which is implemented at various administrative levels. China's domestic classification of the different types of ICH, however, do not entirely match the UNESCO designation of ICH domains and categories.

26. Because of the different ways Baolutuo is pronounced and transliterated, it could also be written in Chinese as Bao'ertuo, Buluotuo, and so on. See also Holm (2003, 2013).

27. Holm's interview with Lan Hong'en, Nanning, September 30, 1993 (Holm 2004, 46n66).

220   NOTES TO PAGES 77–87

28. The original script only reads "twelve Baolutuo," but the translations by the Bumo making reference to mythical tales depict Baolutuo having twelve disciples.

29. A more recent interpretation by one of the Wu brothers concerning Baolutuo is indicative of how it has become strongly attached to mythical tales influenced by Han Chinese culture. Backed by details from Buyi ritual props and performances, the Wu brother suggested that Lutu was the teacher of Emperor Zhuanxu (2513–2435 BC) and the grandson of Huangdi, the common ancestor of the Chinese nation/people (*Zhonghua minzu*) according to common legend. Zhuanxu was the grandfather of the legendary Emperor Yu (the first emperor of the Xia dynasty) who was supposedly renowned for water management and who, according to the Wu brother, has also been worshipped by the Buyi and the Zhuang people (Wu Zhonggang and Wu Kaifeng 2014, 51–52). Baolutuo—or Elder Lutu, *bao* indicating "elder male" in Buyi—was thus the most prestigious priest offering ritual teaching to Emperor Zhuanxu. The Wu brother later told me that this occurred at a time when politics and rituals were one (*zhengjiao heyi*).

30. Narratives about Molujia were scarce in the scripts found in Guizhou (Zhou Guomao 2006, 5) and turned out to be more controversial. While some conjecture that the figure of Molujia bears traces of a female chief figure from the ancient matriarchal system, there are also Bumo who think that he (not she) is one of the twelve disciples of Baolutuo (Yang Zhibin 2012, 84).

31. There is one Wu-surnamed man in Wuyang who understands a little of the Mo rituals but is allegedly not competent enough to perform them. The relatively better educated Wu family members have all moved from the village to the county seat or to other towns and cities nearby.

32. For the Buyi in Zhenning, Mo masters worship Baolutuo on the ninth day of the first lunar month. See Kao (2014) for one of the Baolutuo worship events in Guangxi's Zhuang regions.

33. At present-day Buyi festivals, organized activities often include what was traditionally called *langshao*, during which male and female youths invited each other out to sing and socialize, resembling a dating party.

34. Practical believers, who hold an attitude of "half trust and half doubt" (*ban xin ban yi*), constituted the great majority of Harrell's (1974) interviewees among Taiwanese villagers.

35. Zhou Guomao (2012, 7) states that "Mo is the common belief among the Buyi and the Zhuang, and among the Shui and the Yao, there are also beliefs in *leduo* [or *lutuo*]."

36. For a discussion of the theme parks in Shenzhen as a constructed and consumed space epitomizing the country's cultural business and globalization, see Pinggong Zhang (2007) and Ren (2013).

CHAPTER THREE. FEMALE PERFORMERS AND THE SPECTACULAR STATE

1. The calculus of cultural purity and authenticity at work is seen in many other contemporary indigenous experiences (cf. de la Cadena and Starn 2007). Kendall (2017) and Tenzin (2017), for instance, have discussed how continuing disputes about authenticity and competition for resources in cultural production ensue from differentiations between and even within ethnic groups in the Chinese context.

2. Minorities in China are often sexualized in popular discourse as either hypermasculine or hyperfeminine, which situates locals in an inferior position to the Han (Tenzin 2013; see also Schein and Luo 2016). In considering the inequality that has underlain the civilizing center's claim to superiority, Harrell (1995, 10–17) distills the cultural tropes about "the peripheral peoples" into three metaphors: minorities as women (the sexual metaphor), as children (the educational metaphor), and as ancient and primitive (the historical metaphor).

3. Translation of the lyric from Buyi into Chinese was done with the help of female villagers who composed the song. "Young and old, brothers and sisters" is a typical way to start or end a Buyi song in this region.

4. With influences from traditional Chinese *fengshui* geomancy, Buyi burial rituals entail a ceremony featuring a sod-turning procedure offering apologies to the deities who were disturbed by people breaking ground to build a tomb and a completion ceremony to settle the spirit of the dragon (*longqi*) back to where it belongs after the coffin has been placed into the tomb (Wu Zhonggang and Wu Kaifeng 2014, 137).

5. In Chinese-language books compiling ethnic literature or folk arts, minority folk songs are normally grouped into categories such as ancient songs, narrative songs, love songs, wine songs, and labor songs (e.g., Huang Delin 2014).

6. There were videodiscs delineating a Buyi lineage that traced back the sixteen major Buyi surnames of the area, listing their ancestors and the locations the descendants have spread out to, which, at the same time, were interestingly attached to the Chinese landscape (*jiangshan*) derived from the metaphorical origins of the Yellow and Yangtze Rivers.

7. Many Han villagers residing proximately with Buyi or having maintained trade relations with them could understand basic Buyi expressions.

8. See the appendix of Friedman's (2006) book for instances of folk songs with a propaganda purpose.

9. Media reports by Xu (2014) and Ma Jialu (2020) provide the historical context in which "Good Flowers Are Red" has become politicized over time.

NOTES TO PAGES 108–130

10. Folk singing (*minzu* genre) in Chinese music categorization refers to a professionalized style that often draws on musical elements from ethnic minority songs and folk operas but tends to stress techniques and incorporate training methods of Western music (Kendall 2017).

11. Steinmüller (2013) suggests that gambling, having become one of the most prevalent leisure activities in rural China with the economic growth of the last decades, reveals local expressions and negotiations around desired and acceptable forms of sociality; however, in government and media discourses, gambling is presented as a residue of "backward" peasant culture, in the same category as lack of hygiene and "feudal superstition."

12. See also chapter 5 about the cultivation of human quality as in improving infrastructure development and living conditions, as well as how it relates to healthy forms of consumption in the context of tourism.

13. Translated from a document circulated among village cadres, titled "Grading Criteria for the 2013 'Thousand-Year-Old Buyi Village' Arts and Sports Competition," February 19, 2013.

14. "Vanishing natives" has been a visual trope in some indigenous media representations, first deployed in the colonial practice of salvage ethnography with a primitivist connotation and then welcomed by native cultural activists as a means to restore a sense of identity with continuity from the past (Faulhaber and Forline 2008, 268; see also Prins 2002).

15. In the lists of cultural heritage, the folk songs are categorized as folk music, and the ancient songs are categorized as folk literature. These songs are distinguished from Buyi musical dramas and bronze drums alike, which all contain some components of singing and oral performances.

16. *Lusheng* is a popular musical instrument in southwest China and neighboring Southeast Asian countries. Several ethnic groups besides the Miao in Guizhou also play *lusheng*, and in fact, some Buyi (not in Zhenning) have practiced it as well.

CHAPTER FOUR. HERITAGE AND IDENTITY POLITICS ON DISPLAY IN THE VILLAGE MUSEUM

1. In contemporary cultural industry development, an affinity has begun to form between what used to be public-sector museums and private-sector heritage tourist attractions: the former are now increasingly promoting their entertainment value to be economically competitive in the tourism economy, while the latter frequently advertise their educational value in order to appeal to a more diverse audience and reinvent their identities beyond sites of leisure.

2. English translations of *minzu bowuguan* include "ethnic nationality museums,"

"ethnological museums," "ethnographic museums," and "museums of ethnic cultures." For the sake of coherence, I use "*minzu* museums" to connote museums themed around China's *minzu* groups and cultures. Most of these museums have been related to the disciplinary development of Chinese ethnology and anthropology since the twentieth century.

3. For example, the Musée d'Ethnographie du Trocadéro was established in 1878, the Ethnologisches Museum zu Berlin in 1873, and the Pitt Rivers Museum at Oxford in 1884.

4. See Claypool (2005) and Denton (2014) for the origins of the museum's role in configuring a reformed, modern China.

5. A similar case is the Ethnographic Department of the Russian Museum, which Hirsch (2003) has examined as a venue for virtual tourism, where Soviet ethnographers and activists attempted to work out an idealized narrative about the socialist transformation of the Soviet Union and museumgoers became acquainted with that narrative through mass participation.

6. The State Council promulgated regulations for the preservation of *wenwu* with "historical, artistic, and scientific value, and also those of memorial significance" in 1963. These regulations were replaced by the first law on cultural relics in 1982 (Ho 2018, 227).

7. The term "ecomuseum" was coined in 1971 at the Ninth International Museum Congress held in France.

8. "Heritage" in English, used primarily in its singular form, refers to whatever is inherited from the past (such as valuable possessions and qualities), whereas the Chinese term *yichan* can indicate a single item.

9. For Confucianists, the past still lives in the present, and things made in the present are just as valid representatives of the heritage as those made in the past; even for Mao, the past could be used to serve the present, while the foreign could be used to serve China (Harrell 2013, 287–89).

10. According to Anderson (1991), the nation can be considered an imagined political community as it implies deep horizontal comradeship that knits together all citizens irrespective of race, color, or class.

11. The semimythical figure considered to be the creator of the Mo rituals and the Buyi people's common ancestor is Baolutuo (see detailed introduction in chapter 2).

12. As introduced in chapters 1 and 2, a few of Chairman Yang's brothers-in-law, originally from Wuyang Village, collectively contributed to a book manuscript on the Buyi people in Zhenning County, which was published in 2014. Family photos were also incorporated into a book that one of the Wu brothers, in collaboration with his daughter, published on their research findings related to Buyi clothing (see Wu Kaifeng and Wu Zhonggang 2022).

224 NOTES TO PAGES 147–163

13. Many Miao groups are seen as having practiced slash-and-burn agriculture. The imagery of the Miao with many silver ornaments is also mostly a stereotype, reproduced through festival performances and handicraft exhibits.

14. Scott (2009) argues that sedentarized agriculture has been easier to control by the state, as opposed to the mobility of slash-and-burn or swidden agriculture.

15. In southern China, delayed transfer marriage was a custom of women remaining in natal homes after marriage; the wife only stayed temporarily with the in-laws when important events, festivals, or busy farming seasons required her presence or assistance (Siu 1990b).

16. When I chatted with villagers, there were also some doubts about whether the village itself would charge an entrance fee and whom they would pay. Some villagers had already started referring to Chairman Yang and anyone associated with him as the boss (*laoban*)—the business manager who came to develop (*kaifa*) "our village."

17. Jing Wang (2001) has underscored the role of the elite by suggesting that analytical questions concerning officialdom need to be reinserted and reconfigured in Chinese cultural studies, which has been increasingly dominated by the trope of the market and transnationalism.

CHAPTER FIVE. MODERNIZING RURAL INFRASTRUCTURE AND BRANDING A HISTORICAL VILLAGE

1. In 2005, the politburo of the Communist Party announced that it would make rural development one of its foremost priorities for the Eleventh Five-Year Plan (2006–11) with the Building a Socialist New Countryside (Jianshe Shehuizhuyi Xin Nongcun) initiative. See Hillman and Unger (2013). However, as Perry (2011) points out, the notion of a Socialist New Countryside is not new. Promulgated by Mao himself, this idea was integral to the Communist revolution and socialist construction, aiming to revitalize rural China.

2. The central objectives of this policy are to promote "modern agriculture and local industry" through "scientific research and innovation," to "ensure the steady increase of rural incomes by abolishing rural taxes and optimizing land use rights," and "to deliver more efficient and adapted public services such as healthcare, education, financial services, and environmental protection" (Ye 2006, 12).

3. Wilczak (2017, 111) refers to one Chengdu official saying that "rural urbanization . . . is meant to make the city more like the city and the countryside more like the countryside."

4. Donaldson and Yang (2022) note that Guizhou has witnessed a shift in policy roughly between 2005 and 2010, from a micro-oriented state approach that favors smaller-scale, low-tech opportunities and facilitates the direct participation of

NOTES TO PAGES 164–169   225

poorly educated farmers to a developmentalist approach that reduces poverty through larger-scale urbanization and industrialization. This changing development policy ensued from a battle between the province's top leaders with divergent strategy and background experience.

5. In 2012, the county government also invited the Urban Planning Institute at East China Normal University to design a development plan for cultural industries in the entire Zhenning County.

6. In her discussion of developmental projects in Qinghai, Ptáčková (2020, 56) points out that lack of funds often led to a major curtailment of the project's implementation goals.

7. Case-by-Case (*yishiyiyi*) involves a financial subsidy for village projects on public welfare after rural tax reform in the 2000s.

8. From an internal document, "Facilitating the Beautiful Countryside Campaign," drafted by the county government and party committee, July 2015.

9. In Wuyang Village, water supply had already been ensured through the county's 2008 Drinking Water Safety project.

10. In Dalakoglou's (2010) ethnographic study of the Albanian-Greek cross-border highway, the newly rehabilitated road section emerges as a space that is seen by most people in the region as one of the most proximate, visible, and tangible consequences of the otherwise abstract and distant processes of globalization and post-socialism. Scholars working on Asian countries have pointed out how roads have formed a crucial element in the social organization of space that underpins village morphology (e.g., Harms 2011; Kim 2020). In the Chinese context, Zhou Yongming (2010) suggests that the field of roadology could contribute to a deeper understanding of spatial reconfigurations and landscape transformations brought by road construction and extension.

11. Historically, Guizhou was the thoroughfare that had to be traversed to reach the strategic borderlands on the Chinese frontier. In an essay marking the 590th anniversary of the founding of the province, historian Long Zhiyi (2003, 144) coined the term "passageway culture" to capture Guizhou's cultural identity: "The most revealing feature of this culture is that it is unfixed; it is dynamic. Cultures from all over have mixed here throughout history. All have left their mark like layers of sediment."

12. The slogan hung by the high-speed railway construction site goes: "Dig roads wherever there are mountains, build bridges wherever there are waters; overcome the karst landscapes, here we manifest our awe-inspiring railway-constructing team."

13. The work-point system was set up to ensure maximum participation in labor during the socialist era, serving as the legitimized measure of contribution

NOTES TO PAGES 176–187

(Hershatter 2011). Chan, Madsen, and Unger (2009) have, however, suggested that work points were awarded more on political performance (such as cooperation and enthusiasm) than on actual labor contribution.

14. Even after moving away from original residences directly next to water, earlier generations of Buyi in Wuyang Village had carried on the traditional methods of constructing stilted (*ganlanshi*) houses typically seen nowadays by the riverside in southwest China and mainland Southeast Asia.

15. The Mo ritual masters have been influenced by rural *fengshui* practitioners. *Fengshui* refers to Chinese geomancy, and *fengshui* masters are often called upon to select auspicious sites for dwellings by viewing, and even recommending interventions in, the general landscape. The Mo practitioners deploy similar techniques to assess a site, such as examining a geomantic compass and calculating a favorable course of action.

16. Chio (2014) discusses a similar case in which obsession over the look and style of local architecture prompted local governments to insist on "old houses," that is, building houses made of wood or that looked so, or using wooden planks to cover up concrete walls visible from major roads.

17. During the 1950s, the Four Pests (Chu Sihai) campaign was intended to eliminate flies, mosquitoes, rats, and sparrows (later changed to cockroaches), stressing the importance of paying attention to hygiene (*jiang weisheng*). Along with managing garbage and wastewater, modifications of toilets and livestock pens were also undertaken in this Mao-era campaign. These projects were largely aimed at improving hygienic conditions and preventing large-scale infectious disease (Renmin Ribao 1958).

18. *Nongjiale* is a Chinese version of rural tourism, which involves peasant families hosting urbanite guests in their farm guesthouses, providing them with rustic food and lodging (Chio 2011; Park 2014).

19. Similar cases are common in rural redevelopment and regeneration projects across ethnic minority regions in southwest China. In 2013, Yu Jianrong, a public intellectual, tried to experiment with his ideas on regenerating a Buyi village in southwest Guizhou. One of the first tasks he undertook was to organize villagers (mostly middle-aged and elderly women who had not left for migrant labor) to clean up the communal areas in the village (Shidai Zhoubao 2013).

20. Anthropologists have examined the sociopolitical orderings generated by everyday discourse related to trash in multiethnic societies, which contribute to interethnic tensions by normalizing and naturalizing the linkage between definitions of personhood and acts of social control (e.g., McKee 2015; Bo Wang 2019).

21. Young villagers who had previously engaged in migrant labor recognized that the socket to which the lamp's cord connected was similar to what they had been making for a Japanese company in eastern China's Zhejiang.

NOTES TO PAGES 187–200   227

22. The households who owned a share of the forest cut down their own trees, and this patch of land was collectively sold to Chairman Yang and the county government to be made into a huge parking lot.

23. Chan, Madsen, and Unger (2009, 290) have similarly documented how new homes in Chen Village encroached on rich paddies after the 1990s, which once retained an aura of rural placidity.

24. Many local governmental plans in China are administered through various bureaucracies with different sources of funding, different timelines, and different incentives and goals for supervising officials (see, for instance, Ptáčková 2020).

25. The concept of suspension is widely discussed by scholars, including Xiang (2021), in the context of Chinese migration and developmentalism, where individuals or groups find themselves trapped by larger structural conditions.

CONCLUSION

1. In discussing the emergence of a "tribal modern" brand in the Gulf states, Cooke (2014) unravels the convergence of the symbolic tribal and the material modern as simultaneous spectacle of identities and cultures.

2. Schein (2013) has noted the rise of a "post-alteric" social imaginary in China, as the crisscrossing of spatial and cultural boundaries has resulted in a proliferation of othering, not starkly binarized but increasingly heteroglot. The resulting symbolic meanings have in turn become increasingly multivalent—not simply associated with the bifurcations of Han and minorities, of center and margins—as all participate in the co-creation of such meanings in the contemporary cultural economy.

3. Feng (2017) has discussed the problems of scaling up in China's tourism industry. To prioritize maximizing profits through an increasing volume of tourists, the overscheduled and standardized mass tours become McDonaldized into an assembly-line production of experience.

4. On the controversy around the ethnic tower complex in Dushan County, see Yuan (2020). For detailed discussion of the Miao goddess statue in Jianhe County, see Bradsher's (2020) report in the *New York Times*. Global Times (2020) has reported on governmental responses at the local and national levels toward these hotly debated projects.

5. "Cultural relic protection unit" (*wenwu baohu danwei*) refers to China's official designation of historical sites and cultural relics—as immovable cultural properties—at three levels: national, provincial, and municipal/prefectural (the state issued its first list of national-level sites in 1961). These sites (to be) protected for their historical and cultural value are identified, cataloged, and managed under government regulations. "The 4A (or AAAA) national tourist attraction"

(*guojia 4A ji lüyou jingqu*) refers to the second tier of the most important and best-maintained tourist attractions in the country. The China National Tourism Administration (now merged with the Ministry of Culture and called the Ministry of Culture and Tourism) started administering the tourist attraction rating categories of China in 1999 to rate the quality of the attraction in terms of safety, sanitation, and transportation.

6. Under China's national government agenda for sustainable development, rural revitalization and poverty alleviation are linked to the notion of ecological civilization (*shengtai wenming*), first raised in 2007, which became the party-state's eco-developmental ideology. General Secretary Xi Jinping's famous quote "Clear waters and green mountains are mountains of gold and silver" has become a foundational theory of ecological civilization in 2017. This is particularly important for Guizhou: to eliminate chronic poverty, governmental plans consider preserving local valuable ecological resources—Guizhou's bountiful assets of clear waters and green mountains—which can be turned into real advantages for development.

REFERENCES

Abu-Lughod, Lila. 1991. "Writing against Culture." In *Recapturing Anthropology: Working in the Present,* edited by Richard Fox, 137–54, 161–62. Santa Fe, NM: School of American Research Press.

Adams, Jeff. 2013. "The Role of Underwater Archaeology in Framing and Facilitating the Chinese National Strategic Agenda." In *Cultural Heritage Politics in China,* edited by Tami Blumenfield and Helaine Silverman, 261–82. New York: Springer.

Adams, Laura. 2010. *The Spectacular State: Culture and National Identity in Uzbekistan.* Durham, NC: Duke University Press.

Ai, Jiawen. 2011. "Selecting the Refined and Discarding the Dross: The Post-1990 Chinese Leadership's Attitude towards Cultural Tradition." In *Routledge Handbook of Heritage in Asia,* edited by Patrick Daly and Tim Winter, 129–38. Milton Park, UK: Routledge.

Aibida. (1752) 2006. *Qiannan shilüe* (A survey of Southern Guizhou). Reprint, Chengdu: Bashu Shushe.

Anagnost, Ann. 1997. *National Past-Times: Narrative, Representation, and Power in Modern China.* Durham, NC: Duke University Press.

———. 2004. "The Corporeal Politics of Quality (Suzhi)." *Public Culture* 16: 189–208.

Anderson, Benedict. 1991. *Imagined Communities: Reflections on the Origin and Spread of Nationalism.* Revised and extended edition. London: Verso.

Anshun Shi Wenhua Ju, ed. 2009. *Jiemi Anshun: Feiwuzhi wenhua yichan* (Unveiling Anshun: Intangible cultural heritage). Guiyang: Guizhou Renmin Chubanshe.

Ashiwa, Yoshiko. 2009. "Positioning Religion in Modernity: State and Buddhism in China." In *Making Religion, Making the State: The Politics of Religion in Modern China,* edited by Yoshiko Ashiwa and David Wank, 43–73. Stanford, CA: Stanford University Press.

Ashiwa, Yoshiko, and David L. Wank. 2009. "Making Religion, Making the State in Modern China: An Introductory Essay." In *Making Religion, Making the State: The Politics of Religion in Modern China,* edited by Yoshiko Ashiwa and David L. Wank, 1–21. Stanford, CA: Stanford University Press.

230 REFERENCES

Bach, Jonathan. 2010. "'They Come in Peasants and Leave Citizens': Urban Villages and the Making of Shenzhen, China." *Cultural Anthropology* 25 (3): 421–58.

Bamo Ayi. 2007. "Growing up Half Yi." In *Fieldwork Connections: The Fabric of Ethnographic Collaboration in China and America*, edited by Bamo Ayi, Stevan Harrell, and Ma Lunzy, 5–12. Seattle: University of Washington Press.

Barnett, Robert. 2015. "DV-made Tibet: Domestic Videos, Elite Films, and the Work of Pema Tseden." In *DV-Made China: Digital Subjects and Social Transformations after Independent Film*, edited by Zhang Zhen and Angela Zito, 119–62. Honolulu: University of Hawai'i Press.

Bateson, Gregory. 1972. *Steps to an Ecology of Mind*. New York: Ballantine.

Bennett, Tony. 1995. *The Birth of the Museum: History, Theory, Politics*. London: Routledge.

———. 2006. "Exhibition, Difference, and the Logic of Culture." In *Museum Frictions: Public Cultures / Global Transformations*, edited by Ivan Karp et al., 47–69. Durham, NC: Duke University Press.

Blum, Susan. 2001. *Portraits of "Primitives": Ordering Human Kinds in the Chinese Nation*. Lanham, MD: Rowman and Littlefield.

Blumenfield, Tami, and Helaine Silverman, eds. 2013. *Cultural Heritage Politics in China*. New York: Springer.

Borchert, Thomas. 2005. "Of Temples and Tourists: The Effects of the Tourist Political Economy on a Minority Buddhist Community in Southwest China." In *State, Market and Religion in Chinese Societies*, edited by Joseph Tamney and Fenggang Yang, 87–111. Leiden: Brill.

Boyer, Dominique. 2008. "Thinking through the Anthropology of Experts." *Anthropology in Action* 15 (2): 38–46.

Bradsher, Keith. 2020. "A Soaring Monument to Beauty in China Is Stirring Passions. Mostly Anger." *New York Times*, November 26, 2020. https://www.nytimes.com/2020/11/26/business/china-statues-economy.html.

Bray, David. 2013. "Urban Planning Goes Rural: Conceptualising the 'New Village.'" *China Perspectives* 3: 53–62.

Breidenbach, Joanne, and Pál Nyíri. 2007. "'Our Common Heritage': New Tourist Nations, Post-'Socialist' Pedagogy, and the Globalization of Nature." *Current Anthropology* 48 (2): 322–30.

Bunten, Alexis Celeste. 2008. "Sharing Culture or Selling Out? Developing the Commodified Persona in the Heritage Industry." *American Ethnologist* 35 (3): 380–95.

———. 2018. "Deriding Demand: A Case Study of Indigenous Imaginaries at an Australian Aboriginal Tourism Cultural Park." In *Indigenous Tourism Movements*, edited by Alexis C. Bunten and Nelson H. H. Graburn, 31–55. Toronto: University of Toronto Press.

Buyizu Jianshi Bianxiezu, ed. 1984. *Buyizu jianshi* (A brief history of Buyizu). Guiyang: Guizhou Renmin Chubanshe.

Cartier, Carolyn. 2005. "Introduction: Touristed Landscapes / Seductions of Place." In *Seductions of Place: Geographical Perspectives on Globalization and Touristed Landscapes*, edited by Carolyn Cartier and Alan A. Lew, 1–19. London: Routledge.

Cattelino, Jessica. 2010. "The Double Bind of American Indian Need-Based Sovereignty." *Cultural Anthropology* 25 (2): 235–63.

Chan, Anita, Richard Madsen, and Jonathan Unger. 2009. *Chen Village: Revolution to Globalization*. Berkeley: University of California Press.

Chau, Adam Yuet. 2006. *Miraculous Response: Doing Popular Religion in Contemporary China*. Stanford, CA: Stanford University Press.

———. 2011. "Introduction: Revitalizing and Innovating Religious Traditions in Contemporary China." In *Religion in Contemporary China: Revitalization and Innovation*, edited by Adam Yuet Chau, 1–31. London: Routledge.

Chen Guo'an, Yan Yong, and Ma Qizhong. 2008. *Zhongguo shaoshuminzu xianzhuang yu fazhan diaocha yanjiu congshu: Zhenningxian Buyizu juan* (Research series on the contemporary conditions and development of Chinese ethnic minorities: The Buyi in Zhenning County). Edited by Hao Shiyuan and Ren Yifei. Beijing: Minzu Chubanshe.

Chen Guojun. (1938) 2004. "Miaozu de fanggu" (The use of poison by the Miao people). In *Guizhou Miao Yi shehui yanjiu* (A study of the society of Miao and Yi peoples in Guizhou), edited by Wu Zelin and Chen Guojun et al., 206–9. Beijing: Minzu Chubanshe.

———. (1940) 2004. "Guizhou Miao Yi zu shehui gaikuang" (An overview of the Miao and Yi societies in Guizhou). In *Guizhou Miao Yi shehui yanjiu* (A study of the society of Miao and Yi peoples in Guizhou), edited by Wu Zelin and Chen Guojun et al., 1–13. Beijing: Minzu Chubanshe.

———. (1942) 2004a. "Beipanjiang Miao Yi de fenbu" (The geographic distribution of Miao and Yi peoples along the Beipan River). In *Guizhou Miao Yi shehui yanjiu* (A study of the society of Miao and Yi peoples in Guizhou), edited by Wu Zelin and Chen Guojun et al., 79–80. Beijing: Minzu Chubanshe.

———. (1942) 2004b. "Duliujiang Miao Yi de fenbu" (The geographic distribution of Miao and Yi peoples along the Duliu River). In *Guizhou Miao Yi shehui yanjiu* (A study on the society of Miao and Yi peoples in Guizhou), edited by Wu Zelin and Chen Guojun et al., 76–78. Beijing: Minzu Chubanshe.

———. (1942) 2004c. "Guizhou Anshun Miao Yi zu de zongjiao xinyang" (Religious beliefs among the Miao and Yi peoples in Anshun, Guizhou). In *Guizhou Miao Yi shehui yanjiu* (A study of the society of Miao and Yi peoples in Guizhou), edited by Wu Zelin and Chen Guojun et al., 198–205. Beijing: Minzu Chubanshe.

Cheung, Siu-Woo. 2012. "Appropriating Otherness and the Contention of Miao Identity in Southwest China." *Asia Pacific Journal of Anthropology* 13 (2): 142–69.

China News Service. 2013. "915ge cunluo lieru di'erpi zhongguo chuantong cunluo minglu cunluo mingdan" (The list of 915 villages designated as the second batch of traditional Chinese villages). *Zhongguo Xinwen Wang*, September 5, 2013. https://www.chinanews.com/gn/2013/09-05/5249331.shtml.

Chio, Jenny. 2011. "The Appearance of the Rural in China's Tourism." *Provincial China* 3 (1): 60–79.

———. 2012. "'Village Videos' and the Visual Mainstream in Rural, Ethnic Guizhou." In *Mapping Media in China: Region, Province, Locality*, edited by Wanning Sun and Jenny Chio, 79–93. New York: Routledge.

———. 2014. *A Landscape of Travel: The Work of Tourism in Rural Ethnic China*. Seattle: University of Washington Press.

———. 2017. "Video Documentary and Rural Public Culture in Ethnic China." In *Asian Video Cultures: In the Penumbra of the Global*, edited by Joshua Neves and Bhaskar Sarkar, 35–53. Durham, NC: Duke University Press.

———. 2018. "From the Stadium to the Screen: Bullfights and Their Mediated Afterlife in Southwest China." *Asian Anthropology* 17 (4): 254–75.

———. 2019. "The Miao Festival Crowd: Mediations of Presence, Body Politics, and an Ethnic Public in 'Minority' China." *Current Anthropology* 60 (4): 536–58.

Chua, Liana. 2007. "Fixity and Flux: Bidayuh (Dis)engagements with the Malaysian Ethnic System." *Ethnos* 72 (2): 262–88.

Claypool, Lisa. 2005. "Zhang Jian and China's First Museum." *Journal of Asian Studies* 64 (3): 567–604.

Clifford, James. 1988. *The Predicament of Culture: Twentieth-Century Ethnography, Literature, and Art*. Cambridge, MA: Harvard University Press.

———. 1999. "Museums as Contact Zones." In *Representing the Nation: A Reader. Histories, Heritage and Museums*, edited by David Boswell and Jessica Evans, 435–57. London: Routledge.

Comaroff, John, and Jean Comaroff. 2009. *Ethnicity Inc.* Chicago: University of Chicago Press.

Conklin, Beth A. 1997. "Body Paint, Feathers, and VCRs: Aesthetics and Authenticity in Amazonian Activism." *American Ethnologist* 24: 711–37.

Cooke, Miriam. 2014. *Tribal Modern: Branding New Nations in the Arab Gulf*. Berkeley: University of California Press.

Cornet, Candice. 2010. "Fieldwork among the Dong National Minority in Guizhou, China: Practicalities, Obstacles, and Challenges." *Asia Pacific Viewpoint* 51: 135–47.

———. 2015. "Tourism Development and Resistance in China." *Annals of Tourism Research* 52: 29–43.

Crossley, Pamela. 1990. "Thinking about Ethnicity in Early Modern China." *Late Imperial China* 11 (1): 1–31.

Crossley, Pamela K., Helen F. Siu, and Donald S. Sutton, eds. 2006. *Empire at the Mar-*

gins: *Culture, Ethnicity, and Frontier in Early Modern China*. Berkeley: University of California Press.

Dalakoglou, Dimitris. 2010. "The Road: An Ethnography of the Albanian-Greek Cross-Border Motorway." *American Ethnologist* 37 (1): 132–49.

Davis, Sara. 2001. *Song and Silence: Ethnic Revival on China's Southwest Borders*. New York: Columbia University Press.

de la Cadena, Marisol, and Orin Starn, eds. 2007. *Indigenous Experience Today*. Oxford: Berg.

Dean, Kenneth. 1998. *Lord of the Three in One: The Spread of a Cult in Southeast China*. Princeton, NJ: Princeton University Press.

———. 2009. "Further Partings of the Way: Daoism in Contemporary China." In *Making Religion, Making the State: The Politics of Religion in Modern China*, edited by Yoshiko Ashiwa and David L. Wank, 179–210. Stanford, CA: Stanford University Press.

Denton, Kirk. 2014. *Exhibiting the Past: Historical Memory and the Politics of Museums in Postsocialist China*. Honolulu: University of Hawai'i Press.

Diamond, Norma. 1988. "The Miao and Poison: Interactions on China's Southwest Frontier." *Ethnology* 27 (1): 1–25.

———. 1995. "Defining the Miao: Ming, Qing, and Contemporary Views." In *Cultural Encounters on China's Ethnic Frontiers*, edited by Stevan Harrell, 92–116. Seattle: University of Washington Press.

Donaldson, John A. 2011. *Small Works: Poverty and Economic Development in Southwest China*. Ithaca, NY: Cornell University Press.

Donaldson, John, and Xiaotao Yang. 2022. "Shifting Strategies: The Politics of Radical Change in Provincial Development Policy in China." *China Quarterly* 249: 139–59.

Dourish, Paul, and Genevieve Bell. 2007. "The Infrastructure of Experience and the Experience of Infrastructure: Meaning and Structure in Everyday Encounters with Space." *Environment and Planning B: Planning and Design* 34: 414–30.

Dove, Michael R., Hjorleifur Jonsson, and Michael Aung-Thwin. 2011. "Debate: *The Art of Not Being Governed: An Anarchist History of Upland Southeast Asia*." *Bijdragen tot de Taal-, Land-en Volkenkunde* 167 (1): 86–99.

Du, Chunmei. 2015. "Manufacturing Naxi's Original Ecological Culture in Contemporary China." *Asian Ethnicity* 16 (4): 549–67.

Du Zaijiang and Yin Xiuling. 2011. "Yang Zhibin: Yigeren de Buyi minsu guan" (Yang Zhibin: The Buyi Folklore Museum of his own). *Zhongguo Minzubao*, August 19, 2011. http://iel.cass.cn/mzwxbk/mzwh/201108/t20110819_2764687.shtml.

Duara, Prasenjit. 1987. "State Involution: A Study of Local Finances in North China, 1911–1935." *Comparative Studies in Society and History* 29 (1): 132–61.

———. 1988. *Culture, Power, and the State: Rural North China, 1900–1942*. Stanford, CA: Stanford University Press.

234 REFERENCES

———. 1995. *Rescuing History from the Nation: Questioning Narratives of Modern China*. Chicago: University of Chicago Press.

Elliott, Mark. 2015. "The Case of the Missing Indigene: Debate over a 'Second-Generation' Ethnic Policy." *China Journal* 73: 186–213.

Elman, Benjamin. 1991. "Political, Social, and Cultural Reproduction via Civil Service Examinations in Late Imperial China." *Journal of Asian Studies* 50 (1): 7–28.

Evans, Harriet. 1999. "Comrade Sisters: Gendered Bodies and Spaces." In *Picturing Power in the People's Republic of China: Posters of the Cultural Revolution*, edited by Harriet Evans and Stephanie Donald, 63–78. Lanham, MD: Rowman and Littlefield.

Farquhar, Judith, and James L. Hevia. 1993. "Culture and Postwar American Historiography of China." *Positions* 1 (2): 486–525.

Faulhaber, Priscilla, and Louis Forline. 2008. "Recollecting Indigenous Thinking in a CD-ROM." In *Global Indigenous Media: Cultures, Poetics, and Politics*, edited by Pamela Wilson and Michelle Stewart, 253–69. Durham, NC: Duke University Press.

Faure, David. 2007. *Emperor and Ancestor: State and Lineage in South China*. Stanford, CA: Stanford University Press.

Faure, David, and T'sui-P'ing Ho, eds. 2013. *Chieftains into Ancestors: Imperial Expansion and Indigenous Society in Southwest China*. Vancouver: University of British Columbia Press.

Faure, David, and Helen Siu. 2003. "The Original Translocal Society and Its Modern Date: Historical and Post-reform South China." *Provincial China* 8 (1): 40–59.

Fei Xiaotong. 1951. *Xiongdi minzu zai Guizhou* (Brother ethnicities in Guizhou). Beijing: Sanlian Shudian.

———. 1988. *Fei Xiaotong minzu yanjiu wenji* (Collection of essays by Fei Xiaotong on the *minzu* question). Beijing: Minzu Chubanshe.

Feng, Xianghong. 2017. *Tourism and Prosperity in Miao Land: Power and Inequality in Rural Ethnic China*. Lanham, MD: Lexington Books.

Fennell, Catherine. 2011. "'Project Heat' and Sensory Politics in Redeveloping Chicago Public Housing." *Ethnography* 12 (1): 40–64.

Formoso, Bernard. 2010. "Zomian or Zombies? What Future Exists for the Peoples of the Southeast Asian Massif?" *Journal of Global History* 5 (2): 313–32.

Frangville, Vanessa. 2012. "The Non-Han in Socialist Cinema and Contemporary Films in the People's Republic of China." *China Perspectives* 2: 61–69.

Friedman, Sara L. 2006. *Intimate Politics: Marriage, the Market, and State Power in Southeastern China*. Cambridge, MA: Harvard University Asia Center, Harvard University Press.

Gaskin, Sam. 2014. "China's Aggressive Museum Growth Brings Architectural Wonders." *CNN*, April 30, 2014. https://www.cnn.com/2014/04/29/world/asia/china-museums/.

Giersch, C. Patterson. 2006. *Asian Borderlands: The Transformation of Qing China's Yunnan Frontier*. Cambridge, MA: Harvard University Press.

Ginsburg, Faye. 2002. "Screen Memories: Resignifying the Traditional in Indigenous Media." In *Media Worlds: Anthropology on New Terrain*, edited by Faye Ginsburg, Lila Abu-Lughod, and Brian Larkin, 39–57. Berkeley: University of California Press.

Gladney, Dru. 1994. "Representing Nationality in China: Refiguring Majority/Minority Identities." *Journal of Asian Studies* 53 (1): 92–123.

Global Times. 2020. "County Government Denies Using Poverty Alleviation Funds for 88-Meter-High Statue." *Global Times*, October 21, 2020. https://www.globaltimes.cn/content/1204171.shtml.

Gong Yin. 1992. *Zhongguo tusi zhidu* (The Tusi system in China). Kunming: Yunnan Minzu Chubanshe.

Goodman, David. 2004. "The Campaign to 'Open Up the West': National, Provincial-Level and Local Perspectives." *China Quarterly* 178: 317–34.

Gorfinkel, Lauren. 2012. "From Transformation to Preservation: Music and Multi-Ethnic Unity on Television in China." In *Music as Intangible Cultural Heritage: Policy, Ideology, and Practice in the Preservation of East Asian Traditions*, edited by Keith Howard, 99–112. Burlington, VT: Ashgate.

Gros, Stéphane. 2004. "The Politics of Names: The Identification of the Dulong (Drung) of Northwest Yunnan." *China Information* 18 (2): 275–302.

Guang Chong. (1940) 2004. "Shuo 'manyanzhangyu'" (On the "mist and miasma in the barbarian lands"). In *Guizhou Miao Yi shehui yanjiu* (A study on the society of Miao and Yi peoples in Guizhou), edited by Wu Zelin and Chen Guojun et al., 298–301. Beijing: Minzu Chubanshe.

Guizhou Liushan Liushui Buyizu Juan, Guizhou Sheng Minzu Shiwu Weiyuanhui, Guizhou Sheng Minzu Yanjiusuo, eds. 2008. *Guizhou "liushan liushui" minzu diaocha ziliao xuanbian: Buyizu juan* (Edited volumes of Guizhou "six-mountain six-water" ethnic survey: The volume of the Buyi). Guiyang: Guizhou Minzu Chubanshe.

Guizhou Ribao. 2014. "Hao hua hong" (Good flowers are red). *Guizhou Ribao*, November 7, 2014.

Guizhou Sheng Guangbo Dianshi Tai. 2020. "Ni bu zhidao de Guizhou: Cong Huishui changdao Beijing cheng, Guizhou zheshou Buyi minge zhende tai haoting le" (The Guizhou you don't know: From Huishui to Beijing, this Buyi folk song from Guizhou is truly beautiful). Guizhou Radio and Television Station, October 23, 2020.

Haddad, Mary Alice, and Stevan Harrell. 2020. "The Evolution of the East Asian Eco-Developmental State." In *Greening East Asia: The Rise of the Eco-Developmental State*, edited by Ashley Esarey, Mary Alice Haddad, Joanna I. Lewis, and Stevan Harrell, 5–31. Seattle: University of Washington Press.

Hale, Charles R. 2006. *Más Que un Indio (More Than an Indian): Racial Ambivalence*

236 REFERENCES

and the Paradox of Neoliberal Multiculturalism in Guatemala. Santa Fe, NM: School of American Research Press.

Handler, Richard, and Eric Gable. 1997. *The New History in an Old Museum: Creating the Past at Colonial Williamsburg*. Durham, NC: Duke University Press.

Harms, Erik. 2011. *Saigon's Edge: On the Margins of Ho Chi Minh City*. Minneapolis: University of Minnesota Press.

Harrell, Stevan. 1974. "Belief and Unbelief in a Taiwan Village." PhD diss., Stanford University.

———, ed. 1995. *Cultural Encounters on China's Ethnic Frontiers*. Seattle: University of Washington Press.

———. 2001a. "The Anthropology of Reform and the Reform of Anthropology: Anthropological Narratives of Recovery and Progress in China." *Annual Review of Anthropology* 30: 139–61.

———. 2001b. *Ways of Being Ethnic in Southwest China*. Seattle: University of Washington Press.

———. 2013. "China's Tangled Web of Heritage." In *Cultural Heritage Politics in China*, edited by Tami Blumenfield and Helaine Silverman, 285–94. New York: Springer.

Harrell, Stevan, and Li Yongxiang. 2003. "The History of the History of the Yi, Part II." *Modern China* 29 (3): 362–96.

Harris, Clare. 2012. *The Museum on the Roof of the World: Art, Politics, and the Representation of Tibet*. Chicago: University of Chicago Press.

Harvey, David. 2001. *Spaces of Capital: Towards a Critical Geography*. New York: Routledge.

Harwood, Russell. 2013. *China's New Socialist Countryside: Modernity Arrives in the Nu River Valley*. Seattle: University of Washington Press.

Hathaway, Michael. 2010. "The Emergence of Indigeneity: Public Intellectuals and an Indigenous Space in Southwest China." *Cultural Anthropology* 25 (2): 301–33.

———. 2016. "China's Indigenous Peoples? How Global Environmentalism Unintentionally Smuggled the Notion of Indigeneity into China." *Humanities* 5 (54): 1–17.

He Junfang. 1998. *Zhongguo shaoshu minzu shuangyu yanjiu: Lishi yu xianshi* (Research on bilingualism among China's ethnic minorities: History and reality). Beijing: Zhongyang Minzu Daxue Chubanshe.

Herman, John. 2007. *Amid the Clouds and Mist: China's Colonization of Guizhou, 1200–1700*. Cambridge, MA: Harvard University Asia Center, Harvard University Press.

Hershatter, Gail. 2011. *The Gender of Memory: Rural Women and China's Collective Past*. Berkeley: University of California Press.

Herzfeld, Michael. 1991. *A Place in History: Social and Monumental Time in a Cretan Town*. Princeton, NJ: Princeton University Press.

Hillman, Ben, and Jonathan Unger. 2013. "Editorial: The Urbanisation of Rural China," *China Perspectives* 3: 3.

Hirsch, Francine. 2003. "Getting to Know 'The Peoples of the USSR': Ethnographic Exhibits as Soviet Virtual Tourism, 1923–1934." *Slavic Review* 62 (4): 683–709.

Ho, Denise. 2018. *Curating Revolution: Politics on Display in Mao's China.* Cambridge: Cambridge University Press.

Holm, David. 2003. *Killing a Buffalo for the Ancestors: A Zhuang Cosmological Text from Southwest China.* DeKalb: Southeast Asia Publications Center, Northern Illinois University.

———. 2004. *Recalling Lost Souls.* Bangkok: White Lotus.

———. 2013. *Mapping the Old Zhuang Character Script: A Vernacular Writing System from Southern China.* Leiden: Brill.

Hostetler, Laura. 2001. *Qing Colonial Enterprise: Ethnography and Cartography in Early Modern China.* Chicago: University of Chicago Press.

———. 2006. "Introduction: Early Modern Ethnography in Comparative Historical Perspective." In *The Art of Ethnography: A Chinese "Miao Album,"* translated by David M. Deal and Laura Hostetler, xvii–lxvii. Seattle: University of Washington Press.

Huang Delin. 2014. *Wenhua shengtai shiye xia Buyizu guge shengcun jiazhi yanjiu* (A study of the existential value of Buyi ancient songs in a cultural ecology perspective). Beijing: Zhongguo Shehui Kexue Chubanshe.

Huang, Fei. 2014. "The Making of a Frontier Landscape: The 'Ten Views of Dongchuan' in Eighteenth-Century Southwest China." *Late Imperial China* 35 (2): 56–88.

Huang Zhenbang and Stephen Hoff (Huo Guanlun). 2006. *Buyi Mojing: Muzhuwen* (Buyi Mo script). Guiyang: Guizhou Renmin Chubanshe.

Ingram, Catherine. 2011. "Echoing the Environment in Kam Big Song." *Asian Studies Review* 35 (4): 439–55.

———. 2012. "Tradition and Divergence in Southwestern China: Kam Big Song Singing in the Village and on Stage." *Asia Pacific Journal of Anthropology* 13 (5): 434–53.

Jacka, Tamara. 2009. "Cultivating Citizens: Suzhi (Quality) Discourse in the PRC." *Positions* 17 (3): 523–36.

Jing Xiaoyan. 2013. "Zhenning Gaodang Cun: Buyi wenhua de yangben" (Gaodang Village in Zhenning: The exemplar of Buyi culture). *Guizhou Ribao,* May 10, 2013, 10.

Joniak-Lüthi, Agnieszka. 2013. "The Han 'Minzu,' Fragmented Identities, and Ethnicity." *Journal of Asian Studies* 72 (4): 849–71.

———. 2015. *The Han: China's Diverse Majority.* Seattle: University of Washington Press.

Jonsson, Hjorleifur. 2010. "Above and Beyond: Zomia and the Ethnographic Challenge of/for Regional History." *History and Anthropology* 21 (2): 191–212.

Kao, Ya-ning. 2014. "Religious Revival among the Zhuang People in China: Practising 'Superstition' and Standardizing a Zhuang Religion." *Journal of Current Chinese Affairs* 43 (2): 107–44.

238   REFERENCES

Karp, Ivan. 1991. "Culture and Representation" and "Festivals." In *Exhibiting Cultures: The Poetics and Politics of Museum Display*, edited by Ivan Karp and Steven Lavine, 11–24, 279–87. Washington, DC: Smithsonian Institution Press.

Kaup, Katherine. 2000. *Creating the Zhuang: Ethnic Politics in China*. Boulder, CO: Lynne Rienner.

———. 2018. "Ethnic Studies beyond Tibet and Xinjiang." In *The SAGE Handbook of Contemporary China*, edited by Weiping Wu and Mark W. Frazier, 760–78. London: SAGE.

Kendall, Paul. 2017. "The Location of Cultural Authenticity: Identifying the Real and the Fake in Urban Guizhou." *China Journal* 77: 93–109.

———. 2019. *The Sounds of Social Space: Branding, Built Environment, and Leisure in Urban China*. Honolulu: University of Hawai'i Press.

Keyes, Charles. 2010. "Book Reviews: *The Art of Not Being Governed: An Anarchist History of Upland Southeast Asia* by James C. Scott." *Journal of Peasant Studies* 37 (1): 237–54.

Kim, Chung Ho. 2020. "Sustainability of Korea's First 'New Village.'" In *Greening East Asia: The Rise of the Eco-Developmental State*, edited by Ashley Esarey, Mary Alice Haddad, Joanna I. Lewis, and Stevan Harrell, 150–63. Seattle: University of Washington Press.

Kipnis, Andrew. 2006. "Suzhi: A Keyword Approach." *China Quarterly* 186: 295–313.

———. 2012. "Constructing Commonality: Standardization and Modernization in Chinese Nation-Building." *Journal of Asian Studies* 71 (3): 731–55.

Kirshenblatt-Gimblett, Barbara. 1998. *Destination Culture: Tourism, Museums, and Heritage*. Berkeley: University of California Press.

Klein, Naomi. (2000) 2010. *No Logo*. New York: Picardo.

Kreps, Christina. 2008. "Indigenous Curation, Museums, and Intangible Cultural Heritage." In *Intangible Heritage*, edited by Laurajane Smith and Natsuko Akagawa, 193–208. London: Routledge.

Lam-Knott, Sonia. 2020. "Consuming the Past in Contemporary East Asia: An Introduction." *Journal of Intercultural Studies* 41 (3): 253–61.

Larkin, Brian. 2008. *Signal and Noise: Media, Infrastructure, and Urban Culture in Nigeria*. Durham, NC: Duke University Press.

———. 2013. "The Politics and Poetics of Infrastructure." *Annual Review of Anthropology* 42: 327–43.

Lash, Scott, and John Urry. 1994. *Economies of Signs and Space*. London: SAGE.

Latour, Bruno. 1993. *We Have Never Been Modern*. Translated by Catherine Porter. Cambridge, MA: Harvard University Press.

Lavine, Steven, and Ivan Karp. 1991. "Introduction: Museum and Multiculturalism." In *Exhibiting Cultures: The Poetics and Politics of Museum Display*, edited by Ivan Karp and Steven Lavine, 1–10. Washington, DC: Smithsonian Institution Press.

Leach, Edmund. 1954. *Political Systems of Highland Burma: A Study of Kachin Social Structure*. Cambridge, MA: Harvard University Press.

Lee, James. 1982. "The Legacy of Immigration to Southwest China, 1250–1850." *Annales de Démographie Historique* 1982: 279–304.

Leibold, James. 2007. *Reconfiguring Chinese Nationalism: How the Qing Frontier and Its Indigenes Became Chinese*. New York: Palgrave Macmillan.

Levenson, Joseph R. 1968. *Confucian China and Its Modern Fate: A Trilogy*. Berkeley: University of California Press.

Li Hanlin. 2001. *Baimiaotu jiaoshi* (Explanation of the Miao Albums). Guiyang: Guizhou Minzu Chubanshe.

Li, Tania Murray. 1999. "Marginality, Power and Production: Analysing Upland Transformations." In *Transforming the Indonesian Uplands: Marginality, Power, and Production*, edited by Tania M. Li, 1–44. London: Routledge.

———. 2000. "Articulating Indigenous Identity in Indonesia: Resource Politics and the Tribal Slot." *Comparative Studies in Society and History* 42 (1): 149–79.

———. 2007. *The Will to Improve: Governmentality, Development, and the Practice of Politics*. Durham, NC: Duke University Press.

Li Zhiren. (1941) 2004. "Miaozu fanggu de gushi" (The stories of Miao poisons). In *Guizhou Miao Yi shehui yanjiu* (A study on the society of Miao and Yi peoples in Guizhou), edited by Wu Zelin and Chen Guojun et al., 210–13. Beijing: Minzu Chubanshe.

Litzinger, Ralph. 2000. *Other Chinas: The Yao and the Politics of National Belonging*. Durham, NC: Duke University Press.

Liu, Xin. 2001. *In One's Own Shadow: An Ethnographic Account of the Condition of Post-reform Rural China*. Berkeley: University of California Press.

Long Zhiyi, ed. 2003. *Kouxiang Guizhou lishi zhi men: Jinian Guizhou jiansheng 590 zhounian* (Knocking on the door of Guizhou history: Commemorating the 590th anniversary of the founding of Guizhou). Guiyang: Guizhou Renmin Chubanshe.

Looney, Kristen E. 2015. "China's Campaign to Build a New Socialist Countryside: Village Modernization, Peasant Councils, and the Ganzhou Model of Rural Development." *China Quarterly* 224: 909–32.

———. 2020. *Mobilizing for Development: The Modernization of Rural East Asia*. Ithaca, NY: Cornell University Press.

Lowenthal, David. 1985. *The Past Is a Foreign Country*. Cambridge: Cambridge University Press.

Lu Yongchun. 2010. "'Meide zai nongjia' huodong: Zhenning zizhi xian funü lianhe-hui" ("Virtue in rural households" activities by the Women's Federation in Zhenning Autonomous County). In *Zhenning nianjian* (Zhenning yearbook), edited by Wu Zhongshi, 157. Beijing: Fangzhi Chubanshe.

240   REFERENCES

Ludlow, Francis, Lauren Baker, Samara Brock, Chris Hebdon, and Michael R. Dove. 2016. "The Double Binds of Indigeneity and Indigenous Resistance." *Sustainability* 5: 53–71.

Lujan, James. 2005. "A Museum of the Indian, Not for the Indian." *American Indian Quarterly* 29 (3–4): 510–16.

Luo, Yu. 2018a. "Alternative Indigeneity in China? The Paradox of the Buyi in the Age of Ethnic Branding." *Verge: Studies in Global Asias* 4 (2): 107–34.

———. 2018b. "An Alternative to the 'Indigenous' in Early Twenty-First-Century China: Guizhou's Branding of Yuanshengtai." *Modern China* 44 (1): 68–102.

———. 2021. "Safeguarding Intangible Heritage through Edutainment in China's Creative Urban Environments." *International Journal of Heritage Studies* 27 (2): 170–85.

Luo, Yu, Tim Oakes, and Louisa Schein. 2019. "Resourcing Remoteness and the 'Post-Alteric' Imaginary in China." *Social Anthropology* 27 (2): 270–85.

Luo Zhengfu. 2009. "Tiaoshi yu yanjin: wu wenzi minzu wenhua chuancheng—yi Buyizu wei ge'an de yanjiu" (Adaptation and evolution: Cultural inheritance of non-literate ethnic groups through the case of Buyi). PhD diss., Xiamen University, China.

———. 2010. "Zhongguo minzushi yanjiu fanshi fansi: Yi mingqing xinan 'Zhongjia' kaolun wei zhongxin, jiantan tazhe shuxie de juxian" (Reflection on the paradigm of Chinese ethnic studies: Zhongjia in China's Southwest during the Ming and Qing dynasties and the limitations of representation by others). In *Xinan diqu duominzu hexie gongsheng guanxi yanjiu xueshu huiyi lunwenji* (Proceedings of the International Conference on the Harmonious Coexistence of Multiple Ethnicities in Southwest China), 140–54. Guiyang: Guizhou University.

Ma Guojun. 2010. *"Qingshigao dilizhi Guizhou" yanjiu* (Research on the geographical records on Guizhou in the "Draft History of the Qing Dynasty"). Guiyang: Guizhou Renmin Chubanshe.

Ma Jialu. 2020. "16guo zhengyao canjia de zhongyao huiyi, weihe zheshouge neng dandu zhan liangfenzhong" (Why could this song take up two minutes alone at an important meeting attended by dignitaries from sixteen countries). *Nanfang Dushibao*, September 25, 2020. https://m.mp.oeeee.com/a/BAAFRD 000020200924366625.html.

Macdonald, Sharon. 1996. "Theorizing Museums: An Introduction." In *Theorizing Museums: Representing Identity and Diversity in a Changing World*, edited by Sharon Macdonald and Gordon Fyfe, 1–18. Oxford: Blackwell.

Manning, Paul. 2010. "The Semiotics of Brand." *Annual Review of Anthropology* 29: 33–49.

McCarthy, Susan. 2009. *Communist Multiculturalism: Ethnic Revival in Southwest China*. Seattle: University of Washington Press.

McKee, Emily. 2015. "Trash Talk: Interpreting Morality and Disorder in Negev/Naqab Landscapes." *Current Anthropology* 56 (5): 733–52.

REFERENCES 241

McLaren, Anne, Alex English, Xinyuan He, and Catherine Ingram. 2013. *Environmental Preservation and Cultural Heritage in China*. Champaign, IL: Common Ground.

Meiu, George Paul, Jean Comaroff, and John L. Comaroff. 2020. "Introduction: Ethnicity, Inc. Revisited." In *Ethnicity, Commodity, In/Corporation*, edited by George Paul Meiu, Jean Comaroff, and John L. Comaroff, 1–35. Bloomington: Indiana University Press.

Meyers, Richard. 2019. "Native Anthropology, to Be a Native Scholar, or a Scholar That Is Native: Reviving Ethnography in Indian Country." *Anthropology Now* 11: 23–33.

Michaud, Jean, ed. 2000. *Turbulent Times and Enduring People: Mountain Minorities in the South-East Asian Massif*. Richmond, UK: Curzon Press.

———. 2006. *Historical Dictionary of the Peoples of the Southeast Asian Massif*. New York: Scarecrow.

———. 2010. "Editorial: Zomia and Beyond," *Journal of Global History* 5 (2): 187–214.

———. 2013. "Comrades of Minority Policy in China, Vietnam, and Laos." In *Red Stamps and Gold Stars: Fieldwork Dilemmas in Upland Socialist Asia*, edited by Sarah Turner, 22–39. Vancouver: University of British Columbia Press.

Michaud, Jean, Meenaxi Barkataki-Ruscheweyh, and Margaret Byrne Swain. 2016. *Historical Dictionary of the Peoples of the Southeast Asian Massif*. 2nd ed. Lanham, MD: Rowman and Littlefield.

Mueggler, Erik. 2001. *The Age of Wild Ghosts: Memory, Violence, and Place in Southwest China*. Berkeley: University of California Press.

Mullaney, Thomas. 2010. *Coming to Terms with the Nation: Ethnic Classification in Modern China*. Berkeley: University of California Press.

———. 2012. "Critical Han Studies: Introduction and Prolegomenon." In *Critical Han Studies: The History, Representation, and Identity of China's Majority*, edited by Thomas Mullaney, James P. Leibold, Stéphane Gros, and Eric Bussche, 1–20. Berkeley: University of California Press.

Myers, Fred. 1994. "Culture-Making: Performing Aboriginality at the Asia Society Gallery." *American Ethnologist* 21 (4): 679–99.

———. 2006. "The Complicity of Cultural Production: The Contingencies of Performance in Globalizing Museum Practices." In *Museum Frictions: Public Cultures / Global Transformations*, edited by Ivan Karp et al., 505–35. Durham, NC: Duke University Press.

Narayan, Kirin. 1993. "How Native Is a 'Native' Anthropologist?" *American Anthropologist* 95 (3): 671–86.

Nitzky, William. 2012. "Mediating Heritage Preservation and Rural Development: Ecomuseum Development in China." *Urban Anthropology and Studies of Cultural Systems and World Economic Development* 41 (2–4): 367–417.

———. 2013. "Community Empowerment at the Periphery? Participatory Approaches to Heritage Protection in Guizhou, China." In *Cultural Heritage Politics in China*, edited by Tami Blumenfeld and Helaine Silverman, 205–32. New York: Springer.

242 REFERENCES

Notar, Beth. 2006. *Displacing Desire: Travel and Popular Culture in China*. Honolulu: University of Hawai'i Press.

Nyíri, Pál. 2006. *Scenic Spots: Chinese Tourism, the State, and Cultural Authority*. Seattle: University of Washington Press.

———. 2009. "Between Encouragement and Control: Tourism, Modernity and Discipline in China." In *Asia on Tour*, edited by Tim Winter, Peggy Teo, and T. C. Chang, 153–69. Milton Park, UK: Routledge.

Oakes, Tim. 1998. *Tourism and Modernity in China*. London: Routledge.

———. 1999. "Selling Guizhou: Cultural Development in an Era of Marketization." In *The Political Economy of China's Provinces*, edited by Hans Hendrischke and Chongyi Feng, 27–67. London: Routledge.

———. 2000. "China's Provincial Identities: Reviving Regionalism and Reinventing 'Chineseness.'" *Journal of Asian Studies* 59 (3): 667–92.

———. 2006. "Cultural Strategies of Development: Implications for Village Governance in China." *Pacific Review* 19 (1): 13–37.

———. 2009. "Resourcing Culture: Is a Prosaic 'Third Space' Possible in Rural China?" *Environment and Planning D: Society and Space* 27: 1074–90.

———. 2012. "Looking Out to Look In: The Use of the Periphery in China's Geopolitical Narratives." *Eurasian Geography and Economics* 53 (3): 315–26.

———. 2020. "Leisure as Governable Space: Transcultural Leisure and Governmentality in Contemporary China." In *Testing the Margins of Leisure: Case Studies on China, Japan, and Indonesia*, edited by Rudolf G. Wagner, Catherine V. Yeh, Eugenio Menegon, and Robert P. Weller, 13–41. Heidelberg: Heidelberg University Press.

Oakes, Tim, and Donald Sutton. 2010. "Introduction." In *Faiths on Display: Religion, Tourism, and the Chinese State*, edited by Tim Oakes and Donald Sutton, 1–26. Lanham, MD: Rowman and Littlefield.

Oakes, Tim, and Zhenting Zuo. 2022. "Remoteness and Connectivity: The Variegated Geographies of the Yunnan-Guizhou Plateau." In *Routledge Handbook of Highland Asia*, edited by Jelle J. P. Wouters and Michael T. Heneise, 418–29. London: Routledge.

Ong, Aihwa, and Li Zhang. 2008. "Introduction." In *Privatizing China: Socialism from Afar*, edited by Li Zhang and Aihwa Ong, 1–19. Ithaca, NY: Cornell University Press.

Park, Choong-Hwan. 2014. "Nongjiale Tourism and Contested Space in Rural China." *Modern China* 40 (5): 519–48.

Pedersen, Morten Axel. 2011. *Not Quite Shamans: Spirit Worlds and Political Lives in Northern Mongolia*. Ithaca, NY: Cornell University Press.

Perdue, Peter. 1987. *Exhausting the Earth: State and Peasant in Hunan, 1500–1850 A.D.* Cambridge, MA: Harvard University Press.

Perry, Elizabeth J. 2011. "From Mass Campaigns to Managed Campaigns: Constructing a 'New Socialist Countryside.'" In *Mao's Invisible Hand: The Political Foundations of Adaptive Governance in China*, edited by Elizabeth J. Perry and Sebastian Heilmann, 30–61. Cambridge, MA: Harvard University Press.

Povinelli, Elizabeth. 2002. *The Cunning of Recognition: Indigenous Alterity and the Making of Australian Multiculturalism*. Durham, NC: Duke University Press.

Prins, Harald E. L. 2002. "Visual Media and the Primitivist Perplex: Colonial Fantasies, Indigenous Imagination, and Advocacy in North America." In *Media Worlds: Anthropology on New Terrain*, edited by Faye Ginsburg, Lila Abu-Lughod, and Brian Larkin, 58–74. Berkeley: University of California Press.

Ptáčková, Jarmila. 2020. *Exile from the Grasslands: Tibetan Herders and Chinese Development Projects*. Seattle: University of Washington Press.

Rees, Helen. 2012. "Intangible Cultural Heritage in China Today: Policy and Practice in the Early Twenty-First Century." In *Music as Intangible Cultural Heritage: Policy, Ideology, and Practice in the Preservation of East Asian Traditions*, edited by Keith Howard, 23–54. Burlington, VT: Ashgate.

———. 2016. "Environmental Crisis, Culture Loss, and a New Musical Aesthetic: China's 'Original Ecology Folksongs' in Theory and Practice." *Ethnomusicology* 60 (1): 53–88.

Ren, Hai. 2013. *The Middle Class in Neoliberal China: Governing Risk, Life-Building, and Themed Spaces*. London: Routledge.

Renmin Ribao. 1958. "Zhonggong Zhongyang Guowuyuan guanyu chu sihai jiang weisheng de zhishi" (Instructions from the Central Committee of the Communist Party of China and the State Council on Eliminating the Four Pests and Promoting Hygiene). *Renmin Ribao*, February 13, 1958. https://cn.govopendata.com/renminribao/1958/2/13/1/.

Riegel, Henrietta. 1996. "Into the Heart of Irony: Ethnographic Exhibitions and the Politics of Difference." In *Theorizing Museums: Representing Identity and Diversity in a Changing World*, edited by Sharon Macdonald and Gordon Fyfe, 83–104. Oxford: Blackwell.

Rofel, Lisa. 2007. *Desiring China: Experiments in Neoliberalism, Sexuality, and Public Culture*. Durham, NC: Duke University Press.

Rosenberg, Lior. 2013. "Urbanising the Rural: Local Strategies for Creating 'New Style' Rural Communities in China." *China Perspectives* 3: 63–71.

Ryang, Sonia. 1997. "Native Anthropology and Other Problems." *Dialectical Anthropology* 22 (1): 23–49.

———. 2005. "Dilemma of a Native: On Location, Authenticity, and Reflexivity." *Asia Pacific Journal of Anthropology* 6 (2): 143–57.

Sautman, Barry. 2012. "Paved with Good Intentions: Proposals to Curb Minority Rights and Their Consequences for China." *Modern China* 38 (1): 10–39.

244 REFERENCES

Schein, Louisa. 1989. "The Dynamics of Cultural Revival among the Miao in Guizhou." In *Ethnicity and Ethnic Groups in China*, edited by Chien Chiao and Nicholas Tapp, 199–212. Hong Kong: Chinese University Press.

———. 1997. "Gender and Internal Orientalism in China." *Modern China* 23 (1): 69–98.

———. 2000. *Minority Rules: The Miao and the Feminine in China's Cultural Politics.* Durham, NC: Duke University Press.

———. 2013. "Ethnographic Representation across Genres: The Culture Trope in Contemporary Mainland Media." In *Oxford Handbook of Chinese Cinemas*, edited by Carlos Rojas and Eileen Cheng-yin Chow, 507–25. Oxford: Oxford University Press.

———. 2014. "The Edges of Alterity." In "Remote and Edgy: New Takes on Old Anthropological Themes," edited by Erik Harms, Shafqat Hussain, and Sara Shneiderman. *HAU: Journal of Ethnographic Theory* 4 (1): 370–72.

———. 2018. "Wenhua: 'Culture' as Hierarchy, Identity, Commodity." Paper presented at "The Social Lives of Keywords," Wenner-Gren Foundation for Anthropological Research Award Workshop, Hong Kong, January 2018.

Schein, Louisa, and Yu Luo. 2016. "Representations of Chinese Minorities." In *Handbook on Ethnic Minorities in China*, edited by Xiaowei Zang, 263–90. Cheltenham, UK: Edward Elgar.

Scott, James C. 1985. *Weapons of the Weak: Everyday Forms of Peasant Resistance.* New Haven, CT: Yale University Press.

———. 1990. *Domination and the Arts of Resistance: Hidden Transcripts.* New Haven, CT: Yale University Press.

———. 1998. *Seeing Like a State: How Certain Schemes to Improve the Human Condition Have Failed.* New Haven, CT: Yale University Press.

———. 2009. *The Art of Not Being Governed: An Anarchist History of Upland Southeast Asia.* New Haven, CT: Yale University Press.

Shahar, Meir, and Robert P. Weller, eds. 1996. *Unruly Gods: Divinity and Society in China.* Honolulu: University of Hawai'i Press.

Shapiro, Judith. 2001. *Mao's War against Nature: Politics and Environment in Revolutionary China.* Cambridge: Cambridge University Press.

Shidai Zhoubao. 2013. "'Cunguan' Yu Jianrong de lixiang yu xianshi" (The ideals and reality of "village official" Yu Jianrong). *Shidai Zhoubao*, October 10, 2013. https://www.time-weekly.com/wap-article/22798.

Shneiderman, Sara. 2015. *Rituals of Ethnicity: Thangmi Identities between Nepal and India.* Philadelphia: University of Pennsylvania Press.

Silverman, Helaine, and Tami Blumenfield. 2013. "Cultural Heritage Politics in China: An Introduction." In *Cultural Heritage Politics in China*, edited by Tami Blumenfield and Helaine Silverman, 3–22. New York: Springer.

Siu, Helen F. 1989a. *Agents and Victims in South China: Accomplices in Rural Revolution.* New Haven, CT: Yale University Press.

———. 1989b. "Socialist Peddlers and Princes in a Chinese Market Town." *American Ethnologist* 16 (2): 195–212.

———. 1990a. "Recycling Tradition: Culture, History and Political Economy in the Chrysanthemum Festivals of South China." *Comparative Studies in Society and History* 32 (October): 765–94.

———. 1990b. "Where Were the Women? Rethinking Marriage Resistance and Regional Culture History." *Late Imperial China* 11 (December): 32–62.

———. 2007. "Grounding Displacement: Uncivil Urban Spaces in Postreform South China." *American Ethnologist* 34 (2): 329–50.

Skinner, G. William, ed. 1977. *The City in Late Imperial China*. Stanford, CA: Stanford University Press.

Sleeper-Smith, Susan, ed. 2009. *Contesting Knowledge: Museums and Indigenous Perspectives*. Lincoln: University of Nebraska Press.

Spence, Jonathan. 1990. *The Search for Modern China*. New York: W. W. Norton.

Stalin, Joseph. 1913. "Marxism and the National Question." First published in *Prosveshcheniye*, 3–5. Transcribed by Carl Kavanagh for the Marxists Internet Archive. https://www.marxists.org/reference/archive/stalin/works/1913/03.htm.

Steinmüller, Hans. 2013. *Communities of Complicity: Everyday Ethics in Rural China*. New York: Berghahn.

Su, Donghai. 2008. "The Concept of the Ecomuseum and Its Practice in China." *Museum International* 60 (1–2): 29–39.

Su, Xiaobo, and Peggy Teo. 2009. *The Politics of Heritage Tourism in China: A View from Lijiang*. London: Routledge.

Sum, Chun-Yi, Tami Blumenfield, Mary K. Shenk, and Siobhán M. Mattison. 2022. "Hierarchy, Resentment, and Pride: Politics of Identity and Belonging among Mosuo, Yi, and Han in Southwest China." *Modern China* 48 (3): 568–92.

Tang Landong. 2007. "Zhongguo minzu bowuguan lishi huigu yu xianzhuang fenxi" (Historical review and contemporary analysis of Chinese Nationality Museum). *Zhongnan Minzu Daxue Xuebao* 27 (2): 33–37.

Teng, Emma. 2004. *Taiwan's Imagined Geography: Chinese Colonial Travel Writing and Pictures, 1683–1895*. Cambridge, MA: Harvard University Asia Center, Harvard University Press.

Tenzin Jinba. 2013. *In the Land of the Eastern Queendom: The Politics of Gender and Ethnicity on the Sino-Tibetan Border*. Seattle: University of Washington Press.

———. 2017. "Seeing like Borders: Convergence Zone as a Post-Zomian Model." *Current Anthropology* 58 (5): 551–75.

———. 2022. "Seeing like a Native Anthropologist: A Post-Postcolonial Reflection on the Native Turn in Asian Academia." *American Behavioral Scientist* 68 (3): 389–406.

Tsuda, Takeyuki. 2015. "Is Native Anthropology Really Possible?" *Anthropology Today* 31 (3): 14–17.

246 REFERENCES

Turner, Sarah, ed. 2013. *Red Stamps and Gold Stars: Fieldwork Dilemmas in Upland Socialist Asia*. Vancouver: University of British Columbia Press.

Unger, Jonathan. 1997. "Not Quite Han: The Ethnic Minorities of China's Southwest." *Bulletin of Concerned Asian Scholars* 29 (3): 67–78.

Urry, John. 1995. "How Societies Remember the Past." *Sociological Review* 43 (1): 45–65.

van Schendel, Willem. 2002. "Geographies of Knowing, Geographies of Ignorance: Jumping Scale in Southeast Asia." *Environment and Planning D: Society and Space* 20 (6): 647–68.

Varutti, Marzia. 2008. "A Chinese Puzzle: The Representation of Chinese Ethnic Minorities in the Museums of Kunming, Yunnan Province of China." *International Journal of the Inclusive Museum* 1 (3): 35–42.

Vasantkumar, Chris. 2014. "Unmade in China: Reassembling the Ethnic on the Gansu-Tibetan Border." *Ethnos* 79 (2): 261–86.

Vickers, Edward. 2007. "Museums and Nationalism in Contemporary China." *Compare* 37 (3): 365–82.

Voci, Paola. 2010. *China on Video: Smaller-Screen Realities*. London: Routledge.

Wang, Bo. 2019. "Sacred Trash and Personhood: Living in Daily Waste-Management Infrastructures in the Eastern Himalayas." *Cross-Currents: East Asian History and Culture Review* 8 (1): 224–48.

Wang, Jing. 2001. "Culture as Leisure and Culture as Capital." *Positions: East Asia Cultures Critique* 9 (1): 69–104.

Wang, Jing. 2021. "Sinicizing Islam in Contemporary China." *Allegra Lab: Anthropology for Radical Optimism*, April 30, 2021. https://allegralaboratory.net/sinicizing-islam-in-contemporary-china/.

Wang, Mengqi. 2012. "The Social Life of Scripts: Staging Authenticity in China's Ethno-Tourism Industry." *Urban Anthropology and Studies of Cultural Systems and World Economic Development* 41 (2–4): 419–55.

Wang Ming-ke. 2003. *Qiang zai Han Zang zhijian: Yige huaxia bianyuan de lishi renleixue yanjiu* (The Qiang in between the Han and the Tibetan: A historical anthropological study at China's margin). Beijing: Zhonghua Shuju.

Wang Siming. 1988. "Buyizu minjian wudao de yishu xingshi, fengge tese yu minzu xisu de guanxi" (The artistic forms and styles of Buyi folk dances in relation to ethnic customs). In *Guizhou yishu yanjiu wencong: Yizu Buyizu wudao zhuanji* (Guizhou art research series: Special issue on Yi and Buyi dances), edited by Guizhou Sheng Yishu Yanjiushi, 17–34. Guiyang: Guizhou Sheng Yishu Yanjiushi.

Wang Xiaomei. 2013. "600 nian: Chuanyue lishi de dangdai xushi" (Six hundred years: Contemporary narrative that travels through history). *Guizhou Ribao*, July 12, 2013, B8.

Wang Yugui. 2012. "Buyizu guwenzi guiqulai de sikao" (Reflections on the return of ancient scripts of the Buyi people). In *Buyizu Mo wenhua yantaohui lunwenji* (Proceedings of the Symposium on Buyi Mo Culture), 20–29. Guiyang: Guizhou Sheng Buyi Xuehui.

Watson, Rubie. 1994. "Girls' Houses and Working Women: Expressive Culture in the Pearl River Delta, 1900–1941." In *Women and Chinese Patriarchy: Submission, Servitude and Escape*, edited by Maria Jaschok and Suzanne Miers, 25–44. London: Zed.

Wei Lianzhou. 1981. *Buyizu Miaozu fengtu zhigao* (Buyi and Miao customs and conditions). Edited by Qiannan Buyizu Miaozu Zizhizhou Minzu Shiwu Weiyuanhui Wenyi Yanjiushi. Guiyang: Guizhou Sheng Chubanju.

Weinstein, Jodi L. 2007. "Subsistence and Sedition in Southwest China: Local Responses to Qing Rule in Eighteenth-Century Guizhou." PhD diss., Yale University.

———. 2014. *Empire and Identity in Guizhou: Local Resistance to Qing Expansion.* Seattle: University of Washington Press.

Wengrow, David. 2008. "Prehistories of Commodity Branding." *Current Anthropology* 49 (1): 7–34.

White, Sydney D. 1997. "Fame and Sacrifice: The Gendered Construction of Naxi Identities." *Modern China* 23 (3): 298–327.

Wilcox, Emily. 2019. *Revolutionary Bodies: Chinese Dance and the Socialist Legacy.* Berkeley: University of California Press.

Wilczak, Jessica. 2017. "Making the Countryside More Like the Countryside? Rural Planning and Metropolitan Visions in Post-quake Chengdu." *Geoforum* 78: 110–18.

Wouters, Jelle J. P., and Michael T. Heneise. 2022. "Highland Asia as a World Region: An Introduction." In *Routledge Handbook of Highland Asia*, edited by Jelle J. P. Wouters and Michael T. Heneise, 1–39. London: Routledge.

Wu, Guo. 2014. "Recalling Bitterness: Historiography, Memory, and Myth in Maoist China." *Twentieth-Century China* 39 (3): 245–68.

———. 2019. *Narrating Southern Chinese Minority Nationalities: Politics, Disciplines, and Public History.* New York: Palgrave Macmillan.

Wu, Ka-ming. 2011. "Tradition Revival with Socialist Characteristics: Propaganda Storytelling Turned Spiritual Service in Rural Yan'an." *China Journal* 66: 101–17.

———. 2015. *Reinventing Chinese Tradition: The Cultural Politics of Late Socialism.* Champaign: University of Illinois Press.

Wu Kaifeng and Wu Zhonggang. 2022. *Buyizu fushi wenhua yanjiu* (Study of Buyi clothing and costume culture). Edited by Long Youming. Guiyang: Guizhou Jiaoyu Chubanshe.

Wu Wenyi, Wil C. Snyder, and Yongshu Liang. 2000. *Zhongguo Buyiyu duibi yanjiu* (A comparative study of the Buyi language in China). Guiyang: Guizhou Renmin Chubanshe.

———. 2007. "Survey of the Guizhou Bouyei Language." SIL International, SIL

Language and Culture Documentation and Description 2007-001. https://www.sil
.org/system/files/reapdata/15/19/67/15196744206931885144006477433042575609
/49147_Wu_Survey_of_Bouyei.pdf.

Wu Zhonggang and Wu Kaifeng. 2014. *Zhenning Buyizu* (The Buyi ethnicity in Zhenning County). Edited by Zhenning Buyizu Miaozu Zizhixian Buyixuehui, Zhenning Buyizu Miaozu Zizhixian Minzushiwuju. Guiyang: Guizhou Daxue Chubanshe.

Wu Zhonggang and Wu Zhongshi. 2012. "Mojiao youguan wenti de yanjiu" (Research on issues related to Mo rituals). In *Buyizu Mo wenhua yantaohui lunwenji* (Proceedings of the Symposium on Buyi Mo Culture), 66–70. Guiyang: Guizhou Sheng Buyi Xuehui.

Wu Zhongshi. 2010. "Zhenning zai minzu zongjiao lingyu goujian shehuizhuyi hexie shehui de lishi jincheng" (Zhenning's historical progress in building socialist harmonious society in *minzu* and religious domains). In *Zhenning nianjian* (Zhenning yearbook), edited by Wu Zhongshi, 44–52. Beijing, China: Fangzhi Chubanshe.

———. 2014. *Zhenning jinxiandaishi zhuanti yanjiu* (Specific research on Zhenning County's modern history). Kunming: Yunnan Renmin Chubanshe.

Xiang, Biao. 2021. "Suspension: Seeking Agency for Change in the Hypermobile World." *Pacific Affairs* 94 (2): 233–50.

Xu Ganli and Guo Yue. 2012. "Rentong yu qufen: Minzu fushi de zuqun yuyi biaoda" (Identification and distinguishment: Expression of ethnic costumes). *Minzu Xuekan* 2: 23–31.

Xu Qifei. 2014. "Huishui cunzhai: Yiqu haohuahong chuanchang bainian" (Villages in Huishui County: Singing "Good flowers are red" for hundreds of years). *Guiyang Wanbao*, November 13, 2014.

Yan, Hairong. 2003. "Neoliberal Governmentality and Neohumanism: Organizing Suzhi/Value Flow through Labor Recruitment Networks." *Cultural Anthropology* 18: 493–523.

Yang, Fenggang. 2011. *Religion in China: Survival and Revival under Communist Rule.* Oxford: Oxford University Press.

Yang, Fenggang, and Joseph Tamney, eds. 2005. *State, Market, and Religions in Chinese Societies.* Leiden: Brill Academic.

Yang Tingshuo. 1995. *Xiangji jingying yuanli* (The mechanism of interactive operating among ethnicities). Guiyang: Guizhou Minzu Chubanshe.

Yang Tingshuo and Pan Shengzhi. 2004. *Baimiaotu chaoben huibian* (A collated volume of copies of the Miao Albums). Guiyang: Guizhou Renmin Chubanshe.

Yang Zhibin. 2011a. *Buyizu Mo wenhua yanjiu* (A study on the Mo culture of the Buyi ethnicity). Zhenning: Zhengxie Zhenning Buyizu Miaozu Zizhixian Dishijie Weiyuanhui.

———. 2011b. *Suiyue rensheng* (My life). Zhenning: Zhengxie Zhenning Buyizu Miaozu Zhizhixian Dishijie Weiyuanhui.

———. 2012. "Lun Bao'ertuo" (On Bao'ertuo). In *Buyizu Mo wenhua yantaohui lunwenji* (Proceedings of the Symposium on Buyi Mo Culture), 83–84. Guiyang: Guizhou Sheng Buyi Xuehui.

Yang Zhiqiang. 2009. "From Miao to Miaozu: Alterity in the Formation of Modern Ethnic Groups." *Hmong Studies Journal* 10: 1–28.

———, ed. 2018. *Miaojiang zoulang wenji* (Collected essays on the corridor of the Miao frontier). Guiyang: Guizhou Daxue.

Ye, Jingzhong. 2006. *Nongmin shijue de xinnongcun jianshe* (Construction of a new countryside from farmers' perspectives). Beijing: Shehui Kexue Wenxian Chubanshe.

Yeh, Emily. 2007. "Tibetan Indigeneity: Translation Resemblances, and Uptake." In *Indigenous Experience Today*, edited by Marisol de la Cadena and Orin Starn, 69–97. Oxford: Berg.

———. 2013. *Taming Tibet: Landscape Transformation and the Gift of Chinese Development*. Ithaca, NY: Cornell University Press.

Yin Lixin. 2013. "48zhi Buyi wenyidui 'wuchu' Luobie xiang 'quanguo xianjin'" (Forty-eight Buyi art performance teams achieved national advancement beyond Luobie Town). *Liupanshui Ribao*, May 6, 2013.

Yin Luzhu et al. 2010. "Yang Zhibin: Yigeren ban de minsu guan" (Yang Zhibin: The Folklore Museum run by himself). *Zhongguo Laodong Shibao*, April 1, 2010.

You, Ziying. 2020. *Folk Literati, Contested Tradition, and Heritage in Contemporary China: Incense Is Kept Burning*. Bloomington: Indiana University Press.

Yuan, Ye. 2020. "Unfinished Vanity Projects a Debt Trap for Guizhou County." *Sixth Tone*, July 14, 2020. http://www.sixthtone.com/news/1005931/Unfinished %20Vanity%20Projects%20a%20Debt%20Trap%20for%20Guizhou%20County/.

Zhang, Pinggong. 2007. *Culture and Ideology at an Invented Place*. Newcastle: Cambridge Scholars.

Zhang Shenglan. 2014. "Miaozu fushi yu Miaozu ziwo rentong yishi: Yi Qingchao zhi Minguo shiqi de Guizhou Miaozu gaizhuang yundong wei Zhongxin" (Miao costume and the awareness of Miao identity: From the Qing to the Republic of China in Guizhou). *Minzu Xuekan* 5: 25–33.

Zhang, Yanshuo. 2021. "Entrepreneurs of the National Past: The Discourse of Ethnic Indigeneity and Indigenous Cultural Writing in China." *Positions* 29 (2): 423–50.

Zhenning Buyizu Miaozu Zizhixian Gaikuang Bianxiezu. 1985. *Zhenning Buyizu Miaozu zizhixian gaikuang* (An overview of Zhenning Buyi and Miao Autonomous County). Guiyang: Guizhou Renmin Chubanshe.

Zhenning Buyizu Miaozu Zizhixianzhi Bianzuan Weiyuanhui, ed. 2009. *Zhenning Buyizu Miaozu zizhixian minzuzhi* (Zhenning Buyi-Miao Autonomous County Minzu Gazetteer). Guiyang: Guizhou Renmin Chubanshe.

Zhongguo Difangzhi Jicheng Bianji Gongzuo Weiyuanhui, ed. (1948) 2006. *Minguo Guizhou tongzhi* (Republican-era Guizhou Gazetteer). Chengdu: Bashu Shushe.

Zhongguo Diyi Lishi Dang'an Guan, Zhongguo Renmin Daxue Qingshi Yanjiusuo, Guizhou Sheng Dang'an Guan, eds. 1987. *Qingdai qianqi Miaomin qiyi dang'an shiliao huibian* (Edited volume of the archives on Miao rebellions in the early Qing dynasty). Beijing: Guangming Ribao Chubanshe.

Zhou Guomao. 1995. *Mojiao yu Mo wenhua* (Mo ritual and Mo culture). Guiyang: Guizhou Renmin Chubanshe.

———. 2006. *Yizhong teshu de wenhua dianji: Buyizu Mojing yanjiu* (A special cultural script: Study of the Mo ritual texts of the Buyi ethnicity). Guiyang: Guizhou Renmin Chubanshe.

———. 2012. "Buyizu Mo wenhua yanjiu zongshu" (General review of studies on the Mo culture of Buyi). In *Buyizu Mo wenhua yantaohui lunwenji* (Proceedings of the Symposium on Buyi Mo Culture), 1–8. Guiyang: Guizhou Sheng Buyi Xuehui.

Zhou Guoyan. 1996. "An Introduction to the Kam-Tai (Zhuang-Dong) Group of Languages in China." In *Languages and Cultures of the Kam-Tai (Zhuang Dong) Group: A Word List* (English-Thai version), edited by Zhou Guoyan and Somsonge Burusphat, 1–65. Bangkok: Sahadhammika.

———. 2008. "Guiyang shijiao Buyi zu yuyan shiyong xianzhuang ji tezheng fenxi" (A study of the uses and features of the Buyi language in the suburbs of Guiyang). *Guizhou Minzu Xueyuan Xuebao* 4: 139–45.

Zhou Yongming. 2010. "Daolu yanjiu yu 'luxue'" (Studies on roads and "roadology"). *Er'shiyi Shiji* 120: 71–79.

INDEX

Page numbers in *italics* refer to illustrations.

A You Duo, 124

acculturation, 11, 18, 46. *See also* assimilation

agricultural production, xv, xvi, 43–44, 61, 90, 170

agriculture, 30, 107, 111, 158, 166, 175, 176, 193, 224n2; Buyi, 10, 28, 112; political/moral valence of, 10; sedentarized, 33, 214n16, 224n14; swidden, 11, 210n9, 224n14

ancestral worship, 11, 49, 58, 76–77, 98, 213n12, 219n20

animistic beliefs, 72–73, 78

Anshun City, 75, 80

anthropology, 7–8, 136, 209n5, 223n2; decolonization in, 7, 202

architecture, 199–200; stone, 158, 162, 171; traditional, 181

artifacts, 44; Buyi, 129, 201; cultural, 16, 134, 139, 143; historical, 195

assimilation, 46, 47, 95, 214n15. *See also* acculturation

Association for Buyi Studies, xv, 85; County, 56, 57, 63–64; Guizhou Provincial, 45, 68, 70, 77

Association for Zhuang Studies, 68, 85

authenticity, 86, 129, 132–33, 146, 149–50, 164, 185, 199, 209n2, 221n1

Bamboo King, 79

bao, 61, 78, 220n29

Baogendei, 73, 78, 82

Baolutuo, 55–57, 72, 219n26, 220n28, 220n29, 220n30; Bao'ertuo/Buluotuo, 219n26; Mo rituals and, 78–79, 81–82, 86; portrait of, 79, 83; signboard of, *80*, 87; statue of, *88*; visualizing, 75–82

batik, ix, x, 16, 89–91, 95, 146, 194

Beautiful Countryside campaign, 159

Beijing, 64, 79, 107, 141, 180

Beipan River, 29, 78

Biandanshan Buyi Autonomous District, 37

Big Bastion, 23, 191

birth control, 115, 188

branding, ix, 4, 19–20, 24–25, 51, 52, 88, 108, 158, 161, 182, 197, 209n2, 227n1; contemporary, 54; cultural, 11, 122–24, 188; effective, 53; identity and, 196; local, 162; place, 131, 150, 160, 199; self-, 8; village, 125, 163

252 INDEX

Brief History of Buyizu (National Ethnic Affairs Commission), 94

bronze drums, 2, 86, 125, 141–43, 145, 222n15

Buddha, 79, 81

Buddhism, ix, 58, 62, 71, 213n12, 217n6, 218n9

Building a New Socialist Countryside campaign, 98, 157–59, 163–64, 177, 181, 187, 224n1

Bumo, 61, 64, 69, 72–73, 76–77, 81, 86, 217n7, 218n7, 220n28

Buna, 38, 39, 128, 148, 152; Bunong and, 42, 148

Bunayi, 31, 37

bungalows, *178*, 181, 194. *See also* houses

Bunong, 37–39, 89, 90, 128, 147–48, 152, 170, 215n26; Buna and, 42, 148

Bunongyi, 31, 37

Bureau of Cultural Relics, 133

bureaucracy, 38, 60, 167, 227n24

Buyi, 3, 12, 15, 37, 39, 59, 66, 80, 90–92; belonging by, 117–22; bilingualism and, 34, 47; contemporary, 140–41; depiction of, ix, 19; ethnohistorical terminology/populations related to, 31; ethnonym of, 30–31; flexibility of, 11, 52; geographical distribution of, *40*; Han and, xi, xiii–xiv, xvii–xviii, 9–11, 13, 20, 28, 49, 50, 54, 73, 106, 140, 172; identifying as, x, 29; local, 4, 7, 8, 38, 144; Miao and, 9, 16, 17, 30, 48–49, 50, 51, 147, 216n28; naming and transcription, ix, 38, 215n25; origins of, 5, 75; population of, 5, 209n1; regional history and, 9; self-appellations for, 31; spiritual world of, 87; story of, 25, 203–4; understanding of, 5–6; villages, xv, xvi, 2, 20–21, 23, 69, 163, 200–201; 217n6; Zhuang and, 41–42

Buyi ancestors, 31, 33–34, 36, 56, 73, 82; altar for, 44, 76, 145, 214n19; reciprocal exchanges by, 32

Buyi elites, 9, 12–13, 21, 31–32, 57–68, 70, 71, 76, 92, 97, 126, 184, 189, 201; cultural revival and, 65; disappearing Buyi and, 48; education and, 51; ethnic identity and, 81; Mo culture and, 66, 72, 75; past and, 201; reliance on, 84; road improvements and, 169; support from, xvi; Wuyang and, 24, 137

Buyi Ethnicity in Zhenning County, The (Wu Kaifeng and Wu Zhonggang), 64, 70, 73, 94–95

Buyi Folklore Museum, 139–44

Buyi language, ix, 22, 31, 58, 74, 89, 105, 117, 188, 189; Chinese language and, 218n15, 221n3; Han language and, 106; phonetics of, 27, 62; speaking, xv, 47, 218n8; standardizing, 41; studying, xviii, 130; understanding, 48

Buyi-Miao Autonomous County, 37, 98, 124

Buyi women: carsickness and, 172; clothing and costumes for, 50, 90, 92, 97, 99, *99*, 100, 152; content/scripts by, 93; double burden of, 122–27; ethnic branding and, 94; performances by, *80*, 89, 93, 107–8, 112, 119, 124; state discourse and, 127; traditions and, 100, 201; weddings and, 98

Buyiness, xiv, xvii–xviii, 7, 24–25, 54, 92–93, 200

Buyizu, 12, 39–40, 48, 90; socialist transformation and, 35–39, 41–43

Case-by-Case (financial subsidy), 165, 186, 187, 225n7

celebrations, 50, 55, 82–83, 89, 115–17, 152, 163, 183; media and, 117–20

ceremonies, 93; burial, 92, 104, 106;

life-cycle, 32, 92; marriage, 92; welcoming, 198

Chau, Adam Yuet, 65, 87, 113, 218n13

Chinese characters, 79; imitating, 61–62; modified, 62, 65

Chinese Communist Party (CCP), 35, 60, 96, 101, 107, 180, 200, 215n22, 224n1; Buyi and, 109

Chinese Folk Literature and Art Society, 71, 219n19

Chinese language, xi, 27, 34, 61; Buyi language and, 218n15, 221n3; using, 47, 218n9. *See also* Chinese characters

Chineseness, 17, 196, 211n14

Chinese People's Political Consultative Conference (CPPCC), 22, 55, 64, 103, 139, 140, 212n24; Zhenning County Committee, 68, 140

Chio, Jenny, 190, 211–12n20, 226n16

Chongqing, 103

citizenship, 18, 96, 99, 110, 116, 159–60, 167, 183, 197, 212n22

civilization, 17, 46, 49, 94, 159, 163, 210n11; arrival of, 183; Confucian, 11; connotation of, 184; ecological, 228n6; moral, 215–16n27; spiritual, 75, 98, 115

class, xvi, 20, 109, 137, 144, 145, 223n10

clothing, 142; Buyi, 91, 94–101, 109, 110, 116, 126, 139, 191, 200, 223n12; Buyi women and, 90, 92, 97, 99, 99; ethnic, 95; Han, 96; identity and, 100; preserving, 140–41; traditional, 92; women's, 90–91, 100, 147. *See also* costumes

collaboration, 58, 126, 165

collectivization, 43, 96, 112

commodification, 6, 18, 53, 125; cultural, 130, 136, 138, 144

community: environment and, 135; imagined, 141, 223n10; indigenous, 136, 212n22; participation by, 111–17

competition, 6, 18, 51–52, 59, 90, 150, 190, 196, 221n1

"Conferences of the Gods," 69

Confucianism, ix, 10, 24, 34, 43, 56–58, 74, 75, 138, 214n12, 223n9

conservation, 18, 147, 181; development and, 189. *See also* preservation

Constitution of the People's Republic of China (1982), 212n2

construction, 46, 103, 172, 189, 193–94; cultural, 70–71; housing, 176, 180, 182; identity, 203; infrastructure, 162–64, 167, 182; road, 169, 170, 171, 174; social, 29; socialist, 97; urban-rural, 166

consumerist economy, 15, 136, 138

contact zones, 30, 148–49

cosmology, 58, 64, 73, 104, 213n12, 218n9

costumes, 92; Buyi, 51, 89, 90, 94, 95, 116, 139, 143, 198; Buyi women and, 50, 100, 152; ethnic, 99, 142; Miao, 124. *See also* clothing

County Gazetteer Office, 55, 60, 163

County Red Cross, 151, 165, 188

CPPCC (Chinese People's Political Consultative Conference), , 22, 55, 64, 103, 139, 140, 212n24

crafting, 6, 19, 24, 53, 71, 75, 76, 195, 200, 201

cultivation: body-mind, 114–15; *suzhi*, 111–17, 187; wet-rice, 11, 39, 210n9, 213n9

cultural attractions, 51, 52, 130, 199

cultural changes, 46, 121, 210n11

cultural economy, 100, 125, 139, 196, 197, 227n2

cultural forms, 14, 82, 93, 109, 122, 134, 141

cultural heritage, 15, 57, 68–69, 75, 94, 108, 124, 129, 138, 141, 150, 153, 204; awareness of, 135; ethnic minorities and, 131; preservation of, 131. *See also* heritage; intangible cultural heritage

254 INDEX

cultural industries, xv, 86, 108, 203, 222n1, 225n5

cultural practices, 33, 45, 72, 109, 119, 123, 202

cultural production, 4, 59, 109, 137, 138, 155, 203

cultural promotion, 53, 75, 88, 197; Buyi and, 19; ethnic branding for, 19

cultural purity, 17, 196, 221n1

cultural relic protection unit, 200, 227n5

cultural revival, 60, 65, 71, 113, 134; Buyi, 82–88; post-Mao, 122

Cultural Revolution, 12, 13, 44, 56, 60, 63, 66, 69, 85, 140, 145, 201

cultural workers, 66, 126, 217n2

culture, ix, xviii, 83, 92, 101, 126, 144, 195; advance toward, 34; Buyi, 8, 12–13, 22, 24, 27, 42, 44, 46–48, 53, 64, 85–86, 93, 95, 113–15, 129, 139, 141, 147, 149, 151–53, 156; Chinese, 62, 71, 72, 75; commercial, 155; commodification of, 121, 125; consumerist, 186; ethnic, 5, 6, 94, 132, 136; exotic, 132; folk, 100, 112, 156; Han, 7, 10–11, 46, 116, 140; heritage and, 94; history and, 188; local, 58, 81; material, x, 134; Miao, 53, 116; minority, 86; minzu, 11–15, 56, 77, 126, 138, 141; Mo, 56, 57, 67, 68, 72, 78, 84, 85; museums and, 154; passageway, 168; socialist, 116; traditional, 71, 197; urban, 117; of water, 51, 53–54

customs, 15, 34, 59, 66; Buyi, 75, 124; folk, 81; marriage, 94, 98, 150; Miao, 124; social, 96, 105

Dai, 124, 209n6

Dali, 16

dances, 89, 90, 100; Buyi, 101, 116, 118, 127; communal participation and, 111–17;

Miao, 1, 124; performing, 80, 121, 126; as recreational activity, 116–17; suzhi cultivation, 111–17, 187

Daoism, ix, 58, 62, 213n12, 217n6

dazao, 6

decollectivization, 98, 112, 113

deity, 69, 73, 77, 81

development, xv, 24, 53, 127, 159, 182; conservation and, 189; cultural, 139, 165, 203; economic, x, 168; infrastructural, 158, 165–67, 171, 175, 181, 183, 189, 191–92; local, 17, 167; modern, 179; preservation and, 161, 189; protective, 164; regional, 154; road to, 168–72, 174–75; rural, 159–60, 224n1; social, 46–47; socioeconomic, 19, 164, 192, 197; tourism, 92, 125, 139, 162, 200; village, 159, 165, 182

difference, 6, 118, 122, 141, 147, 150, 211–12n20; celebrations of, 18, 116, 125; cultural, 12, 15, 16, 19, 29, 133, 195; ethnic, 4, 8, 70, 184; generational, 94, 100; paradox, 15–19; politics of, 131

discourse, 39, 45, 71, 107, 184, 201, 210n11; civilizing, 9; popular, 38, 221n2; public, 15; state, 12, 71, 83, 87, 98, 115, 138

domestic economy, 185, 186

Dong, 4, 5, 23, 135; cultural brand for, 123–24; stereotype of, 209n6

ecological niches, 32–33, 38

ecomuseums, 135, 150, 223n7

economic growth, 14, 32, 37, 189, 222n11

education, 8, 20, 24, 34, 37–38, 47, 51, 62, 65, 93, 105, 115, 133, 203; bilingual, 216n36; development of, 159; primary, 218n8; socialist, 12

Eleventh Five-Year Plan, 158, 224n1

elites, 59; local, 143; minority, 137–38;

political, 139, 140; rituals and, 71;
subalterns and, 137. *See also* Buyi elites;
minzu elites
environment, 15, 16, 160, 188; built, 176,
177; community and, 135; physical, 161;
sanitary, 183; visual, 167
environmental protection, 164, 166, 187
ethnic groups, xv, 4, 8, 13, 15, 28, 29, 68,
90, 121, 123, 141, 143, 150, 197, 211n15,
216n38, 221n1; identification of, 36;
interactions among, 19; unity/equality
of, 36
ethnicity, 29, 52, 81, 85, 88, 94, 122, 137,
147, 149; bridging, 33; Buyi, 9, 51;
nature of, 53; study of, 202–3
ethnic minorities, 12, 13, 19, 29, 72, 90, 93,
132, 135, 193; cultural heritage and, 131;
regional autonomy for, 212n2
ethnic population, 25, 34, 87, 132
ethnic traditions, 4, 17, 44–45, 71, 140;
women and, 94–101, 201. *See also*
traditions
ethnocentrism, 27, 50, 52
ethnography, xi, 8, 19, 20–25, 222n14
ethnolinguism, 37, 39
ethnology, 12, 13, 37, 223n2
ethnonyms, 30, 38, 141; endonyms, 31;
exonyms, 31

Fei Xiaotong, 36, 43, 134, 211n14
fengshui, 163, 176, 179–80, 221n4, 226n15
fengshui xiansheng, 217n6
festivals, 117, 123, 200, 213n3; Buyi, xviii,
98, 220n33; Miao, 98; religious, 69
fetishism, 144, 192
folk arts, 92, 122, 221n5
folklore, xvi, 5, 66, 124, 130, 152
folk songs: Buyi, 107, 109, 124; *minzu*,
222n10. *See also* songs

funerals, 64, 66, 67, 72, 76, 84, 104, 106,
117

Gelao, 37, 213n9
gender, xvi, 106; ambiguity of, 20, 212n23;
inequality, 96; social vision of, 114. *See
also* Buyi women
gexing, 5, 6, 7, 15–16, 19, 79
globalization, 16, 86, 220n36, 225n10
Golden Autumn Art Festival, 123
"Good Flowers Are Red" (song), 107, 108,
124
governance, 74, 154; paternalistic nature
of, 194; self-, 94, 114–15, 126
Grand Song of the Dong, 123
Great Leap Forward, 150
Guangdong, 157
Guangxi, 30, 68, 76, 78, 142, 214n12,
220n32; Guizhou and, 42
Guiyang, xiv, 2, 41, 64, 70, 132; urbanization in, 47
Guizhou, 2, 3, 7, 13, 15, 16, 21, 23, 27, 29, 33,
37, 41, 51–53, 62, 64, 75, 76, 95–96, 103,
108, 110; attention for, 199; award from,
22; Buyi in, 24, 68, 150, 151, 219n23;
described, 4, 30; development in, 169,
211n17; ecomuseum and, 135; ethnic
branding in, 20, 161; ethnic inhabitants
of, 66; houses in, 177; hybridization in,
34; identity of, 168; investigation tour
of, 134; *kaifa* in, 189; Miao in, 96; minority regions for, 39; remoteness of,
17–18; research in, 4–5; road building
in, 168; Schotter and, 131, 132; social
engineering in, 190; taking care of, 74
Guizhou Agriculture College, 169
Guizhou Miao Studies Association, 45
Guizhou Minority Nationalities Classic
Archives, 84

256 INDEX

Guizhou Minzu Delegation, 108
Guizhou Nationalities Affairs Commission, 37
Guizhou Normal University, 139
Guizhou Provincial Communist Party Committee, 157
Guizhou Provincial Population Census, 215n23
Guizhou Provincial Radio Station, 107
Guizhou Provincial Song and Dance Troupe, 107
Guizhou Provincial Television, 1
Guizhou University, 169, 213n8

Han, ix, 7, 19, 24, 29, 37, 46, 53, 62, 82, 90, 96, 99, 101, 116, 125, 127, 135–36; Buyi and, ix, xiii–xiv, xvii–xviii, 9–11, 13, 20, 28, 49, 50, 54, 73, 106, 140, 172; encounters with, 10, 47; Miao and, 3, 137; migration by, 33; minorities and, 13, 155, 184, 190; modernity of, 93–94; settlements of, 33; Yi and, 34
Han language, xv, xvii, 7, 117, 146, 216n35; borrowing from, 27; Buyi language and, 106
handicrafts, Buyi, xvi, 5, 45, 142, 150, 156, 224n13
hanhua, 11, 45, 210n11. *See also* sinicization
heritage, xv, 15, 95, 135, 136, 140; Buyi, 121; Chinese, 138; commodification of, 144; identity politics and, 144–49; local, 154; museums, and, 154–55; preservation of, 22, 130, 138, 211n18; territorialized, 154; tourism and, 67, 92, 130, 136, 144, 149, 153, 155, 200. *See also* cultural heritage; intangible cultural heritage
historiography, 72, 133, 134, 210n7
history: Buyi, xviii, 20, 95, 139, 141, 201;

community, 94; culture and, 188; Han-centric, 73; Marxist- Leninist narrative of, 134; *minzu*, 14; national, 17, 196; oral, 28, 31, 63, 96; regional, 85; village, 125
Hmong, 52
houses, 159, 166, 174; chaotic, 181; completing, 182; concrete, 177, 179, 182, 191; construction of, 176, 180, 182; dilapidated, 179, 181; good-looking, 17, 177; guest, 185; old/new, 175–77, 179–82; stilted, 176, *178*, 226n14; stone, 158, 177, 179; wooden, 176. *See also* bungalows
Hu Jintao, 110
Huangguoshu Waterfall, 23, 110, 188
Hui, 36
Hui'an, 96–98
Huishui County, 107–8, 124
Hundred Flowers Campaign, 27, 213n4
Hundred Yue tribes, 30
hygiene, 159, 183, 186, 187, 222n11, 226n17

identity, 25, 29, 36, 130, 197, 202; branding, 8, 196; Buyi, xiv, xvi, 7, 8, 33, 53, 95, 100, 121, 202; Chinese, 71; clothing, 100; collective, 86; crisis, 140; cultivating, 110; cultural, 4, 18, 130, 225n11; as difference, 6; essence of, 28; ethnic, 4, 7, 18, 24, 30, 47, 54, 81, 93, 111, 116, 197, 202–3; Han, 210n11; highland, 14; local, 122, 196, 203; markers, 16, 92; Miao, 52; minority, 13; mixed, 8; multiplicity of, 28; national, 16, 133; nature of, 19; rural, 47; self-, 38; shifting, 8
ideology, 71, 74, 83, 87, 107, 109, 116, 144, 149, 150, 155; eco-developmental, 228n6; Maoist, 66; revolutionary, 35; socialist, 140
imperialism, Western, 45–46

Impression Lijiang, 122

Impression Liu Sanjie, 122

impression management, 130, 152

indigenous population, 4, 15, 18, 19, 141,
212n22, 213n9

industry, 22, 203, 225n4; local, 224n2;
rural-based, 201

infrastructure, 110, 161, 166; connectivity,
190; construction of, 162–164, 167, 182;
cultural, 130; development of, 158, 165,
167, 171, 175, 181, 183, 189; government-
organized, 170; improving, 159, 169,
192; investment, 158, 163, 175; public,
167, 187, 191, 192; recreational, 188;
rural, 193; socialist modernism and,
183; tourism, 144–45; village, 159

intangible cultural heritage (ICH), 15,
68, 69, 75, 92, 108, 124, 138, 141, 150,
219n25; and UNESCO, 123, 211n18

"Inter-Ethnic Unity as Hundred Blossoms" (song), text of, 26

invisibility: politics of, 48–53. *See also*
visibility

Jinba, Tenzin, 7, 202, 221n1

kaifa, 161, 164, 167, 170, 175, 177, 179; process of, 189–94

kinship, xvi, 44, 60, 65, 112, 116

knowledge, 6, 18, 36, 59, 62, 65, 91, 123,
129, 138, 143, 155, 211n13, 214n12; *fengshui*, 176; production of, 8, 14, 45, 58,
136, 149, 209n5; ritual, 63, 70, 84

Kuan, Uncle, 26–28, 32, 34, 50, 114, 115,
121, 190, 212n1

labor, 97, 168, 172, 186; contribution,
226n13; migrant, xiii, 47, 90, 98, 158,
179, 226n21; outflow of, 47

land reform, 36, 43, 44, 109

landscapes, 154, 158, 159, 190, 194, 221n6;
developing/improving, 160; heritage, 138; karst, 225n12; local, 25, 164;
multiethnic, 29; natural/cultural,
22; original, 182; re-ethnicization of,
160; rural, 160, 181, 193; social, 42, 60;
state-managed planning of, 162–67;
village, 161, 162–67

langshao, 106

languages, 92, 210n12; of change/loss,
43–48; minority, 27, 41; national, 47;
ritual, 67; shift in, 47. *See also* Buyi
language; Chinese language; Han
language; Miao: language; Tai language

laojia, 143, 200

leisure, 92, 115, 125, 130, 143, 159, 160, 164,
190; commercialization of, 150

Libo County, 62, 68, 218n18

life cycle, 50, 60, 213n12

lifestyles, xv, 9, 98, 114, 115, 121, 122, 149,
156, 172, 184, 195; Buyi, 27; rural, 15;
traditional, 163

literacy, 65; level of, 45, 64, 93, 95; ritual,
74, 83

Liuyueliu, 45, 55–57, 74, 78, 81, 82, 84,
98; celebration of, 152; event, 99; Mo
rituals and, 83

living standards, 162, 179, 222n12

Long March, 35

Lu, Master, 57, 61, 64, 67, 84

Lunar New Year, 47, 55, 89, 90, 91, 101, 115,
120, 129, 145, 163, 174, 183, 200

Luodian County, 41

lusheng, 51, 124, 222n16

Mandarin, xiv, 216n35. *See also* Chinese
language; Han language

INDEX

Mao Zedong, 42, 93, 107, 110, 133, 141, 169, 223n9, 224n1; death of, 12, 27, 118; Great Leap Forward and, 150; land reform and, 44; socialism of, 53; Soviet legacy and, 112

marginalization, 52, 92, 131, 204

marriage, 30, 47, 95, 99, 106, 117, 119, 150; Buyi and, 20, 94, 97, 98

matriarchy, 77, 220n30

media: engaging, 117–22; mass, 11, 47, 49, 99, 109

memory, 154–55; collective, 94, 106, 130, 152, 203; crisis, 144; entrepreneurs, x, 59, 84; historical, 63, 73, 146

Miao, ix, 2, 4, 5, 10, 23, 29, 33–37, 45, 46, 66, 79, 82, 89, 90, 96, 116, 124, 137, 195, 199, 204n3; Buyi and, 9, 16, 17, 30, 48–49, 50, 51, 147, 216n28; conflicts/disputes with, 48; core identity of, 52; Han and, 3; language, xv, 49; residence of, 11; skills of, 32; stigmatization of, 48

"Miao Albums," 31, 66, 95

migration, xvi, 8, 22, 140, 193; Buyi, 49; Miao, 49; trade and, 30. *See also* labor: migrant

minban, 134

Ming period, 29, 216n27; assimilation and, 214n15; civil service, 216n33

Ministry of Culture, 133, 227n5

minorities, 18, 41, 204; ethnic, 89, 95–96, 105, 154; Han and, 13, 155, 184, 190; historical origin of, 134; semigovernmental association for, 13; training of, 37–38

minzoku, term, 210n12

minzu, xiv, 27, 28, 30, 31, 35, 51, 52, 72, 141, 152, 183; categories, 12, 38–42, 45; characteristics, 177; cultural tradition of, 84; groups, 12, 85, 134, 204; identification, 216n32; issues, 44–45;

70; policy, 37, 45; scheme, 11–12, 29, 43; worship, 79

minzu elites, 57, 65, 85

Minzu University of China, 67, 79, 145

Mo: Baolutuo and, 78; beliefs, 72, 76–79, 83, 86, 213n12, 220n35; Buyi and, 74–76; celebration of, 83; introducing, 56; legacy, 77; legitimacy of, 82; masters, 56–57, 61, 62, 64, 67–70, 72, 78, 83, 84, 119, 217n6, 218n9; *Mojing*, 56, 61; origin of, 61; process of, 75; as religion, 72; revival of, 87; superstition, 66, 69, 87; symbol of, 57; valorizing, 71–75

"Mo Culture of the *Buyizu*" (symposium), 70, 72, 77

modernity, 176; arrival of, 183–89; driving toward, 168–72, 174–75; Han, 93–94; production of, 154; socialist, 169; state-driven, 175; tradition and, 161

modernization, 21, 53, 86, 111, 138, 158, 162, 176, 190, 193; timelessness versus, 181

Molujia, 76, 77, 220n30

multiculturalism, 13, 136, 212n22

museology, Chinese, 130, 134

museumification, 136, 138, 151, 155, 188

museums, 128, 146, 194, 195, 201; Buyi, 25, 129, 130, 137, 139, 149–56; community-based, 131, 149; culture and, 154; development of, 136–37; ethnic, 149, 222n2, 223n2; ethnographic, 133, 136, 223n2; ethnological, 131, 132, 135, 223n2; European, 144; folklore, 150, 152, 154–56, 165; heritage and, 130, 154–55; *minzu*, 130, 131–39, 223n2; nationalist/culturalist disseminations of, 132; as platform, 152; politics of, 131–39; practical life and, 146; subject-object formation and, 131; tourism and, 130, 150; village, 149, 150, 155, 156. *See also* ecomuseums music, 89, 100, 116, 123; dance, 117; folk, 210n10, 222n15; pop, 121

Nanpan River, 29
National Ethnic Affairs Commission, 94
National People's Congress, 108
National Rare Manuscript List, 68
National Youth Singing Contest, 123
nationalism, 27, 46, 109, 132
Nationalist Party, 35, 109
nationalities, 47, 89; Stalinist model of, 36, 210n12
nation-building, x, 15, 17, 27, 130, 133, 189, 196
nation-state, 124, 133, 140, 210n7, 210n12
New Socialist Countryside, 157–59, 166
nongjiale, 185, 194, 226n18
non-Han groups, 4, 35, 50, 53, 133, 196. *See also* minorities
nostalgia, xviii, 5, 113, 135, 140, 143, 191, 201, 203

Oakes, Tim, 74, 154, 190
Open Up the West campaign, 161, 211n17
othering/otherness, 39, 48, 125, 137, 154, 227n2; ethnic, 29; exotic, 93; rural, 121

party-state, 12–13, 75, 104, 110, 145, 175
patriarchy, 10, 76, 77, 95, 153
Pearl River, 29
People's Liberation Army (PLA), 35, 218n15
People's Republic of China, 35, 63, 107, 141; anniversary of, 108; establishment of, 97, 211n13; ethnic populations of, 132
performances, 188; Buyi, 93, 126; cultural, 195; ethnic, 92–93, 100; folk art, 122; group, 121; life-cycle, 117; modern art, 122; oral, 107; preparation for, 121;

reviewing, 119–20; self-governed, 127; song-and-dance, 111–17, 119, 125
personhood, 115, 226n20; naming, 214n19
planning, 153, 201; state-managed, 162–67; urban-rural, 160, 164
politics, 7, 54, 109, 133; cultural, 19, 51, 131; ethnic, 8, 13, 19, 197, 211n16; heritage and, 144–49; identity, 131, 136, 144–49, 155; local, 85; *minzu*, 58, 66; racial, 211n16; regional, 66–71; representational, 130
poverty, 5, 204, 225n4; alleviating, xv, 14, 139, 199, 203, 228n6; reducing, 164, 166, 169, 189, 211n17, 224–25n4
power, 8, 65, 202; cultural nexus of, 59; discursive, 92, 201; ideological, 60; institutional, 60; local, xvi; negotiations of, 131, 155, 166; political, 35; socialist state, 83
preservation, 57, 70, 131, 137, 138, 163, 164, 175, 177, 183, 185; cultural, 119, 142, 162; development and, 153, 161, 189; heritage, 22, 75, 130, 136, 155, 211n18; historical, 189; obstacles to, 181; village-based, 162. *See also* conservation
pride, 4, 28; and artifacts, 129; ethnic and cultural, 21, 81, 126, 144, 147, 201; expressing, 90–91, 104, 110, 200; and housing projects, 176; local, 21, 51; and mobility, 174; and profit, 150
propaganda, 45, 78, 107, 115, 133, 147, 154; Communist Party, 211n13; posters, 99; socialist, 125; state, 16, 109, 111
publicity, 53, 125, 199, 200

Qin Yuezhen, 107
Qing period, ix, 79, 95, 180, 214n12, 215n23, 216n27, 216n28; assimilation and, 214n15; civil service, 216n33; Han and, 214n18

260 INDEX

railways, 30, 169, 225n12
Red Army, 35
Red Cliff Inscriptions, 80
Reform and Opening Up, 27, 45; song about, 170
Regional Minzu Autonomy Law, 213n2, 215n24
religion, 59, 65, 69, 73, 85, 134, 166, 195; appeal of, 86; Buyi, 76; framing of, 71; local, 58; *minzu*, 72
representation, xviii, 93–94; cultural, 71, 96, 137–38, 155; self-, 122; strategies for, 199
Republican era, 35, 43, 60, 66, 95, 133, 176, 213n10, 214n12, 216n27
rituals, 9, 16, 44, 59, 93, 195; academicizing, 69; Buyi, 50, 61, 64, 118, 119, 150, 220n29, 221n4; childbirth, 106; death, 74, 104, 106, 221n4; event production, 82–88; folk, 83; indigenous, 58; life-cycle, 50, 60, 105–6, 117, 118; marriage, 106; Mo, 24, 32, 55, 56–58, 60–68, 71, 74–77, 79, 83–86, 95, 142, 201
ritual specialists, 57, 58, 59, 69, 217n6; organization of, 64–65. *See also* Mo: masters
roads, 30, 175, 177; construction of, 169, 170, 171, 174; improving, 168, 172
Roxburgh rose (*Rosa roxburghii* Tratt), 107

safety, 174, 198, 201, 228n5
sanitation, 159, 172, 183, 185, 187, 228n5
sanlao sishao, 84
Schotter, Aloys, 131, 132, 135
scripts, 32, 34, 41, 42, 69, 81, 93, 219n21; Buyi, 58, 68, 80, 216n29, 218n17, 219n18; Mo, 61–63, 70, 73, 146, 214n12; oracle bone, 80

scriptures: Mo, 56, 66, 67, 69, 70, 73, 77, 79, 219n22; ritual, 75, 219n23, 220n28; Zhuang, 61, 76
self-consciousness, 6, 13, 93, 211n14
self-protection, 44, 63, 101
Shanghai, 103, 110, 180
Shenzhen, 87, 220n36
Shui, 68, 199, 213n10, 220n35
Shuijia, 31, 37
sinicization, 11, 13, 17, 45–46, 184, 210n11. See also *hanhua*
Siyueba, 98
Small Bastion, 23, 86
"Small Bastion, The" (song), 101, 104, 113, 120
social changes, ix, 12, 83, 95, 210n11. *See also* transformation
social groups, 29, 65, 217n3
social life, 87, 124, 136
social mobility, 49, 216n33
social stratification, 14, 43
socialism, 12, 14, 27, 38, 46, 53, 96
socialist market, 159, 170
socialist modernism, 183, 216n39
socialist transformation, 60, 98, 133; coming to terms with, 35–39, 41–43. *See also* transformation
socioeconomic progress, 24, 39, 164, 175, 196, 201, 204
Song period, 214n12, 216n27, 219n22
songs, 113, 117, 123; Buyi, 100, 101, 103–6, 108–9, 111, 114, 116, 118, 119, 124, 127; creation of, 121; ethnic minority, 222n10; lyrics, 112; performing, 121. *See also* folk songs
spiritual civilization, 75, 98, 115
Spring Festival, 200. *See also* Lunar New Year
State Council, 58, 68, 80, 219n18, 223n6
Steinmüller, Hans, 176, 222n11

stereotypes, 9, 33, 54, 131, 154, 209n6, 224n13
stone path, 171, *173*
Stone Village, 23
subjectivity, 6, 28, 94, 113, 122, 126, 202; Buyi, 53, 100; ethnic, 203; gendered, 114; local, 110
Su Donghai, 135
Suoluo River, 188–89
suzhi, 159, 182, 183, 187, 188; cultivation of, 111–17, 192

Tai language, ix, xiv, 3, 10
Tai speakers, 30, 33, 42, 213n10, 214n14, 218n9
Tang period, 214n12
Tang-Song period, 73
Taoism, 71, 218n9
technology, 118, 121, 182
Tenzin Jinba, 7, 202, 209n5, 221n1
textile arts, Buyi, 94–101
"Thousand-Year Buyi village," xvi, 2, 5, 23, 104, 150, 163, 171, 174, 180, 189, 203; promoting, 77–78
"Thousand-Year-Old Village" (song), 110, 125
Tian Shulan, 36
tourism, xv, xvi, 5, 14, 17, 18, 53, 86–87, 94, 131, 143, 156, 170, 180, 183, 195, 197–98; commodification of, 99; cultural, 125; development of, 92, 111, 125, 139, 159, 160, 162, 200–201; domestic, 190; ethnic, 2, 6, 16, 212n20; Han, 153; heritage and, 67, 92, 130, 136, 144, 149, 153, 155, 190, 200; importance of, ix; income from, 4; industry, 23, 77, 109–10, 150, 152, 227n3; museums and, 150; promoting, 29; rural, 226n18; supporting, 203
traditions, 12, 14, 65, 127, 130, 136, 138, 140, 196, 201, 203; Buyi, 75, 119, 150;

cultural, 59, 84, 112, 123, 126, 135, 153; modernity and, 161; oral, 93, 95, 101, 103–11. *See also* ethnic traditions
transformation, 5, 30, 60, 66, 96, 98, 109, 111, 140, 191, 203, 217n4; economic, 111; moral, 46, 210n11; political, 53, 110; rural, 122; social, 147; socioeconomic, 46, 176; sociopolitical, 65; spatial, 161, 225n10. *See also* social changes; socialist transformation
transportation, xv, 35, 164, 166, 168, 228n5
tudigong, 73

UNESCO, 68, 123, 138, 219n25
urbanization, 22, 30, 47, 158, 162, 190, 193, 225n4
urban planning, 159, 160, 187, 225n5

videos, 114, 117–22
Vietnam, 14, 29, 161, 210n10
village gate, 103, 165, *166*
visibility, 4, 6, 17, 54, 78, 90, 91, 122, 129, 134, 138, 196, 225n10, 226n16; politics of, 48–53. *See also* invisibility

Wang Ming-ke, 49
Wang Qinhui, 107
Wangmo County, 41
WeChat, 197, 198, 200
Wei, Teacher, 78–79, 145
wenhua, 13, 24, 51, 62, 68–71, 164, 168, 211n14
wenwu, 133, 139, 143, 223n6
West River, 29
Window of the World, 87
Wu brothers, 36, 44, 63, 64, 66, 73, 77, 95, 200
Wu, Director, 55–58, 60, 61, 63, 70, 77; *kaifa* and, 183; Mo and, 74; village branding and, 163

262 INDEX

Wu family, 21, 26, 32, 41, 44, 55, 63, 64, 70, 72–73, 95, 98, 101, 128–29, 194, 200, 220n31; ancestors of, 180; experience of, 43; history of, 34, 218n11

Wu, Grandpa, 146

Wu, Ka-Ming, 122, 212n13

Wu, Senior Grandma, 60, 61, 101, 105, 113, 115, 120–21, 157, 194; electronic appliances and, 117; video collection of, 121; women's clothing and, 90–91

Wu, Senior Grandpa, 115, 174

Wu, Uncle, 51

Wuyang Barbecue, 198

Wuyang Village, xiii, xvi–xviii, 1–3, 17, 20, 23, 23–24, 32, 37, 38, 41, 44, 51, 67, 77, 78, 80, 84, 86, 90–92, 101, 106, 114, 115, 117, 200, 203, 212n24, 214n20, 225n9; appearance of, 187; architecture of, 87, 199–200; attention for, 21–22; Baolutuo signboard in, 87, 167; Baolutuo statue at, 88; bastion above, 102; branding of, 24, 79, 82, 158, 182, 199; Buyi and, ix, 47, 81, 96, 97, 110, 129, 147, 148, 191, 195, 226n14; celebration in, 55; communal playground in, 55; construction of, 46, 103, 193–94; culture and, 7, 47, 89, 100, 129, 147; described, xvi, 5, 19; development of, 164–66, 181, 189, 191, 192, 196, 200; exhibit in, 128–30; historic feel of, 161; houses in, 158, 175, 177, 191; impression management by, 25, 152; jurisdiction for, 103; kaifa in, 161, 164, 167; landscape of, 139, 182; map of, 22; Miao and, 11, 48; Mo and, 61, 83, 87; modernity in, 183–89; museumification of, 150, 155–56; preservation of, 137, 164, 177, 185; publicity/popularity for, 200; road improvement for, 168, 170, 174; settling in, 27; socioeconomic transfor-

mation of, 176; story of, 196–97, 203–4; tourism and, 67, 139, 144, 149, 180, 197, 198; visiting, 1, 105, 156, 180, 193; Yang and, 142, 145, 147, 151–52

Xi Jinping, 16, 108, 110, 228n6

Xiamen University, 132

xiansheng, 61, 81, 217n6

xiaokang, 166

Xijiang Thousand-Household Miao Village, 16–17, 177, 195

Yang, Chairman, 56, 57, 93, 131, 145, 148, 149; autobiography of, 68; Baolutuo and, 77–79; Buyi and, 72, 77–78, 81, 128, 152, 156; civilizational hierarchy and, 155; collection of, 17, 139–44, 146; CPPCC and, 55, 64, 67, 103, 139, 140; cultural pride/state interest and, 147; cultural resources and, 140; death ritual and, 74; ethnic pride of, 144; kaifa and, 183; lesson from, 130; minority elites and, 137; Mo culture and, 69, 72, 78, 86; monograph by, 79; museum and, 128–29, 143, 150, 151, 155–56, 194; Red Cliff Inscriptions and, 80; research by, 67–68; ritual specialists and, 64–65; self-reflection and, 152; tourism and, 149; transformation and, 184; vision/investment by, 187; Wei and, 79, 145; Wuyang Village and, 137, 142, 147, 151–52, 200

Yang, Cousin, 171, 172

Yang family, xiii, 1, 44, 119, 145, 171, 172, 193, 200

Yang, Fenggang, 219n20

Yang Liping, 122

Yang, Uncle, 1, 11, 110

Yao, 49, 209n6, 220n35

Yi (Lolo) people, 7, 36, 213n9, 215n21, 216n28, 219n24; Han and, 34; writing of, 219n21

yichan, 68, 223n8

Yu, Jianrong, 226n19

yuanshengtai, 15, 86, 122, 123, 124

Yun (daughter-in-law), 157, 158, 159

Yun-Gui Plateau, 30, 213n7

Yunnan, xv, 13, 16, 18, 68, 213n7, 213n8, 217n4

Yunnan Reflections, 122

Zelin, Wu, 132

zhailao, 84

Zhang, Yanshuo, 217n2

Zhang Yimou, 122

Zhenning Buyi Folklore Museum, 139–44

Zhenning Buyi-Miao Autonomous County, xvi, 21, 27, 50

Zhenning County, 1, 2, 24, 30, 35–39, 43–44, 67, 75, 83, 84, 98, 108, 128, 139, 142, 145, 149, 153, 170–72, 179, 215n23, 216n28; agricultural production and, 43; Buyi in, 32, 39, *40*, 42, 90, 108,

139, 143, 151, 220n32, 223n12; cultural industries in, 225n25; government, 45, 165; intellectual history of, 36; map of, 3; Miao in, 79, 124; political economies of, 35

Zhenning County Agricultural Bureau, 169

Zhenning County Bureau of Education, 41

Zhenning County Committee (CPPCC), 68, 140

Zhenning Industrial and Commercial Bureau, 143

Zhenning News Station, 200

Zhenshan Buyi Ecomuseum, 150

Zhongjia, 31, 36, 37, 213n11, 219n24

Zhou brothers, 64

Zhou Guomao, 72, 76, 218n12, 220n35

Zhou Yongming, 225n10

Zhuang, 36, 37, 58, 68, 76, 78, 81, 214n12, 218n7, 220n29, 220n35; Buyi and, 41–42, 84–85; Mo and, 75, 85; stereotype of, 209n6

Zomia, 9, 210n7

zoning, 159, 164, 182

STUDIES ON ETHNIC GROUPS IN CHINA
Stevan Harrell, Editor

Cultural Encounters on China's Ethnic Frontiers, edited by Stevan Harrell

Guest People: Hakka Identity in China and Abroad, edited by Nicole Constable

Familiar Strangers: A History of Muslims in Northwest China, by Jonathan N. Lipman

Lessons in Being Chinese: Minority Education and Ethnic Identity in Southwest China, by Mette Halskov Hansen

Manchus and Han: Ethnic Relations and Political Power in Late Qing and Early Republican China, 1861–1928, by Edward J. M. Rhoads

Ways of Being Ethnic in Southwest China, by Stevan Harrell

Governing China's Multiethnic Frontiers, edited by Morris Rossabi

On the Margins of Tibet: Cultural Survival on the Sino-Tibetan Frontier, by Åshild Kolås and Monika P. Thowsen

The Art of Ethnography: A Chinese "Miao Album," translation by David M. Deal and Laura Hostetler

Doing Business in Rural China: Liangshan's New Ethnic Entrepreneurs, by Thomas Heberer

Communist Multiculturalism: Ethnic Revival in Southwest China, by Susan K. McCarthy

Religious Revival in the Tibetan Borderlands: The Premi of Southwest China, by Koen Wellens

Lijiang Stories: Shamans, Taxi Drivers, and Runaway Brides in Reform-Era China, by Emily Chao

In the Land of the Eastern Queendom: The Politics of Gender and Ethnicity on the Sino-Tibetan Border, by Tenzin Jinba

Empire and Identity in Guizhou: Local Resistance to Qing Expansion, by Jodi L. Weinstein

China's New Socialist Countryside: Modernity Arrives in the Nu River Valley, by Russell Harwood

Mapping Shangrila: Contested Landscapes in the Sino-Tibetan Borderlands, edited by Emily T. Yeh and Chris Coggins

A Landscape of Travel: The Work of Tourism in Rural Ethnic China, by Jenny Chio

The Han: China's Diverse Majority, by Agnieszka Joniak-Lüthi

Xinjiang and the Modern Chinese State, by Justin M. Jacobs

In the Circle of White Stones: Moving through Seasons with Nomads of Eastern Tibet, by Gillian Tan

Medicine and Memory in Tibet: Amchi *Physicians in an Age of Reform*, by Theresia Hofer

The Nuosu Book of Origins: *A Creation Epic from Southwest China*, translated by Mark Bender and Aku Wuwu from a transcription by Jjivot Zopqu

Exile from the Grasslands: Tibetan Herders and Chinese Development Projects, by Jarmila Ptáčková

Pure and True: The Everyday Politics of Ethnicity for China's Hui Muslims, by David R. Stroup

Ethnic Branding in Contemporary China: Buyi and the Paradox of Difference, by Yu Luo